Crisis Resolution: Presidential Decision Making in the *Mayaguez* and Korean Confrontations

Other Titles in This Series

Presidents, Secretaries of State, and Crises in U.S. Foreign Relations: A Model and Predictive Analysis, Lawrence Falkowski

U.S. Policy in International Institutions: Defining Reasonable Options in an Unreasonable World, edited by Seymour M. Finger and Joseph R. Harbert

Congress and Arms Control, edited by Alan Platt and Lawrence D. Weiler

Political Leadership in NATO: A Study in Multinational Diplomacy, Robert S. Jordan

U.S.-Japan Relations and the Security of East Asia: The Next Decade, edited by Franklin B. Weinstein

Communist Indochina and U.S. Foreign Policy: Postwar Realities, Joseph J. Zasloff and MacAlister Brown

National Interests and Presidential Leadership: The Setting of Priorities, Donald E. Nuechterlein

Arms Transfers to the Third World: The Military Buildup in Less Industrial Countries, Uri Ra'anan, Robert Pfaltzgraff, Jr., and Geoffrey Kemp

Westview Special Studies in International Relations

Crisis Resolution: Presidential Decision Making in the Mayaguez *and Korean Confrontations*

Richard G. Head, Frisco W. Short, and Robert C. McFarlane

In the nuclear era, the use of even low levels of force risks catastrophe for all mankind. Yet military force remains an important element of political strategy, and control and coordination of its use with other instruments of national power is of vital importance.

The authors of this book, examining two crises that occurred during the Ford administration—the *Mayaguez* incident and the murder of two U.S. Army officers in the Korean DMZ—describe the crisis communications and coordinative mechanisms used by the president, the Joint Chiefs of Staff, and the Department of State. Summarizing, as well, the literature on crisis management and resolution, they present a comprehensive analysis of how intelligence is gathered and analyzed; how U.S. interests are defined; how diplomatic and military options are developed; how decisions are made (drawing on the actual minutes of National Security Council meetings); and how these decisions are implemented by U.S. diplomatic missions and military forces in the field.

The book is the first to present an authoritative view of how each department functioned internally and externally during the crises. The analysis, based on personal interviews, of what factors loomed largest in the decision-making processes of President Ford, Secretary of State Kissinger, General Scowcroft, and others, is particularly incisive and makes a unique contribution to the literature on crisis resolution.

Richard G. Head is a colonel in the U.S. Air Force and a military fellow at the Council on Foreign Relations. At the time of this research he was a student at the National War College and an associate research fellow with the Research Directorate of the National Defense University. Frisco W. Short, a retired colonel, U.S. Army, was formerly a senior research fellow at the National Defense University. He spent more than two years on the joint staff developing procedures associated with the management of international crisis. Robert C. McFarlane is a lieutenant colonel in the Marine Corps, currently assigned to the National Defense University, where he is a senior research fellow. He spent more than three years on the staff of the National Security Council and a year as a White House Fellow.

Crisis Resolution: Presidential Decision Making in the *Mayaguez* and Korean Confrontations

Richard G. Head, Frisco W. Short, and Robert C. McFarlane

Foreword by Vice Admiral M. G. Bayne

Published in cooperation with the National Defense University

Westview Press / Boulder, Colorado

Westview Special Studies in International Relations

This study has been reviewed and cleared for open publication by the Department of Defense. Opinions, conclusions, and recommendations expressed or implied herein are solely those of the authors and do not necessarily represent the views of the National Defense University, the Department of Defense, or any other government agency.

Published in 1978 in the United States of America by
Westview Press, Inc.
5500 Central Avenue
Boulder, Colorado 80301
Frederick A. Praeger, Publisher

Library of Congress Cataloging in Publication Data
Head, Richard G.
        Crisis resolution.
        (Westview special studies in international relations)
        Bibliography: p.
        1. Mayaguez Crisis, May 1975. 2. United States—Foreign relations—Korea (Democratic People's Republic) 3. Korea (Democratic People's Republic)—Foreign relations—United States. 4. Decision-making. I. Short, Frisco W., joint author. II. McFarlane, Robert C., joint author. III. Title.
E865.H4   353.008'9   78-9514
ISBN 0-89158-163-4

Printed and bound in the United States of America

For Elaine, Jane, and Jonny

Contents

Appendixes

Figures and Tables

Photographs

Foreword

It must count as one of the truly dramatic ironies of policy research that crises—phenomena which if allowed to escalate could threaten mankind's very existence—have received relatively little attention as an area for focused study. This is particularly true among practitioners—officials in government—among whom the incentive for improving our knowledge of crises and our ability to cope with them ought to be highest. Such work as has been done, much of it quite good, has been predominantly by serious students and scholars in the academic world. In a few cases, officials who have experienced crises in public life have left government and written analytically of crisis resolution, and these have been among the most useful contributions to the literature. All in all, however, our knowledge of crises, what causes them, how to prevent them, and how to resolve them, is very primitive. With apologies to Mark Twain, it seems that "everyone talks about crises but no one ever does anything about them" in a procedural sense.

This is not to say that parts of the Washington community haven't learned valuable lessons from past crises. The tremendous effort by the Joint Chiefs of Staff to develop the World Wide Military Command and Control System received its principal impetus from communications breakdowns during the 1967 Israeli attack on the *Liberty* and the 1968 North Korean attack on the *Pueblo*. Other examples could be cited from the intelligence and diplomatic sectors. But these are internal measures taken by one department in isolation from the others. Even today, postcrisis critiques tend to be done by executive departments, or even narrow directorates within departments, and the staff officer or historian often lacks the mandate or the freedom to investigate across organizational boundaries. Seldom to my knowledge has the U.S. government looked at how all the actors—the president, the secretaries of state and defense, the chairman of the Joint Chiefs, and others—all bring their expertise together and collectively go about resolving crises. That's what this book is all about.

The authors' objective has been to advance what we know of low order crisis in several important respects. Their method has been to analyze two specific crises with a view toward defining what factors were most important in shaping the president's decisions. Their work is particularly absorbing in that it is not based upon tenuous extrapolation or inference but on the precise views of the principals involved—President Ford, Secretary Kissinger, General Jones, General Scowcroft and others.

Important questions are raised, questions especially important for the new administration: can crisis decisions and control be decentralized to cabinet officers as President Carter's general statements imply? Where must the buck stop and why?

The notion of differing perceptions is covered in a most realistic way, and leaves one with the feeling that the decision maker of today must consider many interpretations of the situation he faces, rather than simply search for the obvious shining truth. Here pragmatism seems to lay a heavy hand on ideology. There arises the clear implication that intelligent action is not the result of efficient organization, but of the judgment of intelligent people in authority, exercised at times in spite of the organization. The authors draw on a fascinating interview with former President Ford, in which his concern that overreaction be avoided is clearly evident.

Their conclusions and suggestions raise some interesting questions for further study. One concerns the availability of information during crisis management. By whose judgment is information passed to higher echelons? Clearly, some better criteria are needed on which to decide what information should be at the policy level, and what is not necessary.

There is strong justification for continuing control of the

tactical operation in a crisis at a high policy level, since new information may be available only at that level. The authors express the opinion that the founding fathers saw civilian control of the military not only as a concept to prevent imprudent action by the military, but as a way to require the commander in chief to exert control before, during, and after a crisis. It seems quite clear, in light of the evidence set forth here, that 535 members of the Congress cannot exercise crisis management. Such management must be done by the chief executive himself, the War Powers Resolution notwithstanding.

This book deserves careful study, and surely will give rise to much discussion and some argument concerning the lines of authority during a national crisis. Clearly evident, and not subject to argument, is the indication that in no other country on earth is there such an awareness of one's own nation's strength, or such care and moderation exercised in the use of that strength.

Vice Admiral M. G. Bayne
U.S. Navy (Ret.)

Preface

History reflects that very few high officials who played a role in decision making during crises had ever read anything about "crisis management" prior to being called upon to perform. That does not necessarily imply a criticism of the individuals or of the literature. Without the benefit of focused study, countless officials have performed extremely well and contributed to the successful resolution of many difficult situations. At the same time, the existing literature contains a substantial amount of analysis which might have served as useful background for all those involved.

The problem with much of the crisis literature is that the state of the art from the perspectives of both analysts and practitioners is sufficiently underdeveloped to preclude precise prescription. The purpose of this book is to advance our knowledge of crises by the development of a descriptive model, drawing on those elements of past analysis that seem most relevant to contemporary circumstances and then applying the model to two case studies of recent low-intensity crises. Relevancy, of course, is the rub. What is relevant to the theoretician is often esoteric to the empiricist.

We have attempted to make this volume relevant to public officials in actual crisis conditions by developing the components of our model from the conditioned attitudes of high-level participants. That is, through a series of interviews with the president, the secretary of state, the assistant to the president for national security affairs, the acting chairman of the Joint Chiefs of Staff, and other policy-level officials, we have sought to determine what factors loomed largest in their individual decision-making calculations. Any value which emerges is the result in large measure of the candor with which these principal figures treated their individual and collective experiences. We believe that their willingness to treat recent events forthrightly is unique in our time. The freshness of their recollections—validated by and large by consistency among their separate treatments of events—should enhance confidence in the data base. The conclusions, of course, are only as good as our analytical treatment of their views.

None of the officials interviewed avoided criticism or hesitated to criticize. None sought to rationalize his judgments or differences with others in the light of outcomes. We are extremely grateful for this candid cooperation and believe it represents an intellectual trust. Each of the viewpoints referred to in the work is documented in our interview notes; however, we have not footnoted many of them out of respect for the privacy our subjects should enjoy and from our conviction that individual consistency makes the results intellectually defensible without specific personal reference. This book on crisis resolution has been written after access to NSC source material and first-hand interviews. In the nuclear age, the study of crisis factors and of alternative approaches to controlling crisis escalation is a moral imperative. We hope that the results justify the very substantial trust they have been given.

The study was written with a view toward two distinct but interdependent audiences—the scholars and the policy makers. For this reason a word about the organization of the book may be appropriate. Chapter 1 reviews the academic literature on crisis behavior. Chapter 2 draws on the literature and existing organizational procedures to develop a descriptive model of crisis behavior. The purpose of Chapter 3 is to outline the written and unwritten crisis guidelines promulgated by the National Security Council, the Joint Chiefs of Staff, and the Department of State. It also summarizes important personality factors among key policy makers involved in the *Mayaguez* and Korean tree crises. The communications available to the president and executive agencies are discussed in Chapter 4. Chapters 5 and 6 are devoted to case studies of the *Mayaguez* and Korean DMZ crises respectively, using the descriptive model developed in Chapter 2. Chapter 7 compares the two crisis decision systems and presents our conclusions and evaluation. For those interested in the state of crisis research, the first two chapters are important; policy makers and those whose main interests lie in influencing crisis behavior may find it more useful to begin with Chapter 3 or even Chapter 5.

We would like to express our appreciation to the many officials and staff members who contributed so greatly to our research. We are especially grateful to former President Gerald R. Ford for his support of our request for access to source material from his administration and for his devotion of time to answering questions on crisis management during his stewardship. Similarly, we express our appreciation to Secretary of State Henry A. Kissinger; General Brent Scowcroft, assistant to the president for national security affairs; General David C. Jones, chief of staff, USAF; General Richard G. Stilwell, commander in chief of United Nations forces in Korea; Honorable William G. Hyland, deputy assistant to the president for national security affairs; Lieutenant General C. J. LeVAN, JCS director of operations; Assistant Secretary of State Arthur W. Hummel, Jr.; Deputy Assistant Secretary of Defense Morton I. Abramowitz; Peter Rodman of the NSC staff; Mrs. Jeanne Davis, staff secretary of the National Security Council; Major General Kenneth Houghton, USMC, and Lieutenant Colonel Randall W. Austin, USMC, commanding general of the Third Marine Division and commanding officer of the Marine assault force on Tang Island during the *Mayaguez* recovery respectively; Lieutenant Colonel Victor S. Vierra, commander of the U.S. forces in the Joint Security Area; and the many professionals within the departments of State and Defense, the Joint Staff, and the Central Intelligence Agency, without whose help this book would not have been possible. At the Council on Foreign Relations, senior research fellows William J. Barnds and John C. Campbell read the final drafts and added comments.

We are deeply indebted to Colonel Andrew J. Dougherty, USAF, director of research at the National Defense University, whose technical support and scholarly criticism have been invaluable in assuring comprehensiveness in our approach and integrity in our analysis. We are, as well, grateful to the staff at the National War College, to Dr. William C. Hamilton, Colonel Whitney Hall, and Lieutenant Colonels John R. Nevins and Peter B. Lane, each of whom read and critiqued preliminary drafts. Lieutenant Colonels John C. Fryer and Richard L. Reynard and Mr. Leonard L. Quiram contributed valuable comments on Chapter 2 and the Korean case. Mr. George C. Maerz and Messrs. Art Hewitt, Greg Caruth, and Dick Thompson of the National Defense University staff shaped the book with their professional attention to editorial and graphics matters, respectively. The portraits were provided by White House photographer David Hume Kennerly; the other illustrations by the Operations Directorate of the Joint Chiefs of Staff. Miss Mary Threadgill, librarian at the National War College, eased the research burden greatly through her knowledge and facility in locating source material. Thanks are also due to Commander Fred Daly, assistant director of the Research Directorate, for his administrative support and effective counsel in resolving numerous problems related to clearance and publication of the manuscript. Ms. Evelyn Lakes performed herculean tasks as research assistant, editorial critic, and executive secretary. The authors take full responsibility for the judgments in the book.

R.G.H.
F.W.S.
R.C.McF.

Abbreviations

ABCCC	Airborne Command and Control Center
ADP	Automatic Data Processing
AID	Agency for International Development
ANMCC	Alternate National Military Command Center
AUTODIN	Automatic Digital Network
AUTOSEVOCOM	Automatic Secure Voice Communications
AUTOVON	Automatic Voice Network
CAS	Crisis Action System
CIA	Central Intelligence Agency
CINCPAC	Commander in Chief, Pacific
CINCPACFLT	Commander in Chief, Pacific Fleet
CINCUNC	Commander in Chief, United Nations Command
CJCS	Chairman, Joint Chiefs of Staff
CONUS	Continental United States
CRIMREP	Crisis Management Report
C³	Command, Control, and Communications
DAO	Defense Attaché Office
DCA	Defense Communications Agency
DCI	Director, Central Intelligence
DCS	Defense Communications System
DIA	Defense Intelligence Agency
DMZ	Demilitarized Zone
DOD	Department of Defense
DPRK	Democratic People's Republic of Korea (North Korea)

DRP	Defense Review Panel
GAO	Government Accounting Office
IG	Interdepartmental Group
INR	Intelligence and Research Bureau of the Department of State
ISA	International Security Affairs/Office of the Secretary of Defense
JCS	Joint Chiefs of Staff
JOPS	Joint Operations Planning System
JSA	Joint Security Area
KCNA	Korean Central News Agency
KPA	Korean People's Army
MAC	Military Armistice Commission
MDL	Military Demarcation Line
MINIMIZE	Procedures established by Defense Communications Agency to restrict communications traffic in specific areas of the world during emergencies
NATO	North Atlantic Treaty Organization
NCA	National Command Authority
NCNA	New China News Agency
NEACP	National Emergency Airborne Command Post
NMCC	National Military Command Center
NMCS	National Military Command System
NSC	National Security Council
NSDM	National Security Decision Memorandum
NSSM	National Security Study Memorandum
OAG	Operations Advisory Group
OMB	Office of Management and Budget
OP	Observation Point
OPREP	Operational Reporting System
PACOM	Pacific Command
PRC	People's Republic of China
ROK	Republic of Korea
SAC	Strategic Air Command
SIOP	Single Integrated Operations Plan
SRG	Senior Review Group
UNC	United Nations Command

USIB	United States Intelligence Board
VP	Verification Panel
WPR	War Powers Resolution
WSAG	Washington Special Actions Group
WWMCCS	Worldwide Military Command and Control System

1
Approaches to the Study of Crisis

On May 12, 1975, the S.S. *Mayaguez,* a commercial container ship of U.S. registry, was boarded and seized off the coast of Cambodia by Khmer soldiers. The crew was detained for four days and then released unharmed. Fifteen months later, two U.S. military officers were brutally attacked and murdered while supervising the trimming of a tree in the Joint Security Area (JSA) between North and South Korea. The United States responded to the seizure of the *Mayaguez* with a Marine assault on a Cambodian island and air attacks on the port of Kompong Som and nearby installations. In the Korean case, the United States decided to conduct a major show of force and to reassert its authority in the JSA by cutting down the tree at which the incident occurred.

Why were these two events, which both became international crises, treated in such different ways? Were the international or domestic contexts so different? Or did the differences derive from changes among the actors? What were the United States' goals in each crisis, and how did it go about the process of achieving these goals? How did policy making in these crises differ from more routine types of policy making in Washington? This book is an attempt to answer these and other questions about international crises by exploring the fundamental nature of crisis decision making and by examining in detail the *Mayaguez* seizure and the Korean demilitarized zone killings.

THE VALUE OF STUDYING CRISIS DECISION MAKING

There has been an increasing concern on the part of policy makers, the public, and the Congress with the subject of crisis decision making since the Cuban missile crisis of 1962. This concern often centers on fears of involvement in situations that could embroil the United States in another Vietnam, a limited war over Middle Eastern oil, or even—in the worst case—escalation to general war with the Soviet Union. What is the nature of international political crises that they create such fears in modern man?

Crises in the international system are a frequent phenomenon. Every nation has crises, but the feeling is widespread that no bureaucratic formula exists for controlling them. International crises appear to defy analytical forecasting; they seem to be unpredictable in time, scope, and outcome. They threaten individuals with disruptive stress and psychological breakdown. They threaten organizations with communications overload and failure. They threaten nations with embarrassment, violence, and potential escalation to nuclear conflict. And further, they appear, in the U.S. context, to be increasingly handled by a small group of unelected officials, with little opportunity for citizen comment or congressional advice and consent. They are mysterious, ominous, and ill-understood.

Government officials deal with crises and impending crises frequently. President Eisenhower complained that he attended to at least one crisis every day; Dean Rusk, while secretary of state, related to a Senate subcommittee that the world had averaged eight and one-half international political crises per year since 1961.[1] A 1976 study by the Brookings Institution listed 215 political uses of U.S. military forces since 1945, most of which were responses to crisis situations.[2]

The conventional Western view is that crises are unique events caused by sudden and abrupt changes in the international environment which are to be avoided and, when unavoidable, are best resolved quickly as short-term, high-risk, no-win situations.[3] The view that crises are undesirable neglects their positive aspects. Crises present opportunities not available in routine policy making. They provide the chance to motivate and mobilize citizens and the bureaucracy to action, to unify, to organize interest groups, and to move forward in areas where such progress might not be possible otherwise.

The problem for the policy maker, and thus for students of the process, is how best to organize to cope with international crises. But reorganization should be based on analysis of past performance. How do the policy makers search for alternatives? How do government agencies bring past experience, advice, and information into the decision-making arena? Does the tremendous demand for information overload the capacity of communications channels and overworked policy makers who handle it? How do U.S. government agencies organize to meet a crisis, and how do they comply with White House requirements? What role does the president play? Does he really decide, or are decisions left to lower-ranking officials? To what degree have congressional activism and the War Powers Resolution affected executive decisions? Academic theory is underdeveloped and provides no concrete answers to these and other important questions. Yet crisis theory and empirical data interact to tell us much about the nature of this partially open and partially mysterious policy process. The purposes of this book are to examine what we know about crisis, to provide a framework for analysis, to describe some crisis decisions, to analyze crisis behavior, and to suggest several conclusions.

DEFINITIONS OF CRISIS

There has been a multitude of uses of the term "crisis" in the twentieth century. Most of these have been indiscriminate, nonanalytical, and broad-gauged, and thus not very useful in any systematic study. Crises have been variously defined in the *American Heritage Dictionary of the English Language* as (1) "a crucial point or situation in the course of anything"; (2) a "turning point"; (3) "an unstable condition"; (4) "a sudden change"; and (5) "a tense state of opposition." People talk of crises in education, urban affairs, racial integration, the economy, the Congress, every institution of the executive branch, international relations, and the United Nations. The major common thread that can be discerned in these disparate usages is a vague sense of perceived threat or risk. This threat may be caused by internal changes within the organism or by a gathering of external forces. These changes bring a challenge to the fore and thereby create a situation of conflict. Any discussion of the concept of crisis should also encompass the related terms of change, stress, tension, panic, catastrophe, and disaster.

Definitions of crisis in the international political scene, however, tend to cluster around two basic elements—the system and the individual actor. Systemic definitions of crisis tend to use macroanalysis, a global view of the interactions of states as they would appear to an observer in earth orbit. Crisis is seen as a threat to system stability, as a disruption. Thus, crisis is defined as "an extraordinary situation which results from unusual extensive and intensive inputs to the international system,"[4] "some kind of boundary or turning point,"[5] or "a set of rapidly unfolding events which raises the impact of destabilizing forces in the general international system or any of its subsystems substantially above 'normal' (i.e., average) levels and increases the likelihood of violence occurring in the system."[6] Systemic definitions tend mainly to focus on the international characteristics of crises.

The second group of definitions tends to be oriented more toward the effect of crises on the individual, and there has evolved substantial agreement on a definition. This group represents microanalysis, with a focus on the backgrounds and motivations of individual government officials, their perceptions of threat, and their reactions to time pressure. James Robinson in 1962 proposed a basic definition of crisis that had three components: origin—internal or external; decision time available for response—short, intermediate, or long; and relative importance to officials of the values at stake—low or high.[7]

Subsequently, Charles Hermann, a colleague of Robinson's at Ohio State University, deleted the origin component and defined crisis as "a situation that (1) threatens high-priority goals of the decision-making unit, (2) restricts the amount of time available for response before the decision is transformed, and (3) surprises the members of the decision-making unit by its occurrence."[8] Although Hermann in his 1969 and 1972 definitions specified surprise as a characteristic, subsequent research findings did not support surprise as a necessary property. In a 1975 article, he dropped the requirement for surprise, although it may still be considered an important component of the threat.[9]

Michael Brecher and his colleagues at a Jerusalem "crisis seminar" during 1975-1976 developed a consensus around the basic Hermann/Robinson construct, but elaborated a more precise conceptual definition:

> . . . a foreign policy crisis is a situational change in the external or internal environment which creates in the minds of the incumbent decision-makers of an international actor a perceived threat from the external environment to basic values to which a responsive decision is deemed necessary.[11]

Another (and official Department of Defense) definition of crisis is that of the Joint Chiefs of Staff (JCS). It states that "a crisis is . . . an incident or situation that rapidly develops, external to CONUS [continental U.S.], and creates a condition of such diplomatic, political, or military importance to the U.S. Government that commitment of U.S. military forces is contemplated to satisfy national objectives." This definition substitutes the concept of "diplomatic, political, or military importance" for threat, but the meaning is virtually the same. Further, the JCS notes that the crisis could develop with "little or no prior warning" (surprise) and it "may require accelerated decisions" (short time for response). This bureaucratic definition was developed independently of the academic definitions we have discussed, but it has much in common with them.

In summary, despite the wide variance in the general usage of the term crisis, in the field of foreign and defense policy there appears to be substantial consensus on a working definition. The main thrust of this definition can be traced back at least fifteen years and has been incrementally refined by the contributions of many individuals. These definitions represent cumulative knowledge and can be used as foundations for further research.[11] In the second chapter of this volume, we will develop a definition of crisis for the purposes of this study which will be a variation of the Robinson/Hermann/Brecher version.

MAJOR ACADEMIC APPROACHES TO THE STUDY OF CRISIS

There have been essentially two approaches to the study of crisis as a policy problem: rational/analytic and decision making. A note of caution needs to be expressed at the very beginning, however, that this categorization of the many and diverse studies and research materials into only two broad areas is somewhat arbitrary and is only for purposes of simplification for the reader. As is true with most attempts to simplify, this effort may easily suffer from the error of reductionism—the failure to fully represent the variety and richness of the original. The effort is made with the purpose of guiding the interested student into the diversity of the original material as it meets his requirements.

Before outlining the approaches, it is necessary to address two categories of classification that affect the approaches. The first is the level-of-analysis problem, which roughly divides foreign affairs inquiry into two broad areas—international politics and foreign policy.[12] The international politics approach leads the researcher to a global systemic view of crisis, while the foreign policy approach generally leads to a national, organizational, or individual perspective. Although the international and national are the two basic classifications, there is really a spectrum of approaches which relate to the level-of-analysis problem. These approaches can be listed in descending order of size of aggregation:

> the international system
> the regional subsystem
> the nation-state
> the organizational system
> the small group
> the individual

The second problem concerns the differing methodological approaches that can be used with any of the above levels of analysis. Studies have been written on a single case, on several comparative cases within the same nation, and on cases compared among nations. There have also been numerous simulations of crises acted out by college students and government officials.[13] Thus, in theory, one could have a study with any one of the hierarchical classifications and any number of cases or simulations.

Rational/Analytic Approaches

Rational/analytic approaches are characterized by an international orientation where the actors are nation-states, the crisis "problem" originates from the actions of other states, and the crisis "solution" consists of the selection from among a list of ordered alternatives of that outcome which maximizes the values of the decision maker. The critical assumptions of the rational/analytic approach are that: (1) the values of the decision maker can be rank-ordered; (2) the decision alternatives will each produce a different outcome; (3) the costs and benefits of each alternative can be calculated directly; and (4) the calculations and analysis will be actively updated with pertinent information.[14]

The rational/analytic approach is at the heart of most economic theories of consumer behavior and theories of the business firm, where the constraints on goal achievement are characterized as external to the decision maker. In international political studies, three major groups share the rational/analytic approach: "power school" researchers; sovietologists; and strategic studies analysts. Strategic studies, in particular, have contributed greatly to our knowledge of crisis signaling techniques and have formed the basis for most prescriptions for crisis management.

The Strategic Studies Approach

The field of strategic studies had its origins in the late 1950s, when the development of mathematical (and especially computer) techniques made the integrated analysis of interdisciplinary factors possible, and when an awareness of the growing complexity and risks of international affairs in the nuclear age made the application of interdisciplinary approaches to public policy necessary. Pioneered by such scholars as Thomas

Schelling, Herman Kahn, Bernard Brodie, and Henry Kissinger, this new field incorporated the latest in decision theory and game theory methodology, blossomed quickly, and had a profound impact on public policy. It has tended to have a universal focus on the behavior of the international political system and the maneuvers of states within that system. It has also tended overwhelmingly toward a rational/analytic explanation of events, decisions, and actions.[15] That is, national behavior has most often been analyzed as the purposeful choice from among a wide list of alternatives. States are assumed to select that option which will maximize the nation's strategic goals and objectives.

The methodology for the application of game theory to the deterrence problem, although not necessarily a crisis situation, was elaborated by Glenn Snyder in 1961:

> [The] probability of any particular attack by the aggressor is the resultant of essentially four factors which exist in his "mind." All four taken together might be termed the aggressor's "risk calculus." They are (1) his valuation of his war objectives; (2) the cost which he expects to suffer as a result of various possible responses by the deterrer; (3) the probability of various responses, including "no response"; and (4) the probability of winning the objectives with each possible response.[16]

After making the requisite calculations, the game theorist can then predict the action of the parties involved. (For example, "The deterrer will select the response which minimizes his expectation of cost or maximizes his expectation of gain.")[17]

A recent example of the use of the rational/analytic approach and game theory to produce propositions about crisis choices can be seen in Charles Hermann's "cost calculation model." In this formulation, he describes policy makers as weighing the respective costs and benefits of any action against the criterion of national survival.[18] This model hypothesizes, briefly, that if national survival is perceived to be threatened, policy makers will tend to exercise extreme caution, negotiate to seek settlement, and avoid physical acts of violence. Conversely, if national existence is not perceived to be threatened, policy makers will be motivated to manipulate the risks in the crisis, avoid settlement, and commit military forces. Although Hermann treats only survival this way, the model is obviously adaptable to less threatening consequences.

An emphasis on bargaining has been one of the enduring concepts of the strategic studies approach, starting with Thomas Schelling's excellent work *The Strategy of Conflict* in 1960.[19] Schelling's unique contribution was to identify the concept of "tacit" bargaining and to show how nations have used it to reach agreement, despite their continuing divergent interests. Oran Young, in two of his studies, has carried Schelling's work forward and focused it specifically on crisis.[20] Young's contribution, especially in *The Use of Force,* was in relating the international interaction processes described by Schelling to important contextual factors such as the force of events, communications, resolve, asymmetries, and restraints on the use of violence. As opposed to Schelling, who mainly used examples as asides, Young described several cases in some detail. However, his overall view was still from the perspective of the international system, and he treated nations as subsystems and participants.

Another work from the strategic perspective is Albert and Roberta Wohlstetter's *Controlling the Risks in Cuba,* which analyzed the 1962 missile crisis in terms of the strategic interests and influence of the Soviet Union and the United States.[21] Their joint work on the missile crisis was paralleled by Roberta Wohlstetter's comparative study on Cuba and Pearl Harbor, and followed her earlier classic on the intelligence aspects of the Pearl Harbor attack.[22]

A use of the strategic approach strictly from the Soviet view is the Triska and Finley work *Soviet Foreign Policy.* These authors looked at twenty-nine crises in the 1945-1963 time period and concluded that the Soviets tended to be conservative, cautious, deliberate, and unwilling to engage in activities that have high risk. Further, there seemed to be only minimal differences between Stalin and Khrushchev, and the tendency of the Soviet Union to accept risk was markedly higher in relations with other Communist states than in those with the West.[23] Hannes Adomeit, writing in 1973, evaluated such Soviet risk-taking determinants as ideology, military power, and domestic factors, but was inconclusive with regard to the future. He argued the Soviet Union was not a status quo power with a goal of "stability," but retained an ideological commitment to approaching crisis with the objective of coming out on top—of "winning."[24] He also rejected the assumption that Soviet growth in military power would reduce their risk-taking propensities by making them more responsible. But in the final analysis, he noted that the Soviet Union had not fulfilled Western worst-case predictions that increased military power would lead to an increase in expansionist behavior and risk acceptance.

Many of the previously discussed works contain elements of other approaches, but the bridge between strategic studies and the nonrational approaches that follow is perhaps best seen in the writing on perception. Still basically a strategic analyst, Robert Jervis, in an excellent book, discussed the role of signals in crises.[25] He noted that sincerity can be communicated by using special channels or channels that have been especially trustworthy in the past. Moreover, the role of personality and personal trust intensifies interpersonal contact such that signals given directly to another individual are perceived as more reliable than written messages.

Thus, discussions of signaling and bargaining continue to be important strategic contributions to the literature on international crises, but they also tend to use a rational/analytic approach. The link between rational/analytic and decision-making approaches can be seen in the transfer from a focus on signals to signal perception and misperception. Errors in perception of threats are widespread and primarily due to three categories of problems: intellectual difficulties, human predispositions, and bureaucratic routines. To examine these aspects of crisis, we will have to change our focus from the strategic studies approach to the decision-making approach.

In summary, the rational/analytic approach has been a valuable framework in the study of crisis. It tends to use the analysis on the international level to define the "crisis problem" and to view the constraints on states' actions as being external to the nation—in the actions of adversary states. The approach assumes a unitary calculus of values, alternatives, cost/benefit ratios, and value-maximizing choices, and requires aggressive

updating with new information. Its primary purposes have been
the evaluation, prescription, and prediction of crisis decisions,
and as such, the approach provides normative judgments about
how governments *should* act in the process of crisis management. The approach has been used widely in designing command, control, and communications systems as will be described
in Chapter 4. However, most of the rational/analytic assumptions have been challenged by alternative formulations. The
basic criticisms are that rational theory assumes sophisticated
information-processing systems that are beyond human cognitive capability, that it neglects intra- and inter-organizational
bargaining, and that observed government behavior does not
correspond with the requirements of the rational/analytic
model. In short, the rational/analytic approaches tend to treat
national decision-making processes as heroic simplifications
and tend to be optimistic with regard to human and organizational abilities to cope with the crisis situation.

Decision-making Approaches

There have been many alternative formulations to the
rational/analytic approach. In this section we will survey the
main body of literature associated with the decision-making
approach to crisis study and note some of the contributions of
two converging approaches—the analysis of bureaucratic politics
and the social-psychological perspective. The decision-making
approach in political analysis traces its lineage to Thucydides'
The Peloponnesian War and Machiavelli's *The Prince*. The
broadest treatment of the approach in political science literature is Snyder, Bruck, and Sapin in *Foreign Policy Decision-
Making.*[26] The approach is based on the assumption that the
nation-state is going to continue to be the dominant actor on
the international scene. There are six major components of
decision-making study: (1) the actors; (2) the situation; (3) the
organizational system; (4) the decision-making process; (5) the
decisional unit; and (6) choice.[27] Decision making takes place
in an environment of external (international) and internal
(domestic political) factors that strongly affect actors and
decisions. Decision making lends itself to the development and

use of case studies, and many have been written on either single or multiple cases. In a classic example of the single case study, Glenn Paige in _The Korean Decision_ introduced two further aspects—crisis decision stages and single versus sequential decisions.[28]

Like the strategic approach, early decision-making theory was almost entirely dominated by the assumption of rationality. Even Snyder, Bruck, and Sapin adopt one of the main determinants of the rational/analytic model when they define the state as its official decision makers and state action as decisions by those acting in the name of the state.[29] This rational/analytic model formed the basis for most studies because alternative theories were underdeveloped and more pessimistic with regard to the future. Most decision-making theories still tend toward some sort of rationalism, as can be discerned from the following prescription in a leading political science textbook: decisions "ought to be a calm ordering of national values and necessities, of rationally perceived interests and prudently framed objectives, of long-term goals and short-term exigencies."[30] The authors proceed to advocate the application of mathematical decision theory and probabilities to obtain the "maximization of expected utility."

The difficulties of putting operation into this idealistic rational/analytical model of decision making in the complex, political policy-making process have been extensively treated elsewhere.[31] The impact of these collective attacks on the assumptions of rationalism in policy making has been to modify analytical approaches and to increase the number of studies sensitive to nonrational modes and factors of decision making. Some of these studies will be treated further under the heading of the bureaucratic politics approach.

There are at least four basic limitations to the decision-making approach. First, there are problems with obtaining and handling the quantity and quality of data required for adequate analysis. Second, there is the difficulty of specifying which of the multitude of possible variables really influenced the decision. Third, there is too little known about the effects of national cultural values on the political process. Many of our theories may be more ethnocentric than we suspect, and thus not applicable to the analysis of other nations' policy processes. Fourth, there are the problems of uniqueness, simultaneity, and accident that operate to preclude accurate separation of factors from their background.[32] These difficulties and recent advances in organization theory have broadened the decision-making approach with an awareness of what has been called bureaucratic politics.

The bureaucratic politics approach. Many theories in the social and physical sciences arise out of opposition to long-held, conventional views of the universe. This situation creates an adversary relationship between those with a vested interest in the maintenance of the old order and those revolutionaries who see a vision of the new. In a sense, this is the case with the bureaucratic politics approach to foreign policy study. The approach was not in itself so different from decision-making studies that had preceded it, but the emphasis was different, and it tended to make some people defensive. The conventional wisdom that bureaucratic politics challenged was of two types. First was the widely accepted view that there was a separation between policy (which was defined as controlling all the important decisions) and administration (which provided support and only made implementing decisions).[33] The second institutionalized doctrine was the linkage between hierarchy and authority, a view which still ascribes authority to those high in private and public organizations because of their alleged superior wisdom and control of resources. In the U.S. government these two views converged to focus on the presidency and to create expectations of leadership and control that would properly emanate from this office.

This hierarchical view of policy making has been challenged increasingly since World War II, first by Herbert Simon, then progressively by Warner Schilling, Richard Neustadt, Roger Hilsman, and many others.[34] The major argument of these challengers was that power (defined as the ability to influence decisions) is dispersed over a wide range of individuals and organizations, each with their own subunits and each possessing clearly discernible institutional interests, often opposed to those of the president. While many participants and close observers of the policy process conceded the truth of this view, the more unitary, authoritarian approach tended to dominate analyses of the policy process, and strategic analysis continued to be the predominant mode of explaining crisis behavior.

A watershed in the study of both crisis management and foreign policy occurred in 1969 with the publication of Graham Allison's article on the Cuban missile crisis.[35] The article was not only an excellent case study of a crisis, it outlined three different approaches to policy analysis, each with unique data requirements and each producing unique explanations for what happened. His Model 1 was entitled the rational policy model, and is basically what has been outlined here as the strategic studies approach; Model 2 was an organizational process model, which emphasized the role of sub-units and standard operating procedures. Model 3 was the bureaucratic politics model, with "actors," "action channels," and bargaining. Although several other researchers had described the same aspects as Allison, his unique contribution was in his organization and outlining of the distinctions among the various conceptual approaches.[36]

There are five basic tenets of the bureaucratic politics approach. First, as we have discussed, governmental power is not seen as unified, but as dispersed among a wide range of institutional players. Second, these players characteristically define *their* problem in terms of individual and organizational interests or perspectives as opposed to national or (especially) presidential interests. Third, institutional players differ in resources and, therefore, power. They differ in the amount and quality of information they command, in communications capabilities, in skilled personnel, in allies among the bureaucracy and the press, and in access to action channels. Fourth, the manner in which decisions are made is not primarily through elaborate arrays of alternatives and cost/benefit calculations, as required by the rational/analytic model, but by the political process of bargaining. Fifth, traditional decision theory, game theory, and rational models in general have tended to concentrate on *decisions* as the primary unit of analysis. Bureaucratic politics places less emphasis on decisions than on actions, where control of the implementation process is a critical component of political power.[37]

Using the bureaucratic politics model, Allison described the intelligence failure during the Cuban missile crisis as significantly affected by CIA-air force bargaining over the reconnaissance mission. Similarly, the vulnerability of the Kennedy administration to the Cuban issue was partially the result of a domestic political situation involving the congressional election of 1962. The decision to blockade, he argued, was determined as much by *who* favored it as by their arguments. Finally, Allison argued that the implementation of the blockade was not in accordance with the president's direct orders; critical aspects of it were conducted instead according to navy doctrine and standard operating procedures.[38]

There have been many criticisms of the bureaucratic politics approach, but they cluster around four basic views. First, its emphasis on the bureaucracy tends to undervalue the central role and power of the president. Second, the organizational process portion of bureaucratic politics analysis has difficulty in explaining nonincremental change. Third, the approach ignores the influence of belief systems and mind sets among top decision makers. Fourth, although the approach goes far to explain the "slippage" between decisions and implementation, it is less helpful in explaining the decisions themselves. Although many of these concerns have been acknowledged by the advocates of the bureaucratic approach, the explanations do not fully convince the critics.

In summary, what the bureaucratic politics perspective has done is to modify, enlarge, and enrich the traditional decision-making approach without destroying its earlier framework. It has, however, tended to emphasize nonrational behavior almost exclusively, with bureaucratic politics becoming bureaucratic determinism. As such, it tends to be overwhelmingly pessimistic with regard to coping with crisis. Further, bureaucratic politics theory makes little attempt to get deeply into the mind of the decision maker, to examine his cognitive processes and motivation. Theories that attempt to explain events through these internal factors tend to have their roots in sociology or psychology.

The social-psychological approach. The social-psychological approach to crisis study is firmly in the decision-making tradition. Its emphasis on the individual places it at the lower end of the level-of-analysis spectrum. In 1913, J. B. Watson introduced his theory of behaviorism to psychology in an attempt to rid the profession of such subjective data as purposes, motivations, and intentions. He demanded instead concentration on observable, external action ("behavior") and proposed a stimulus-response (S-R) model.

In subsequent years most psychologists came to realize that between external stimulus and observable response, many subjective experiences intervene to influence both the perception of the stimulus and the nature of the response. In their view, this intervention was an important constraint on rational action, and the constraint was an internal one, having to do with the basic nature of the human organism. Thus, the concept of a stimulus-organism-response (S-O-R) model was introduced and rapidly gained a prominent place in the discipline of psychology. As the conduct of interdisciplinary research grew after World War II, psychological theory and concepts began to be adapted for use in political science. One of the early applications of psychological theory to foreign policy by a political scientist was Ole R. Holsti's study of the beliefs of John Foster Dulles. His findings suggested that the secretary of state had a powerful belief system that interpreted aggressive Soviet moves as hostile and attributed decreasing Soviet hostility to necessity and weakness, rather than to good intentions. Thus, there was no move the Soviet Union could take that would have convinced Dulles of its good intentions.[39]

Joseph de Rivera broadened the approach considerably when he published *The Psychological Dimension of Foreign Policy* in 1968.[40] He studied the determinants of perception, resistance to change of a belief, perception as a determinant of the stimulus, distorted perceptions, intelligence failures, selective biases, risk taking, and stress. The most important conclusion de Rivera reached was that decision makers should not be treated as independent variables (being free to make any choice they like with only good or poor judgment), but should be viewed as dependent variables (subject to the forces that affect each of us).[41]

The psychological concept that has been most widely used in relation to crisis research is stress. There is much evidence that links increases in stress with crisis situations. "What is relevant for policy," in a crisis, observed Henry Kissinger, "depends not only on academic truths but also on what can be implemented under stress."[42]

Stress is a concept that defies precise definition, and most attempts describe it in terms of its effects rather than its characteristics. Thus, stress may denote "a relatively temporary emotional condition of tension resulting from external factors,"[43] or it may be "the activation of the individual's coping mechanisms."[44]

Stress can be functional; depending on the level of stress and the nature of the individual experiencing it, stress can be a powerful motivating factor. But beyond a certain threshold, additional stress creates anxiety, apprehension, and disruption of normal physiological and cognitive processes. Specifically, under dysfunctional stress, creativity and initiating behavior tend to decrease, perceptions decrease in accuracy, behavior becomes less adaptive, judgments decrease in quality, aggression increases, untested ideas become fixed, and random (non-goal-directed) behavior increases. In addition, disruptive stress tends to produce regression to simpler modes of response, problem-solving rigidity, reduced span of attention, reduced ability to distinguish the dangerous from the trivial, loss of abstract reasoning, and reduction in tolerance of ambiguity.

Time plays an important part in stress development. In cases where stress has been imposed by increasing the number of decisions required in a given period by a factor of five, the number of decision errors rose fifteenfold.[45] As a crisis is prolonged and stress increases, creative decisions become both more important and less likely.

The relationship between stress and decision alternatives is inconclusive. Holsti cited Paige's Korean study and Snyder's research to tentatively propose that in a crisis the alternatives examined by the decision makers tend to be reduced.[46] Yet other research, including that of Howard H. Lentner, does not confirm this hypothesis. Lentner questioned seventy-nine Foreign Service officers in the State Department in 1966, and only 30 percent thought crisis alternatives were restricted over noncrisis situations.[47] However, this may not fully account for the number of times that the actual number of conceivable alternatives is large, but there is coalescence around a single, dominant alternative. This happened in the 1950 Korean case, in the Japanese decision to attack the United States in 1941, and in the latter stages of the 1914 crisis. It is not uncommon to read or hear of decision makers saying, "We had no alternative; we had to do it."

This perception of a lack of alternatives (in the extreme case the reduction to a simple acceptance or rejection of one proposal) is the classic example of stressful behavior. It denies the fact that there are always alternatives. The perception or argument that there is only one alternative provides the decision maker with a rationalization that lets him avoid a value conflict and its related stress. Instead of resolving or accepting the value conflict, he denies moral responsibility for the action by denying the existence of any alternatives. Another technique of dealing with uncertainty without dealing with the problem is displacement—transfer of the responsibility for the unwanted action (say, initiating a war) to the adversary. This has led to the legal doctrine known as "last clear chance."

Holsti combined the concepts of displacement with perception-reduction to produce several interesting hypotheses. First, he proposed that in a crisis, decision makers will tend to perceive the range of their own alternatives as being more restricted than the range of their adversaries' alternatives. Second, they will perceive the range of alternatives open to the adversary as expanding.[48]

This linkage with the adversaries in an interaction sequence is related to the strategic approach described above, and it leads to one of the groupings of hypotheses that Charles Hermann put together in *International Crises.* He devised a "hostile interaction model" built around three concepts: hostility, expression of hostility, and perception of hostility.[49] The model proposes, basically, that the expression of hostile behavior by one party is related to (1) the previous hostility from the adversary; and (2) its own hostile actions. The model as it is expressed predicts that the interaction process will tend to produce excessive hostility and thus result in escalation. This outcome is widely feared but tends to be refuted in academic research on escalation and in actual crisis behavior.[50] The vast majority of the post-1945 crises just did not escalate as the model would have predicted. Hermann notes, however, that this tendency of perceived hostility to exceed actual hostility does exist, and officials would do well to think about accommodative gestures and other methods to curb the expression of hostility.

In the same volume, Hermann summarizes the hypotheses that discuss stress and proposes what he calls an "individual stress model."[51] In this model, crisis produces disruptive stress, which is exemplified by reduction in cue awareness, rigidity in perceptions, rigidity in cognitive processes, and reduced time perspectives. These characteristics lead in turn to such behaviors as a repetition of prior successful responses (without recognition of differences in the situations); perception of reduced alternatives; regression to simpler forms of behavior; definition of the situation in zero-sum terms; and decreased consideration of domestic political consequences. Thus, the individual stress model as constructed by Hermann strongly suggests ineffective coping behavior.

More recently, however, Hermann broadened his approach to stress and noted that the relationship between stress and performance is related to three conditions: the nature of the task, the nature of the individual, and the setting.[52] He argued that complex tasks are the first casualties of stress, and these are exactly the kinds of tasks that have to be performed by high-level officials in a crisis. Second, high-level policy makers are undoubtedly far above average in their ability to cope with stress, but even they are likely to exhibit differences in tolerance. Third, one's ability to withstand stress varies with the organizational setting and one's orientation with respect to group versus individual decision making.

There has been less research attention paid to the psychology of collective decision making than to the psychology of the individual, most likely because of the greater complexity of the study of groups. Two works will be mentioned here, the chapter on small group theory in the Alexander George volume for the Murphy Commission[53] and Irving Janis' *Victims of Groupthink.*[54] Janis noted that properly organized and managed groups have the potential not only to compensate for the cognitive and stress-related deficiencies of individuals (as in the individual stress model above), but to produce decisions on complex topics with markedly greater insight. Yet, "the advantages of having decisions made by groups are often lost because of psychological pressures that arise when the members work closely together, share the same values, and above all face a crisis situation in which everybody is subjected to stresses that generate a strong need for affiliation."[55] Janis argued that groups in general tend to produce a lack of vigilance and a decreased sense of personal responsibility, while crisis-related stress adds pressure for group cohesion against the external threat. Excessive group cohesion has a tendency to produce stereotyped images of out-groups and excessively risky courses of action. He developed a list of eight major symptoms, which he calls the "groupthink syndrome":

1. an illusion of invulnerability which encourages risks
2. collective efforts to rationalize and discount warnings
3. an unquestioned belief in the group's inherent morality
4. stereotyped views of enemy leaders
5. direct pressure on dissidents
6. self-censorship of deviations
7. shared illusion of unanimity concerning judgments
8. the emergence of self-appointed "mindguards"—individuals who discipline those who exhibit deviant behavior, perceptions, and proposals

In summary, group decision making, which we will find to be characteristic of most crisis situations, is no panacea for the limitations of the individual facing disruptive stress. On the contrary, the dynamics of small groups are exceedingly complex and can either dampen or accelerate tendencies toward escalation and risk taking, depending on the group's composition, motivation, and leadership.

Many advances in small group theory have been applied to crisis study over the past six years. Particularly helpful has been research on stress, information search, information overload, and communications flow. Important policy-related propositions have been developed in the areas of the perception of reduced alternatives, simplified perception of the adversary's motivations, collapsed time perspectives, and excessive concurrence seeking.

As we have noted, social-psychological approaches have combined with bureaucratic politics analysis to broaden and intensify the decision-making perspective in crisis study. Whereas rational/analytic models tend to prescribe how people *should* act, decision-making models are more relevant to how individuals actually behave in crises. The decision-making approach, with its emphasis on human perceptions and organizational processes, appears to be the most relevant for the study of crisis behavior at the national level. Rational/analytic models, with their emphasis on goals and goal-achievement, appear to be more relevant to attempts at crisis management. Research which combines these two basic approaches has been limited.

MIXED MODELS AND MULTIPLE MODELS

Studies of crisis have had to cope simultaneously with two boundary problems—first with the larger field of international politics and then with the field of foreign policy at the national level. It is no wonder that few researchers have had the breadth of vision and energy to tackle the problems of integrating such a vast set of variables.

Although others had examined the underlying assumptions and intellectual paradigms that analysts bring to events, Graham Allison was one of the first to apply multiple models explicitly to an international crisis. His detailed analysis of the Cuban missile crisis from the point of view of a rational model (Model 1), organizational process (Model 2), and a bureaucratic politics paradigm (Model 3) was a distinct advance in the state of the analytical art. In his writing, Allison was careful to state that Models 2 and 3 were advanced as alternatives to, and not replacements for, the basic rational model which remains preeminent in policy analysis as it does in the hard sciences. One is struck, in reading his paradigms, by how these fundamentally unique approaches can lead an analyst to look at the same event and produce three different sequences of observation, description, and prediction. This situation is disturbing for two reasons: first, for other researchers, it produces very little advice about where to look for interrelationships among the models and how exactly to go about predicting when one model is superior. Second, it is disturbing for the policy maker because it destroys his confidence that there is an "objective reality" that can be discovered and used to produce effective decisions. One is reminded of de Rivera's contention that each individual's beliefs in fact "construct reality" for him from the chaos of events.

Allison's models have been widely applied to policy analysis ranging from naval strategy to weapons acquisition,[56] but few analysts have advanced the power of his analysis. One who has is John D. Steinbruner, who combined undergraduate work in psychology with doctoral study in political science at MIT, followed by postdoctoral research at Harvard with Allison, Halperin, and Neustadt and the faculty of the Seminar on Bureaucracy, Politics, and Policy. His publications analyze, rearrange, and sharpen Allison's policy paradigms into two basic models, which constitute a second major attempt at multiple-model analysis.[57] Steinbruner redefines Allison's rational model as an "analytic paradigm," but he goes much further and claims that bureaucratic politics *also* embodies the Model 1 assumptions of individually rational behavior and value-maximizing choices. The major alternative model Steinbruner offers is the "cybernetic paradigm." Cybernetics, he explains, is based on the theory of a very simple decision mechanism that does not activate unless one of its small set of "critical variables" exceeds its tolerable limits. Then, and only then, will the mechanism enter a simple (as opposed to a comprehensive) search pattern, stopping whenever it finds the first "satisfactory" (as opposed to optimal) alternative. The paradigm thus assumes the triple concepts of limited search, bounded rationality, and feedback.[58] Steinbruner supplements the cybernetic paradigm with principles from cognitive theory—principles which analyze how human beings structure their beliefs and make inductive inferences. Steinbruner, like Allison, does not claim supremacy for the cybernetic model, but stresses the benefits of competition. For our purposes, several of his conclusions on crisis decision making are significant:

1. An examination of government decision-making systems under crisis conditions reveals that decision makers

chronically and seriously estimate wrongly the flow of events, particularly the behavior of other governments.

2. There is no theory of decision to be found in the social sciences with established empirical validity across the range of events that one must include in the category of crisis decision making. Steinbruner concludes that both the analytic and cybernetic paradigms provide a coherent structure useful for explanations and predictions, but that the cybernetic paradigm is much less developed. He argues that researchers need to develop their abilities to understand organizational and bureaucratic contexts.

3. Significant benefits can accrue to the foreign policy analyst if he can generate multiple perspectives on the phenomena he examines.[59]

Steinbruner's approach argues strongly for the development of integrated, coherent, general theories to accompany the generation of specific concepts and propositions, but he offers no guidelines as to the relative advantage and appropriate selection of rational/analytic versus organizational/cybernetic frameworks. One of those who has is Raymond Tanter.

Tanter, with his *Modelling and Managing International Conflicts: The Berlin Crises*,[60] produced a major attempt to integrate the international and foreign policy levels of analysis. In this study, he used game theory (rational/analytic) and mediated stimulus-response (psychological) concepts to achieve a synthesis of the strategic studies approach with decision-making and organizational process. He divided each of the several Berlin crises into three phases—precrisis, crisis, and post-crisis. For the pre- and postcrisis stages, he found actor behavior was according to past patterns—the standard operating procedures of the organizational process model. When a crisis intensified, however, he claimed that the routine paths of action did not adequately explain behavior. He observed that organizations increased their search for information, and states adapted their behavior to the crisis events. There were five variables in Tanter's framework: (1) alliance actors: NATO and the Warsaw Pact; (2) conflict; (3) phases of crisis; (4) event/interaction; and (5) organizational process.

While Tanter's mixed model attempts to bridge the gap

between international systemic approaches and foreign policy decision-making approaches, it requires a significant amount of information about the adversary and his action-producing processes. It also tends to neglect several relevant factors such as small group processes, information search, and domestic politics.

In a subsequent study, Tanter and Stein compensated for some of these earlier omissions by developing a process model of choice which incorporates the three hitherto competitive paradigms outlined by Steinbruner—analytic, cybernetic, and cognitive.[61] They hypothesized that the crisis decision-making process may follow one or more paths, using different combinations of rational, programmatic, and cognitive elements. Thus, the model begins with a stimulus which is processed by one of six paths through the three paradigms and results in a decision/choice. The Tanter and Stein research is not conclusive, but it represents a genuine innovation in the integration of multiple decision-making models.

Hermann, in his 1972 study *International Crises,* attempted what we can note as the fifth major effort at producing a mixed-model of crisis. In this study he edited the works of eleven other researchers, made his own contributions, and produced 311 empirically testable propositions. He then grouped them into four general categories and developed four models of crisis analysis. They included an "organizational process model" which related to Allison's Model 2, and three models discussed above: "individual stress"; "hostile interaction"; and "cost calculation." Hermann identified one problem: his models contradict one another because of the diverse origins and purposes of the propositions. Still he went on to create a "series model," which linked the major elements in each of the four models.

There are two problems with this approach. The first, Steinbruner argues, is that by expanding the context of decision making into the broad categories of stress, small group processes, communications, hostility, historical experience, and domestic politics, what one produces is not a coherent theory but a taxonomy. The second problem with Hermann's approach is that the linkage does not resolve the contradictions between the models, but rather attempts to shunt the researcher by simple yes-no options into one or another of the model chains. The resulting flow chart in its current state may be less helpful than his previous four models, each one having at least an internal consistency.

CONCLUSIONS

The general conclusion of this cursory review of the academic literature on crisis is an unsettling one. It is, simply, that there has been a richness and diversity in approaches to the study of crisis, but few agreements have been reached. Rational and decision-making approaches use widely varying assumptions, and few satisfactory attempts have been made to integrate the two approaches. In addition, the following specific conclusions may be drawn:

1. The concept of crisis is used widely in a variety of popular and academic ways, but there is little agreement on an *interdisciplinary* definition.
2. In the field of international politics, definitions tend to cluster around two levels of analysis: the international system and the individual actor.
3. In the subfield of foreign and defense policy, there is substantial consensus among academics and government officials on a working definition that has been incrementally refined over the past decade.
4. The two major academic approaches to crisis policy making can be categorized as rational/analytic and decision making.
5. The decision-making approach, with its emphasis on human perceptions and organizational processes, appears to be the most relevant to the study of crisis behavior at the national level.
6. There currently exists no theory to adequately *describe* national crisis decision making, let alone *prescribe* a model for crisis management.

Substantively, academic contributions to the field of crisis policy making have been greatest when they: (1) argue that officials should not overestimate the manageability of crisis in a stressful environment; (2) integrate the study of option *selection* with the examination of organizational processes for decision *implementation;* and (3) delineate historically the attributes and limitations on the use of force as an instrument of policy.

These substantive and procedural conclusions provide guidelines for our study of crisis decision making. A firm foundation of explanatory concepts is necessary for accurate predictions in public policy. Yet there is no general theory of crisis decision making. The goal of Chapter 2 is to provide a descriptive framework for crisis analysis and explanation.

2
The Outline of a
Conceptual Framework

The purposes of this chapter are to build on the basic approaches to the study of crisis discussed in Chapter 1 and to outline a framework for analysis. Each of the major approaches—strategic studies, decision making, bureaucratic politics, and social-psychological—has its focus of primary interest and is useful for its own purposes. In this chapter, we will develop an integrated framework which will examine factors affecting crisis behavior and attempts at crisis management. In subsequent chapters, we will examine specific cases and apply this framework.

THE APPROACH OF THIS STUDY

The general approach of this book is to bring together strategic, organizational, and domestic factors and to examine their interaction. To accomplish this we will attempt to define an international political/military crisis, to discuss the characteristics that separate it from routine policy making, and to analyze the following factors: *key policy makers*—their interests and concerns; the international and domestic *context*—the situational factors that structure crisis decisions; the role of *surprise*—strategic and tactical; the *crisis event*—crisis recognition and notification; *organization and interdepartmental procedures*—the major departments and their activities; the *decisional unit*—a small, high-level group; the *decisions*—the substantive alternatives and the final choice among them; *operational implementation*—the execution of executive decisions; and *outcomes*—tactical, international, and domestic. An organizational flow model will be developed to illustrate some of the aspects of decision making over time from a perceived crisis to decision implementation.

The level of analysis will be predominantly national because crisis decisions are national decisions—choices taken and implemented in the name of the nation-state. Military action obtains its legitimacy only when it operates under the authority and control of the nation. Similarly, diplomats gather information for and act as representatives of the state. Ideally, they are motivated by the national interest, but this has to be defined by each administration. In the U.S. political system this articulation of national interests is specifically the responsibility of the president in accordance with the Constitution. The nature of the president's power as chief executive and commander in chief, as compared with other principal policy makers in the decision-making process, will be one of the major focuses of the research.

The nation will not be treated as a unitary, undifferentiated actor. The research and analysis will examine the actions of the major departments and components of the national government to discern their organizational procedures to recognize and manage crises. Individual policy makers' interests and motivations will be included based on interviews. The effects of stress on individuals will be noted, but actions, rather than emotions, are the subject of the work.

LIMITATIONS OF THE STUDY

There are three limitations to this study. The first, and most important, is the limitation imposed by classification of written data. The *Mayaguez* and the Korean tree incidents, the cases treated in this study, are both recent; both were handled at the highest levels of the U.S. government. Concern for the security of classified information and the wish to preserve the principle of executive privilege were very keenly felt by persons involved in the crisis. This concern was perhaps heightened by the recent history of congressional disclosures of intelligence information and the unsettled status of executive privilege as a legal concept.

The second limitation is inherent in any post hoc study where participants are the main sources of the data. The records, when they are available, are incomplete sources. Human memory, although consistently richer than the record for the kind of data needed in a policy-making case study, is imperfect, and often displays blind spots and distortion. The written record is a valuable aid in reconstructing events and influences, but it is an imperfect analogue to reality. The Freedom of Information Act and the increased frequency of security breaches have, in themselves, degraded the quantity and quality of what is written down about important and potentially controversial decisions. Another of the major changes in the availability of accurate historical data is the revolution in message transmission—the use of computers, visual display systems, and secure telephones. In fact, the international message traffic that formed the main data base for analysts of the communications leading to the origin of World War I would no longer be sufficient material.[1] Many of the initial reports of crisis development and most high-level military and diplomatic actions are initiated with secure telephones, and there is no sure correlation of telephone instructions with back-up written messages. These electronic communications devices have made the job of the political analyst more difficult.

Problems with the data are only a portion of the study's limitations. There are many limitations on the intellectual side as well. There is no comprehensive theory of decision making, and there is no agreement on the supremacy of either rational/analytical or organizational/bureaucratic/cybernetic paradigms of analysis. The number of variables that can be developed is extremely large, and there are analytical limitations in weighing them. There is no quantitative analysis capable of being applied consistently and uniformly to the subjective data dominating these cases.

From the international point of view, the crisis-bargaining process is highly interactive. One unit's decision and the action output of that decision become another unit's input; our solutions become our adversary's problems. This is also true to a degree among the organizational and individual players in the national decision-making process.

In summary, there is no general theory of crisis decisions that will explain all influences and events. There are few aids that even indicate whether two variables are roughly correlated. The factors we will develop are mostly suggestive, and even those have low levels of reliability. Studies of the relationships among the variables and the major clusters of factors are insufficiently developed, and no algorithm of the decision-making process is thus far possible. But frameworks are necessary and useful to structure empirical data and to categorize knowledge. A definition of crisis serves a similar purpose.

A DEFINITION OF CRISIS

The two crises examined in this study are *international*, in that they involve more than one sovereign nation, *political*, in that they concern power and influence, and *military*, in that they involve the deployment and operation of military forces. Thus, for the purposes of this study, an international political/military crisis is a situation characterized by:

1. a change in the international or domestic environment, which may be abrupt or gradual, but which generates
2. a threat to important national goals or objectives as defined by individuals or policy-making groups experiencing the crisis, with
3. significantly increased probability of military action and war and the perception of
4. a short time for response.[2]

In summary, a crisis is caused by a change in the international or domestic environment that generates a perception in the minds of policy makers of a threat to important goals or values, with significantly increased probability of hostilities, and a short time for response. Although not included in this definition, crises also tend to be characterized by surprise, unusually high levels of uncertainty, and a potential for escalation to higher levels of conflict.

This definition differs from the conventional one—which includes high threat, short time, and surprise—in five ways.

It introduces the possibility of a crisis being initiated by change in the *domestic* environment (such as the election of a new president or the shift of internal political forces), which then modifies the leaders' perceptions of a crisis threat. It deletes the requirement for the threat to be to basic values of a state, but requires only that the threat be to important goals or values. It adds the requirement that the situation include the probability of military action. The crisis conditions do not have to constitute a "high probability of involvement in military hostilities," as required by Brecher,[3] but require only that the probability be significantly increased. Thus, we would argue, the rate of change in the probability of war is as likely an indicator of its potential for escalation as is the absolute level of that threat.

We considered the issue of time and the arguments over whether a crisis required that there be a "short time" or a "finite time" for response. While we can accept that there may be situations in which a government would have a finite time—perhaps up to a year—to respond, our research does not lead us to conclude that such situations are viewed by policy makers as crises. It is only when the demands of the environment and the flow of events require a response within a short time—most often days but certainly not more than months—that our definition of crisis would be satisfied. Finally, our definition removes the requirement that the crisis be a surprise or the result of a single dramatic event, but allows the possibility that it may occur out of a gradual spiral of escalating tensions and hostilities. In our research, policy makers confirmed that surprise could not be dismissed as at least a contributing factor, however, because abrupt changes in the international environment tend to be accompanied by high uncertainty. In turn, this uncertainty tends to increase the perceived level of the threat, and thus the risks of policy making. We would note that crises tend overwhelmingly to be characterized by abrupt changes in the environment, but slower changes also qualify.[4]

As will become apparent in the case histories, changes in the international arena do not automatically present themselves as crisis events. Definitions of crisis do not guarantee that, in practice, crises will be recognized as such, but they can reduce situational ambiguity. In almost every known crisis there has been an initial period of uncertainty concerning: (1) whether the perceived facts constitute a real threat to national objectives or values; (2) the length of time before a response is required; and (3) the necessity of using military forces. In this initial period, the private goals, values, and objectives of policy makers interact with the goals and objectives of the nation as laid out in the Constitution, the political culture, and the most recent declaratory statements of national policy such as documents, treaties, posture statements, and speeches. Because these declaratory statements satisfy a variety of organizational needs and purposes, ranging from policy guidelines to attempts to influence allies, they often indicate only very general guidance for the future. Political crises can arise from situations that were not—and perhaps could not be—anticipated. One obvious example, often cited, is Secretary of State Dean Acheson's speech in January 1950, indicating a line of U.S. security interests in the Pacific that did not include Korea.

In the absence of precise policy, the ambiguity of events offers policy makers considerable discretion in declaring a situation a crisis. At times the detention of a U.S.-owned fishing boat by a foreign power is viewed as an unfortunate by-product of having far-flung economic enterprises, but not as a threat to important U.S. interests. In a different context, the same event can be perceived as an abrupt change in the international environment which threatens U.S. prestige, or important national goals and objectives—even its very status as a superpower.

The definition of these often diffuse national interests is vested with elected and appointed officials, each of whom has his own perception of national and organizational objectives and responsibilities. The result is that an international political situation may exist with all the characteristics of a crisis, but only the appropriate national officials can authoritatively label the situation as such. One of the important questions we will examine is who in the U.S. government is empowered to make this critical judgment. The declaration of a crisis sets in motion a multitude of formal and informal mechanisms for increased intelligence collection, planning, and development of options. For all practical purposes, lower-level officials are more affected by the initiation of these extraordinary procedures than they are by the crisis itself. Thus, once a crisis is so identified by appropriate authorities, it reorients priorities and focuses the attention of many members of that organization, regardless of their personal perceptions. The chief value of a definition of crisis, then, is to identify those characteristics which separate crisis from noncrisis situations and to alert operations centers and policy staffs to the recognition of crisis situations.

A CRISIS DECISION-MAKING MODEL OUTLINED

A model in social science, in order to be useful in the study of public policy, must meet two requirements: it must be relevant (i.e., realistic) when compared with empirical data; and it must be economical (simpler than reality).[5] The primary problem of the analyst is to achieve the goal of simplification without doing violence to the subtlety and diversity of the data. The purpose of the model developed in this study will be to provide a general outline or conceptual framework which will: (1) identify the major components of the decision process; and (2) facilitate the examination of the components in such a way that their interdependence is suggested. This specification of elements and interdependencies is broadly consistent with theories of system functionalism, but no analogy with biological or mechanical systems is intended.[6] Instead, it is the integrated input-output feedback process and the interrelationships among variables suggested by systems theory and structural-functionalism which are most useful in a blend with traditional decision-making concepts. The model's components include a basic unit of analysis and organizing concepts.

Basic Unit of Analysis: Crisis Actions

The escalatory threat of crisis and the short time for response combine to elevate the responsibility for a decision to the president in the United States and to the top of organizational hierarchies elsewhere. The president may be advised by a council, but he bears the final responsibility. He makes decisions based on his judgment of the information flowing to him from the international system, the domestic system, governmental organizations, and his advisory body. Crisis actions can be usefully analyzed in terms of these decisions and their implementation. This is not to say that organizations and individuals do not have influence over what the president selects or what action is finally implemented. It does mean that the president is formally and legally responsible for U.S. crisis behavior, and actions in a crisis are most usefully analyzed as the organizational implementation of presidential decisions.

Organizing Concepts

Key policymakers. The players in a crisis decision-making system are primarily those individuals and organizations that have a legitimate role in making and implementing foreign and defense policy. They include the president, his assistant for national security affairs, members of the National Security Council and its staff, members of the departments of State and Defense, the Joint Chiefs of Staff, the intelligence community, and the major unified and specified military commands. There are also selected individuals in and out of government who often influence the decision process by virtue of a relationship of trust with one of the principals. Outside the executive branch, the Congress plays a variable role—sometimes institutional in accordance with statutory responsibilities (the War Powers Resolution and oversight responsibilities) and sometimes as individual consultants, supporters, or critics. Beyond the Congress, the press and the public are both sources of national values and critics of presidential actions.

Factors influencing the key policy makers should be examined, and this list should include:

- their position and basis of authority
- limits on this authority
- their basic belief systems (if they can be determined)
- their previous crisis experience

Context—the structure of the situation. Despite the natural tendency to examine the crisis event in isolation, it is impossible to fully understand its implications without discovering its background and special circumstances. As an example, the 1961 Bay of Pigs invasion was an especially critical event in the presidency of John F. Kennedy because it influenced the newly elected president and conditioned him to approach intelligence estimates and Joint Chiefs of Staff planning with more than a little skepticism.[7] The invasion's failure also detracted from the U.S. image and decreased U.S. confidence in its political-military planning capability. In the strange way that events and issues become linked, the Bay of Pigs became a part of the context of President Kennedy's 1962 decision to land an American on the moon within the decade and his later response to the Cuban missile crisis. Similarly, the U.S. political system includes presidential elections every four years and congressional elections every two years. Any analysis of a crisis that falls in an election year and does not consider this factor is bound to be incomplete.

The goal of a comprehensive study should not be to include *all* known events, but rather only those events that might have had a significant influence on relevant organizations, decisional units, or key policy makers. At a minimum, discussions of the situational context should include analysis of international and domestic factors such as:

o   major superpower relationships
o   interests of third parties
o   geographical/regional configurations
o   relative military and economic capabilities of the adversaries
o   outcomes of past crises
o   threats to internal security
o   impending changes in domestic political relationships

Surprise. Although, after reflection, we have argued that surprise is not a necessary condition of a crisis, it is a valuable analytical concept. Surprise can be used both descriptively and normatively to examine an intelligence function—the responsibility to provide warning of threatening situations and impending crises. Thus, to analyze surprise, we will seek to discover to what extent the crisis event was anticipated at both the national/strategic level and the unit/tactical level.

Discussions of surprise as an analytical concept should include:

- o the level of political hostility and changes in that level in the period immediately prior to the crisis
- o formal and informal statements of governmental officials which may signify warnings
- o events and actions of military forces that may be indicators
- o verbal or physical warnings at the tactical level
- o the prominence of crisis indicators—the "signal-to-noise" ratio (i.e., strength of the indicator relative to the strength of other, background stimuli)
- o the "cry-wolf" phenomenon (possible nonreceptivity of higher authority)

The crisis event. Crises involving U.S. interests occur as the result either of our actions or of those of others. A nation's peacetime policies are normally produced by a system of bureaucratic routines that attempt to preclude surprise. Thus, even when a crisis erupts as the result of a nation's own actions, the element of surprise tends to make the event nonroutine. When an international adversary provides the ingredients of threat, short time, and possible escalation, the requirements for crisis are satisfied. Most often, however, a nation will tend not to perceive a crisis as emerging out of its own actions. Decision makers tend to see a crisis as an abrupt incident initiated by a foreign state.

Individuals, and organizations especially, tend to conduct their business in a pragmatic, routine fashion, answering those problems that are most pressing each day and delaying the solution of problems that do not demand immediate attention. Thus, in their search for information, ordinary people tend to use certain scanning techniques, depending upon their drive and the necessity to produce. It can be shown that this search is not random. It tends to be concentrated in areas that have been most productive in the past. Mechanisms and individuals habitually monitor a relatively narrow set of parameters which define the limits of acceptable performance and are trained to warn of breaches in these limits.

A cybernetic analogy is useful here. One of the most effective and efficient mechanisms designed by man is the thermostat. Its operation is quite simple, but its conception is ingenious. Its purpose is to maintain the operating temperature of any given area within acceptable limits—whether they be 68°–72°F. in a home or 170°–180°F. in an automobile engine. To do this, the thermostat does not employ a complex device to continually run either the furnace or the air conditioner to maintain one temperature precisely; it uses a simple off-on switch which is activated only when the operating temperature crosses a certain boundary condition, or threshold. The savings resulting from using a thermostat with a wide operating range rather than more precise but more complex mechanisms, is significant.[8]

Of course, each organization and each individual in federal executive departments has a unique set of parameters, so the spread of observation is quite wide. This is so particularly in the intelligence community, where many semiautonomous organizations and agencies have responsibility for monitoring allied and adversary behavior. Any one of them could signal an approaching crisis. When a boundary condition is breached, or even approached, and a warning parameter is perceived, the individual supposedly notifies his organization, and the entire national system of crisis decision making is jarred from routine into a crisis mode.

Questions for consideration in crisis study, then, include:

- ○ the source of the crisis event
- ○ its physical or nonphysical elements
- ○ its duration and intensity
- ○ the recognition and assessment of the event
- ○ the communication lines and notification of key policy makers

Once the conflict situation is stabilized and the crisis terminated, the boundary conditions are reestablished and the national security organizations resume routine behavior, modified only by the results of the crisis action.

Organizational and interdepartmental procedures. As noted in the discussion of the crisis event, crisis management in the United States is not random. It is a process structured by the organizational procedures affecting intelligence gathering, information handling, planning, development of alternative courses of action, decision making, and implementation.[9] Typically, these procedures have been developed over long periods of time and have been tested through many different kinds of policy problems.[10] In noncrisis situations, these procedures are usually designed to permit each part of the organization to express its interpretation of the events and to have its proposals heard, especially if it is to have a role in the implementation of policy. This participatory aspect of large organizations can be likened to an "administrative due process," whereby the search for expertise and the responsibility for consequences are decentralized in the broad base of the organization. Within the overall rubric of organizational procedures are several more specific components: organizational ideology—a generalized view of the environment and basic policy preferences; factored problems—the tendency to divide problems into separate parts to be resolved independently, rather than as a whole; organizational autonomy—the drive for control over resources which often breeds parochialism; standard operating procedures—which may or may not be appropriate for the specific crisis situation; uncertainty avoidance—attempts to reduce conflict by negotiating organizational environments (as in roles and missions agreements); and incremental change—the preference for small modifications on the margin, rather than large, more disruptive changes.

In addition, crisis situations in the United States require an unusually high degree of interdepartmental coordination and cooperation. Having a high-level decision group with departmental representatives is not sufficient to insure coordinated action. Each of the major departments will probably have a crisis task force, and many of the task forces will have interdepartmental membership. The composition and operation of these crisis management bodies is important to effective and successful action.

To examine the influence of organizational and interdepartmental procedures in crisis situations one should discuss:

- ○ operations center notification procedures
- ○ initial actions after notification
- ○ organizational crisis operating procedures
- ○ relationships among organizations
- ○ interdepartmental task force operations
- ○ organizational phases in crisis planning
- ○ field and headquarters relationships
- ○ communications patterns and methods of control

The decisional unit. Solitary decisions by presidents, unaided by recommendations of advisors and departmental officials, are rare in situations of crisis. Postwar presidents from Truman to Carter have used some form of structured decisional unit to gather information, discuss alternatives, and recommend actions. This decision group in a crisis tends to be a small, high-level body of policy makers, varying in size according to presidential style and the magnitude of the threat to the goals and interests of the United States. In past crises, this group has been characterized by three variations: *ad hoc*—as in President Truman's decision to defend South Korea in 1950 and President Kennedy's use of the Executive Committee of the National Security Council in the Cuban missile crisis; *formal/high level*—as in President Nixon's use of the National Security Council in the India/Pakistan war over Bangladesh in 1971; and *formal/lower level*—as in President Nixon's use of the Washington Special Actions Group in the Jordanian crisis of 1970.

For purposes of this study, analysis of the crisis decisional unit will be process-oriented and should include the following:

- ○ structure of the unit
- ○ size and membership
- ○ sources of information
- ○ consultation with field commands and allies
- ○ purposes of various meetings
- ○ communication with the president

Decisions. This section will examine the objectives, alternatives, consequences, and choices of the decision makers. Unlike with models of rational choice, we reject the concept of the unitary, heroic decision maker who stands above the process and selects the alternative that is most value maximizing. Instead we substitute the concept of the harried official, invariably the president, who tries to evaluate a multitude of alternatives, assesses the consequences of each, considers the recommendations of his advisors, and decides because he must. His decisions, however, are not immutable acts, but rather partial choices in a continuum of decisions that can be modified or amplified but rarely canceled. The identification of the key policy makers came under a previous heading; this section will examine the substance of crisis decisions and will include:

- ○ the evaluation of pertinent information by decision makers
- ○ the perception of the character of the adversary
- ○ the discussion of the adversary's intentions or motives
- ○ evaluations of relative power and capabilities
- ○ discussions of U.S. interests in the region
- ○ the enumeration of alternatives
- ○ perceptions of possible reactions of the adversary, third parties, and domestic interest groups
- ○ choice among the options

Operational implementation. Once the decision to act is made, the nation delegates the authority to conduct military and diplomatic operations to units at great distances from Washington. These operations have become increasingly susceptible to highly centralized control by sophisticated long-line communications, and a command and control network can connect the lowest tactical levels directly to the president. This capability presents obvious benefits, but not without costs. While the uniformed military acknowledge the legitimacy of "civilian control," they often interpret that control to stop with the decision to commit or not to commit force and assert that, once this strategic decision is made, the execution of it ought to be left to professional military men. Historically, the constitutional mandate to the president as commander in chief of the armed forces has not been acknowledged by the military to imply *command* in the normal military sense. The question that most military men and many analysts continually ask is: to what degree does presidential direction of tactical matters constitute interference with military commanders and the principle of unity of command?

The discussion and analysis of operational implementation should include:

○ the means of implementation (military, diplomatic)
○ the role of the commander in chief
○ the availability of forces
○ the deployment of forces
○ the role of the field commander
○ command, control, and communications

Outcomes—tactical, international, and domestic. The outcomes of an international political/military crisis can be analyzed on several levels and against numerous criteria. This study will specify three levels and three areas of interest and apply them in a comparative analysis of the two cases. The first level is tactical—the immediate environment of the confrontation of adversaries. Beyond the specific geographical environment there is the general milieu of international politics—relations between the superpowers and with other parties. Finally, there is the level of domestic concerns—interest groups, presidential popularity, and executive-legislative relations.

On the third level, perhaps the most active element has been the Congress. Increasingly, since the Vietnam War, the Congress has articulated a strong public interest in the limitation of presidential power to involve the United States in situations of hostility with foreign powers. This oversight role of the Congress has been expressed in the War Powers Resolution (see Appendix C), and since 1973 each crisis has brought with it discussions about the applicability and desirability of this resolution's provisions.

The three levels of analysis can be evaluated against three areas of interest—substantive outcomes, the techniques of attainment, and the extent of resolution. Thus, the substantive outcomes of each crisis can be evaluated in regard to the tactical situation, international changes, and domestic judgments. The range of outcomes can vary from conclusive to inconclusive, and the techniques of attainment can include compellence, deterrence, the use of force, or negotiations.

The individual outcomes of a crisis can be discussed in a comparative sense, but they are most properly evaluated against the objectives and interests of the key policy makers. Thus, one of the principal questions that one must ask in any international crisis is whether the objective of the decision makers was achieved. However, very few objectives are deemed worthy of unlimited resources, so the real question must be whether the objective was achieved with economy of force. Among the specific factors that deserve attention are:

- o   original objectives and changes in them
- o   substantive international and domestic results
- o   methods of achieving the results
- o   the degree of conclusiveness
- o   any changes in the adversaries' influence

A Concise Verbal Model of Crisis Decision Making

The national security policy-making system for responding to international crises consists of *key policy makers* who live and work in a complex international and domestic *context.* This situational context creates a high level of "background noise," which often precludes the intelligence community from providing strategic or tactical warning to avoid *surprise.* Thus, detection of the *crisis event* and initial notification rely heavily upon *organizational and interdepartmental procedures,* as do the search for information and development of a course of action. The threat to important values and the perceived short time for response have historically led to the rapid emergence of a small, high-level *decisional unit* which discusses and presents alternative courses of action to the president. The president then makes *decisions* and orders *operational implementation,* which is extraordinarily dependent upon human and technical means for command, control, and communications. These actions result in tactical *outcomes,* which in turn trigger international and domestic reactions. The tactical results, the decisions, and the entire decision process then lead into a new cycle of scrutiny by the key policy makers by the bureaucracy, the public, the press, and the Congress, where these outcomes are evaluated against constitutional, strategic, and popular standards.

An Organizational Flow Model

Many of the elements of our framework can be represented visually. The accompanying diagram (Figure 1) displays the essential factors and relates them to the dominant dynamic of crisis—its flow from crisis event to decision to implementation. Represented in the visual model are the following: the situational context (separated into its international and domestic environments); the crisis event (the stimulus, occurring usually by surprise); a perceptual lens (which distorts each actor's image of the situation); a spectrum of actors (the major departments and their principals); the phases of crisis (representing organizational planning procedures); the decisional unit (the small, high-level group); a decision (the choice of a strategic action); implementation (which constitutes state action); signal distortion (because the adversary views the action through his own perceptual lens); and feedback (which can create a reaction and interaction cycle). The visual model is not meant to be conclusive or analytically complete. It is only designed to represent the major crisis elements in a decision-flow network, to be suggestive of crisis relationships, and to be heuristic.

THE SELECTION OF CASES

The *Mayaguez* and Korean DMZ cases were selected for analysis because they: (1) met the definition of crisis established in Chapter 1; (2) involved at least the deployment, if not the use, of military forces; and (3) were recent incidents whose resolution forms part of the environment for future crisis decisions.

The *Mayaguez* case is important because it represents the first major use of offensive military force since the end of the Vietnam War. The *Mayaguez* seizure took place within a few weeks of the fall of Saigon to North Vietnamese forces and the

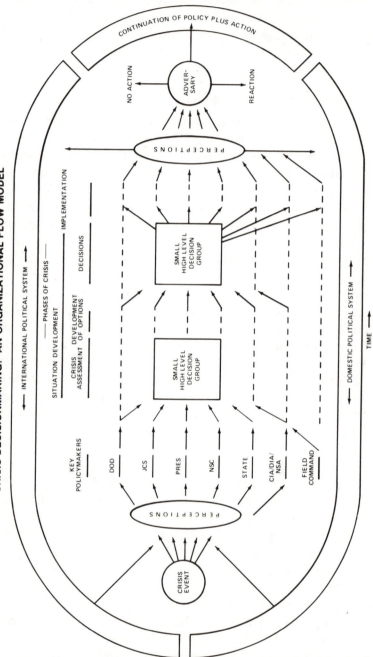

FIGURE 1

CRISIS DECISIONMAKING: AN ORGANIZATIONAL FLOW MODEL

extensive effort taken by U.S. forces to evacuate 145,000 South Vietnamese from the mainland. The *Mayaguez* capture came as a total surprise to U.S. decision makers, who perceived a short time for response if the United States were to prevent the crew from being taken ashore, where any efforts at rescue would have been much more difficult.

There was some question in Congress and among citizens as to what was actually threatened in the *Mayaguez* incident. Although merchant vessels of U.S. registry had been detained before, this seizure was perceived as an unusually hostile act. The president and his top advisors quickly identified a threat to both the prestige and influence of the nation and to their own administrative competence. The fall of Vietnam was seen throughout the world as the coup de grace of a ten-year defeat for the United States. U.S. credibility in the eyes of allies and adversaries was in question. At issue was the status of the United States as a great power, with all that implies in terms of commitments, resolve, and the ability to act decisively.

The episode on the Korean DMZ in which two American army officers were killed by North Korean soldiers is the second case. The threat to the United States that this represented is linked to the three years of war between the United States/ South Korea/United Nations forces on one side and the armies of North Korea and the People's Republic of China (PRC) on the other. The incident was not so threatening in itself (although the killings were deplorable), but it recalled earlier Korean aggression and escalation; and historically, border incursions have been precursors of major conflict. The short time for response was not as critical in this case as in the *Mayaguez* incident, but the participants widely perceived the need for swift action. That the decision makers in Washington were surprised by the incident is not in doubt. The question of whether they should have been warned is an age-old intelligence inquiry that will be examined in this case and in that of the *Mayaguez*. The Korean DMZ crisis, like the *Mayaguez* crisis, represented an immediate increase in the probability of military action; it even posed the possibility of another Korean war.

The information generated in these cases will be organized and integrated into the framework we have developed. The framework's purpose is to channel our thoughts and to lead us into a search for the important explanatory factors in crisis decision-making cases. Before we get to the cases, however, it may be useful to sketch the major organizations involved in crisis management and to review some of their procedures.

3
The National Security Decision-making Process

The ultimate responsibility for formulating U.S. policy in the resolution of a crisis lies with the president. Both the substance and process of how the crisis is resolved will reflect his personality and belief system and those of his key advisors. Automated or standard operating procedures, regardless of their efficiency, are unlikely to supplant this human contribution, which will continue irrespective of the level of technological or organizational sophistication developed for crisis management. As Roger Hilsman stated in response to a question on the Nixon-Kissinger approach to national security decision making:

> I am skeptical of organizational gimmicks. I don't think you can improve foreign policy by up- or down-grading the NSC, or creating a special action group. The way you improve foreign policy is to get good people into key positions.[1]

This use of top level officials and close personal associates as advisors is common to all past presidents. This chapter will not examine in detail past presidential styles or the character of the small advisory groups that contributed so heavily to each president's modus operandi. For illustrative purposes, however, we will briefly describe how some of our recent presidents have managed the bureaucratic process during periods of crisis and how they organized and utilized their advisors in making decisions. This chapter will examine the National Security Council system—its evolution and use during the Nixon and Ford presidencies—the Joint Chiefs of Staff crisis action system, the

Department of State organization for crisis, and the role of Congress and the key policy makers in the 1975-76 time period.

THE NATIONAL SECURITY COUNCIL SYSTEM

The National Security Council (NSC), established by the National Security Act of 1947, consists of the president, the vice president, the secretary of state, and the secretary of defense. The chairman of the Joint Chiefs of Staff was designated as the principal military advisor to the president and historically has attended all NSC meetings. Similarly, the director of the Central Intelligence Agency sits as the senior intelligence advisor. The NSC is assisted in the decision-making process by the NSC staff and the departmental staffs of the sitting members. The NSC "system" refers to the established procedures for acquiring and analyzing facts, the development and presentation of clear policy options for decision, and the delivery of implementing directives.

Each past president has attempted to mold the NSC system to conform to his own management concept, views, and personality. Some have viewed the NSC with disdain or uncertainty, while others have strengthened and solidified the influence of that organization.

Evolution of the NSC System

President Truman did not have complete trust in the NSC and used it only in an advisory role in his dealings with the strong cabinet officers and agencies in his administration. President Eisenhower considered the NSC an organization without sufficient breadth, depth, or management capability to develop the comprehensive foreign and domestic policy evaluations he needed for decision making. He therefore created an elaborate staff structure to coordinate the numerous agencies and bureaus in the federal government. He was convinced that this course of action was necessary to focus the efforts and attention of the NSC on a national strategy for the cold war.

President Kennedy took office in 1961 believing that the

Eisenhower NSC system was overly rigid and inflexible and did not satisfy his more informal manner of doing business. He was convinced that the bureaucratic staff procedures developed by his predecessor were ponderous, stifled creativity, and were not as responsive as would be the informal use of close personal advisors. It is perhaps worth noting that this perception of the NSC staff effectively precluded its members' active participation in the planning of the abortive Bay of Pigs operation.

President Johnson quietly attempted to deemphasize the role of the Kennedy "brain trust" of advisors. His approach was not radically different, although the advisors changed. He placed less reliance on White House associates because he felt that these individuals had preempted the role of the president without assuring that the interdepartmental foundation of the system worked and was exercised to assure consensus within the government. Too, Johnson was faced with a growing problem that would require, in his judgment, substantial presidential involvement—the Indochina war. As the U.S. commitment in Vietnam became larger and more complex, the requirement for more sophisticated and responsive command, control, communications, and intelligence systems increased accordingly. This factor, coupled with President Johnson's propensity for personal involvement at all echelons, led to the creation of a command, control, and communications system which enabled him to participate directly in even the tactical level of operations. His style was characterized by wide-ranging and informal "consultations," which led to some serious problems for the NSC staff and other agencies of the bureaucracy. Often staff members were not informed of his decisions directly, and had to employ back-door methods for determining what had been decided. President Johnson's wish to be very closely involved in directing the course of the war in Vietnam led to the establishment of a very active, but restricted, presidential advisory body called the "Tuesday Lunch Group." It was composed of as many as five of his closest advisors, including the secretaries of state and defense, who met periodically—usually on a Tuesday at lunch— to consider options and to decide national security policy.

President Nixon made perhaps the most comprehensive overhaul of the national security policy process since creation of the NSC in 1947. In his "Report to the Congress on United States Foreign Policy" in February 1970, he set forth his concept and detailed procedures for how the NSC system would operate. The NSC system that he visualized drew heavily on his experience during the Eisenhower administration, his observation of the Kennedy and Johnson administrations, and his personal evaluation of the strengths and weaknesses of each.

President Ford took the NSC mechanism that he inherited and retained it essentially unchanged with respect to its role in crisis planning. He did carry out a thorough analysis of the intelligence community and greatly strengthened the role of the NSC and the director of central intelligence in overseeing and controlling the activities of each element of the community. In addition, he shifted the chairmanship of the Defense Program Review Committee (renamed the Defense Review Panel) to the Defense Department, but this had no impact on crisis planning (see Figure 2). The national security decision-making process as established by President Nixon and continued by President Ford was designed to meet six requirements:

1. *Creativity:* a positive and imaginative foreign policy rather than a reactive one
2. *Determination of facts:* reliable information, intelligently discussed from all points of view
3. *Systematic planning:* thorough and deliberate analysis
4. *Range of options:* alternatives debated and views defended to allow consideration of all implications prior to a decision
5. *Crisis planning:* crises anticipated and prevented whenever possible and supported by a systematic contingency-planning system that would consider all aspects of the problem
6. *Implementation:* effective, coordinated action constantly reviewed for modification in light of new information and other considerations

The previous descriptions highlight the surface factors of greatest influence on past presidents in shaping their organizations for national security decision making. Their goals as well

FIGURE 2
THE NATIONAL SECURITY COUNCIL STRUCTURE

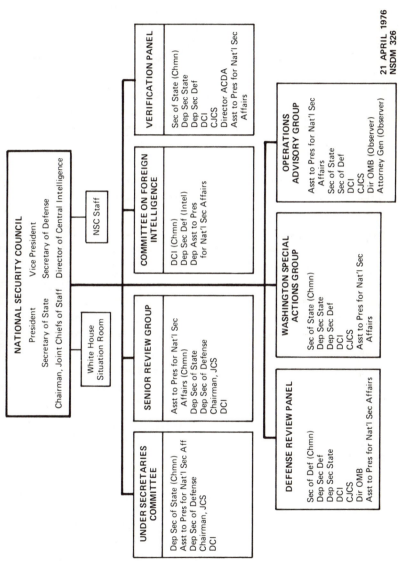

NATIONAL SECURITY COUNCIL

President
Vice President
Secretary of State
Secretary of Defense
Chairman, Joint Chiefs of Staff
Director of Central Intelligence

White House Situation Room

NSC Staff

UNDER SECRETARIES COMMITTEE

Dep Sec of State (Chmn)
Asst to Pres for Nat'l Sec Aff
Dep Sec of Defense
Chairman, JCS
DCI

SENIOR REVIEW GROUP

Asst to Pres for Nat'l Sec Affairs (Chmn)
Dep Sec of State
Dep Sec of Defense
Chairman, JCS
DCI

COMMITTEE ON FOREIGN INTELLIGENCE

DCI (Chmn)
Dep Sec Def (Intel)
Dep Asst to Pres for Nat'l Sec Affairs

VERIFICATION PANEL

Sec of State (Chmn)
Dep Sec State
Dep Sec Def
DCI
CJCS
Director ACDA
Asst to Pres for Nat'l Sec Affairs

DEFENSE REVIEW PANEL

Sec of Def (Chmn)
Dep Sec Def
Dep Sec State
DCI
CJCS
Dir OMB
Asst to Pres for Nat'l Sec Affairs

WASHINGTON SPECIAL ACTIONS GROUP

Sec of State (Chmn)
Dep Sec State
Dep Sec Def
DCI
CJCS
Asst to Pres for Nat'l Sec Affairs

OPERATIONS ADVISORY GROUP

Asst to Pres for Nat'l Sec Affairs
Sec of State
Sec of Def
DCI
CJCS
Dir OMB (Observer)
Attorney Gen (Observer)

21 APRIL 1976
NSDM 326

as their apprehensions were much more subtle, however, than these brief paragraphs indicate. In the United States, presidents come to office for four or eight years. Having served in government and having read thoroughly the history of past administrations, each new president arrives in office with two overriding concerns. The first is an overwhelming drive to reorient the course of U.S. policy by changing goals, priorities, the substance of policy, and/or the modalities through which it is conducted. The second is a clear recognition of the enormity of that task in even an eight-year period, given the historically ponderous pace of the vast governmental bureaucracy.

Presidents arrive at the White House with very mixed feelings toward the bureaucracy. All would acknowledge that it contains creative experts, thoughtful analysts, and experienced diplomats, and most presidents would like to draw this wisdom out of the lower reaches of the departments. The question is how to do it. Experience tells them that even with the best of intentions and total dedication they may fail miserably. Even if their planning system succeeds in getting some new ideas to emerge from the working level, there is no guarantee that those ideas will survive the review of a strong-willed assistant secretary or an even stronger willed secretary. Even if they do survive, will it not have been at the expense of caveats which mask the kernel of truth in the original, or delays which make it irrelevant. This prospect has led some presidents (e.g., Kennedy, and to some extent Johnson) to forsake any effort at a comprehensive, horizontally integrated planning system and to rely predominantly on a small band of high-level officials or aides. The risks of this tendency have been treated at length elsewhere, the most frequently cited example being the Bay of Pigs failure. There are other risks, however, which became more pronounced in the late 1960s, as bureaucrats, disaffected over Vietnam policy, began to voice their dissent to journalists—journalists who were either similarly dissaffected or simply better investigators and less inhibited than their predecessors. Thus, the administration found its ability to maintain "water-tight integrity" (in the naval sense) seriously corroded, with all that implied for policy formulation and implementation. Although originally legitimized by Vietnam-related dissent, the practice of leaking spread to all areas of policy, weapons development and acquisition, and policy implementation. The moral of the period can be summarized in a corruption of the well-known aphorism "Hell hath no fury like a bureaucrat scorned."

This trend was likely to be reinforced for another reason in 1969. By most accounts, the bureaucracy is overwhelmingly non-Republican. This is not to say anti-Republican; however, faced with a request from a Senate Democratic staff member for information on the status of an ongoing, sensitive policy study, the average Defense employee would have found it easy to agree that the Congress should be well informed.

The political coloration of the bureaucracy and the implications of Democratic control of the Congress were thoroughly appreciated by President Nixon. There was no question that a small "band of brothers" approach to national security policy formulation simply would not have worked. To be fair, however, there is no evidence to suggest that such an exclusive approach was ever considered. To the contrary, President Nixon's commitment to a process which elicited the broadest range of options and fullest possible review throughout the government was often stated publicly and was given credibility by the management features of the system which assured that these objectives would be achieved.

The NSC system relied for policy planning upon interdepartmental groups (IGs), chaired at the assistant secretary level, but populated by department and agency representatives at least one and usually two or three levels into the career bureaucracy. For a description of how this procedure worked see pages 55–58.

The role of the NSC staff in making the system work may deserve further treatment, however. NSC staff members can perform two important functions. First, as competent regional and functional experts, they can bring up for the president's consideration those issues which require policy review, noting possible solutions for analysis during the study. Subject to his approval, the studies—the analysis of the issues and development of policy options—would be launched. As mentioned above, the NSC staff officer would serve as a member of the working group. The other important function carried out by these officers is day-to-day oversight and management of the national security community through daily contact with their counterparts in State, Defense, Treasury, Commerce, Agriculture, CIA, ACDA, AID, and USIA. This role is especially valuable in assuring that once policy decisions are made by the president they are implemented in keeping with his intentions.

The men who were brought to the senior positions of the NSC staff in 1969 were eminently qualified to fulfill both of these functions. Most of them had been in government for many years but were notable exceptions to the normal pattern of military or foreign service careers: Helmut Sonnenfeldt, a foreign service mustang who had risen to the upper level of the service by dint of extraordinary knowledge and insight into Soviet history, doctrine, strategy, goals and weaknesses; William Hyland, for more than fifteen years an intelligence specialist in Soviet affairs, a respected author on Soviet internal politics, a master of the complex technology of strategic arms and of Soviet negotiating techniques, a brilliant analyst and extraordinarily effective manager/arbiter/moderator of the interdepartmental policy process. It would be difficult to overstate Hyland's contribution, particularly during the Ford administration, to the progress made in SALT II and to the continuity and coherence of the NSC policy process. Another standout was Lawrence Eagleburger, a foreign service officer who combined extraordinary intellect with uncanny skill in assessing the political feasibility—both domestic and foreign—of policy options spanning the complete spectrum of politico-economic issues. Eagleburger also had the uncommon ability to write eloquently and intelligibly with very little advance notice, on virtually any subject. An equally admirable quality was his courageous irreverence toward blatant incompetence in government. For an example see the excerpt from his letter to the GAO following his investigation of the *Mayaguez* incident, on page 145.

The director of NSC planning was Richard T. Kennedy, a tough senior army colonel who, through lengthy service in the Pentagon and in the field, had developed an extremely thoughtful but forceful ability to define problems and orchestrate the often parochial and dissident departmental players toward workable solutions. There are few, if any, men in Washington who know as much about national security planning, programming, and budgeting as Kennedy (now a commissioner of the Nuclear Regulatory Commission). The director of Middle East plans and operations was Harold Saunders, a veteran of twelve years on the NSC staff, who is an acknowledged and widely respected expert on Middle East matters and ultimately perhaps the key staff contributor to the successful U.S. effort to lead the parties toward a peace after the October 1973 war. The list of highly experienced, thoughtful, talented men who made the system work over the years could continue.

In many ways the president's best appointment—in terms of assuring highly effective performance of the NSC system during the Nixon and Ford administrations—was Brent Scowcroft, who will be discussed in the next chapter.

NSC Organization 1969–1977

The NSC staff performed the staff work associated with decision papers going to the president and acted as the corporate memory for that body. In the 1969–1977 time period, there were two functional subdivisions within the NSC system, each of which was assigned a specific management role. As described in "National Security Decision Memorandum (NSDM) 326," published April 26, 1976, these included planning and operational groups.

Planning Groups

Five types of groups were concerned with planning.

Interdepartmental groups (IG). There were six of these groups, one for each of the five major geographical subdivisions of the world and a politico-military group. These groups, with representation from all appropriate agencies, once asked by the president to study a given area, defined the basic issues requiring decision by the NSC and provided a range of analyzed options for discussion by the Senior Review Group or the full NSC.

Senior Review Group (SRG). A policy-planning group was composed of the assistant to the president for national security affairs (chairman), the deputy secretaries of state and defense, the director of central intelligence, and the chairman, Joint Chiefs of Staff. The SRG reviewed the work of the interdepartmental groups to be sure that the issues, options, and agency views were presented fully and fairly.

Verification panel (VP). A senior group (same level as the SRG) was responsible for strategic and conventional arms limitations and monitoring, the capabilities of potential adversaries, and the means of verifying compliance with possible agreements in this area. This group played a major role in preparation for the Strategic Arms Limitations talks with the Soviet Union and the Mutual Balanced Force Reductions talks in Europe.

Defense Review Panel (DRP). This panel reviewed major defense policy and program issues which had strategic, political, diplomatic, and economic implications in relation to overall national priorities.

Committee on Foreign Intelligence. This group controlled budget preparation and resource allocation for the U.S. foreign intelligence program. It established policy for the management of the program, including priorities for collection and production of national intelligence, and provided continuing guidance to the intelligence community in order to ensure compliance with the policy of the NSC.

Operational Groups

There were three groups which operated within the framework of current events and policy decisions already made by the president.

Operations Advisory Group (OAG). The OAG considered and made recommendations to the president on special sensitive activities in support of U.S. national foreign policy objectives, and conducted periodic reviews of these activities.

Washington Special Actions Group (WSAG). The WSAG was organized to meet the special need for coordination in crisis situations. Its interagency membership served as a management team to assure flexible and timely recommendation and implementation of presidential decisions. During its early years, the WSAG's major objective was to anticipate crises; to do this, it stimulated and reviewed contingency plans prepared by the interdepartmental groups. Its major purpose in a crisis situation was to develop options for NSC or presidential consideration. Its operation will be examined in great detail in Chapter 6.

Under-Secretaries Committee. This group was charged with the responsibility for overseeing implementation of the president's decisions and developing programs and recommendations for carrying out policy decisions.

Operation of the NSC System

During noncrisis periods when an issue was raised which required a presidential decision, a National Security Study Memorandum (NSSM) was written which defined the issue, set out the terms of reference of the study, assigned responsibility for its preparation to a particular group (normally one of the interdepartmental groups described above), set a due date for completion of the study, and indicated which of the intermediate groups would review the study.

The selected interdepartmental group, composed of representatives from all agencies concerned with the issue, responded to the NSSM by outlining specific issues, U.S. objectives, advantages and disadvantages of each objective, the estimated budgetary impact (if appropriate), and some possible consequences that might be expected from a decision along the lines of each option.

This study was then forwarded to the appropriate senior-level group, where it was reviewed to ensure that all viable options had been included and that the options and agency views were fully and fairly stated. If there was agreement among the agencies to recommend a particular option to the president, the issue could be forwarded to the president in a memorandum drafted and coordinated by the NSC staff. If, however, the issue was an exceptionally important one or if there was disagreement among the agencies as to the recommended option, an NSC meeting was scheduled so that the president could hear the views of his senior advisors directly. The issues and the options were carefully presented to the president, and he usually asked each member present for his views and recommendations. These meetings could be long and detailed, with the president asking many questions and the members engaging in considerable debate as to the possible courses of action.

NSC Meeting Format

The formal structure of the NSC extended into the meetings where critical issues and possible options were debated. According to observers, NSC meetings followed a set pattern, whether conducted during crisis or noncrisis periods. The pattern established for NSC meetings was designed to:

○ determine the facts
○ determine the motives behind the issue or crisis that brought it to the attention of the NSC
○ determine U.S. interests and objectives
○ assess possible interests and objectives of third countries
○ discuss options to achieve U.S. objectives, be they diplomatic (bilateral, multilateral, or through international organizations); military (courses of action, relocation of forces, immediate reactions); or economic (domestic and international)
○ discuss possible reactions to the various options by allies, neutrals, and adversaries

Based on the discussion and the papers presented, the president reached his decision, which was formalized in a National Security Decision Memorandum (NSDM). The NSDM informed the appropriate departments and agencies of the president's decision in specific terms and in as much detail as required, and included directives for operational activity and for reporting on implementation. As is evident, the focal point for the NSC system is the president. During crisis and noncrisis periods Presidents Nixon and Ford managed the security of the country through this system.

By law the president is the commander in chief of the armed forces and he bears the ultimate responsibility for their employment and for the security of the nation. The powers and functions of the president's principal advisors are individual matters and largely depend on each president's preference.

Since 1947, all presidents have had an assistant for national security affairs, whose responsibilities and prerogatives have ranged from the essentially administrative (Sidney W. Souers in the Truman administration) to the extremely strong, substantive position enjoyed by Henry Kissinger and Brent Scowcroft under both Presidents Nixon and Ford.[2] Historically, presidents have relied heavily on selected advisors, regardless of their bureaucratic status, in whom they had great confidence and trust. This has, on occasion, led to situations where a cabinet member was completely overshadowed by an advisor. As President Nixon's assistant for national security affairs, Henry Kissinger overshadowed Secretary of State William Rogers. After Rogers' resignation in September 1973, President Nixon relieved part of this structural tension by appointing Kissinger as secretary of state, retaining however his role and title as assistant for national security affairs. President John F. Kennedy used his brother, Attorney General Robert Kennedy, extensively in an advisory role, and Lyndon Johnson similarly called on Clark Clifford and Abe Fortas. Figure 3 depicts the circle of advisors available to the president, although each chief executive develops his own balance of their influences.

Despite the importance of selected individuals, however, it is the president who governs, who is ultimately responsible, and who is situated in a position to control the substance and process of crisis resolution. The role of advisors is important, but the president determines how decisions will be made during times of crisis. Historically, presidents have never hesitated to intervene in operational matters when they felt the various departments were not following the letter or intent of their orders or when they felt it necessary to get information directly from the source. President Kennedy conversed directly with the destroyer commander during the Cuban missile crisis in 1962, and President Johnson bypassed many echelons in his discussions with local commanders during the Dominican Republic crisis. More recently, through satellite communications, President Ford or advisors speaking for him were in frequent contact with the embassies in Phnom Penh and Saigon during the evacuations of Cambodia and Vietnam. It is human nature, no less in presidents of the United States than in other people, to

FIGURE 3
SOURCES OF ADVICE AVAILABLE TO THE PRESIDENT DURING CRISIS DECISIONMAKING

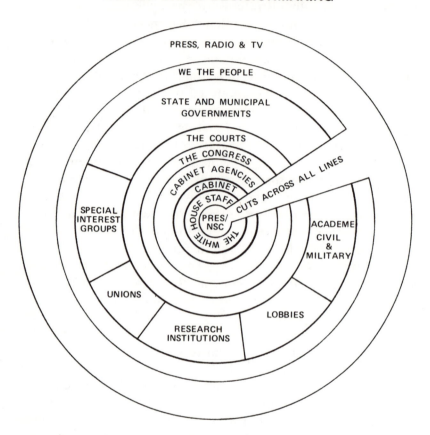

want to be at the center of the action—especially when one is ultimately responsible for success or failure. Instantaneous communications have reinforced the president's capability to personally and intensively manage and direct the agencies and organizations on the crisis scene.

The National Security Council During Crisis

The NSC subcommittee responsible for supporting the president during crises, the Washington Special Actions Group

(WSAG) provided an institutionalized means for information search and decision making. Figure 4 shows the resources available to the president to conduct this search, generate options, make decisions, and carry them out. At first glance, the organization seems to function in a rigid and stereotyped style, and the departments would seem to interact only very formally. This is not completely true. Within the various departments, there are directives and standard operating procedures to guide their actions, but these are simply guides. The departments and agencies interact with each other, both formally and informally, during a crisis, and their internal procedures provide a flexibility designed to react to changing situations. One of these, to be examined in detail later in this chapter, is the crisis action system of the Joint Chiefs of Staff.

The most critical factor determining the extent of the search for information is time. Time, or the lack of it, will always be a factor in the reaction capability of all players involved in the crisis. In many instances, this time restriction may be self-imposed, as when it is decided that if certain events or concessions do not transpire by a designated time, specific retaliatory action will be taken. In other situations there may not be a specified reaction time, only a vague sense of urgency that a solution must be found quickly. In either case, time is perceived as the key factor in the diversification and exhaustiveness of the information search.

The first step in making intelligent decisions during a crisis is to determine as accurately as possible what is going on. There are three key contributors to this process: the director of central intelligence, who as the principal intelligence advisor to the president coordinates the work of the community while concurrently managing the use of the resources of the CIA; the Defense Intelligence Agency, which commands enormous capabilities for collecting and evaluating crisis information of a military nature; and the State Department Bureau of Intelligence and Research (INR), which contributes assessments of a political nature based upon diplomatic message traffic and embassy reports. Depending upon the nature of the crisis (aircraft hijacking, terrorist kidnapping, ship seizure, conventional military attack) important contributions may also be

FIGURE 4

Function Flow Diagram of the
NATIONAL SECURITY COUNCIL CRISIS MANAGEMENT STRUCTURE[1]

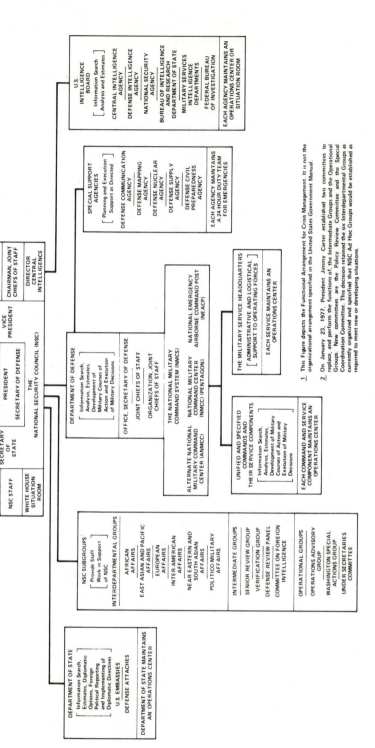

1 This **Figure** depicts the Functional Arrangement for Crisis Management. It is not the organizational arrangement specified in the United States Government Manual.

2 On January 23, 1977, President Jimmy Carter established two committees to replace, and perform the functions of, the Intermediate Groups and the Operational Groups. New committees are the Policy Review Committee and the Special Coordination Committee. This decision retained the six Interdepartmental Groups as currently organized and specified that NSC Ad Hoc Groups would be established as required to meet new or developing situations.

made by the National Security Agency, the FBI, the intelligence unit of the Department of the Treasury and representatives of the Energy Research and Development Administration (now the Department of Energy). This community relies upon technical systems and human information sources in the United States and overseas. In an overseas area, principal information sources include the ambassador, his country team (Foreign Service sources, the defense attaché system, intelligence community representatives, and other special representatives on the scene), and the resources of the military unified command for the area in question. Information is transmitted to the participating agencies by a variety of communications means; many of them are a part of the Worldwide Military Command and Control System, described in Chapter 4. When information arrives in the Washington area, it is disseminated to the various intelligence offices over special dedicated communication subsystems which include a conference call capability linking watch officers and analysts in the Central Intelligence Agency, Defense Intelligence Agency, organization of the Joint Chiefs of Staff (director for operations), the State Department, the White House Situation Room, and the National Security Agency. These networks enable the exchange of raw data, evaluated information, or requests for further information. Currently under development is a new system that would link several of the agencies through the use of interconnected minicomputers. The new system would allow all participants using a computer console to pass, store, edit, or update information, thus allowing messages to be developed and coordinated in a fraction of the time previously spent in the electronic transmission of messages.

Each of the principal agencies providing information and advice to the National Security Council and the president has available an operations center to coordinate the information search and the issuance of orders and directives. In addition to these specialized communications setups devoted to the network of watch officers and analysts, each operations center has an extensive, and often redundant, communications system for support, which includes radio, telephone, teletype, facsimile transmission, and message-handling capabilities. During a major crisis, both interdepartmental and worldwide communications increase significantly.

MILITARY CRISIS MANAGEMENT PROCEDURES

As will be described in Chapter 4, on the Military Command and Control System, the National Military Command System is the single most important element of the system. The National Military Command Center (NMCC), located at the Pentagon in Washington, D.C., is the principal means by which the president may exercise command and control over the military forces involved in a crisis. Through the NMCC, the president orders execution of the response required to attain the national objective in a crisis.

The NMCC operates on a continuous basis and is staffed by operations teams composed of Joint Staff personnel and representatives of the DIA, CIA, NSA, and OSD (public affairs). During minor crises, these teams may be augmented by additional Joint Staff representatives, and Service and State Department personnel. As the intensity of the situation increases, specifically organized teams may be formed to devote full attention to the crisis while the NMCC operations teams continue with their primary responsibility of monitoring the world situation.

The NMCC has detailed procedures for three levels of operation: day-to-day, minor crisis, and major crisis. During day-to-day operations, when nothing unusual enough to invoke crisis procedures is going on, the first of these sets of procedures is in effect. Worldwide situation monitoring is in progress and situation and intelligence reports are being routinely transmitted. The current operations teams conduct communications checks as required to ensure that emergency communications are possible, and test messages are exchanged periodically with the USSR over the Washington-to-Moscow Communications Command hotline. If a situation develops which exceeds the operations team's limited capability, provisions are made to augment the team with Joint Staff and service personnel having expertise in the particular area. When an event occurs somewhere in the world that may develop into a crisis involving the possible use of United States military forces, a crisis-action team is formed.

The crisis-action team is headed by the chief of the Current

Operations Division and the majority of its members are from this group (J-3). The remainder of its members come from the Defense Intelligence Agency, Central Intelligence Agency, the services, and other divisions of the Joint Staff. The crisis-action team has the necessary manning to keep information and orders flowing, to develop courses of action, and to coordinate decisions during minor crises. If a crisis escalates to an intensity requiring greater participation by the Joint Chiefs of Staff personally, the NMCC shifts to a higher gear. For example, planning responsibility might be assigned to a higher-level team chaired by the director of operations himself. Such a group would probably organize on a shift basis for twenty-four-hour coverage; its membership would likely include (per shift): a vice-chairman, a team chief and planners from within Operations, Logistics, and Plans and Policy; and representatives from all agencies with a role to play. This group would perform essentially the same functions as the crisis-action team, but with its higher-ranking members and broader representation, it would carry greater authority and would signal the urgency necessary to expedite action.

The crisis-action system has the capability to distill the information transmitted during the crisis to its essence so as to facilitate the development of military courses of action for consideration at the NSC level and the execution of a decision involving the use of U.S. forces, as directed by the president.

The system envisages a logical sequence of events in the life of a crisis from problem recognition to the execution of an operation order. The six phases are situation development; crisis assessment; course of action development; decision; execution planning; and execution.

JCS CRISIS PHASES

Situation Development

During normal worldwide monitoring, if an event of significance is detected by military personnel, it is reported to the JCS through the operational reporting system or perhaps as a critical information communication report.

If the Joint Chiefs of Staff were to decide that the situation warranted review or if it appeared to be developing the potential for adversely affecting United States' interests, Phase 2 would be entered.

Crisis Assessment

Many means are available to define and understand developing crises. Increased reporting is normally ordered through both military and diplomatic channels. Answers are analyzed, possible solutions are evaluated, and alternative solutions discussed.

At this point, the first White House level meeting (NSC or WSAG) might well occur. At such a meeting, the participants would be briefed on the situation and tasks assigned for the development of diplomatic and military options.

Course of Action Development

This phase involves the analysis of alternative means of achieving the objective; translating these general concepts to plans; and tentatively alerting those forces which might ultimately become involved. Field commanders would be asked for their estimates with appropriate recommendations of military courses of action for consideration by the JCS and the NSC. Once this information is assembled, evaluated, and organized, it is presented to the JCS and ultimately to the president by the chairman of the JCS and the secretary of defense, during Phase 4.

Decision

Once the analytical and planning work has been completed by Defense, State, and possibly other departments, the decision unit (NSC or WSAG) would be called together. At the meeting, the possible combinations of diplomatic, military and/or economic options would be thoroughly discussed. Serious consideration would be given by the NSC to the "signals" sent to friends and potential adversaries by repositioning military forces. During the meeting or soon thereafter, the president would decide what steps the U.S. government should take and would announce these decisions to the officials responsible.

Execution Planning

Once the decision is made to execute a specific military course of action, an operation order is prepared. Such an order translates the concept and overall objective into specific military tactics—phased movement of forces, fire support, communications arrangements, logistic support, etc.—for achieving the objective.

Execution

Once the execution order is issued, the task shifts to monitoring the thousands of political-military actions which take place. As the operation is carried out, the adversary may react, make concessions, or escalate the crisis diplomatically or militarily. For this reason, the president must be able to control events closely. The system has been designed to provide this essential flexibility. It must permit a holding period, if this is deemed appropriate from the national point of view. The situation may be identified and may develop so fast that entire phases may be reduced to a few hours or minutes, or may be skipped entirely.

In summarizing the formal system for information search and crisis planning, several conclusions can be reached:

1. Time is the most critical factor during any crisis.
2. While the president can and does employ the talents of a small, high-level group of advisors during the decision phase of a crisis, and functions in an ad hoc mode during this phase, supporting agencies and departments have established procedures that are followed.
3. The volume of communications takes a dramatic jump, but the established lines of communication and the interaction of agencies do not change appreciably.

DEPARTMENT OF STATE ORGANIZATION FOR CRISIS

Under normal conditions, the responsibility within the Department of State for receipt, evaluation, and distribution of worldwide reporting cables rests with the Operations Center.[3] It is the senior watch officer who has the earliest opportunity to judge the crisis potential of a given report and to activate the department's crisis system. (JCS military representatives, each of whom have had at least one year of duty in the NMCC, are available in the State Operations Center to assist in the interpretation of the military implications of various actions.) Specifically, when a report judged to have immediate crisis impact is received, the senior watch officer determines the level at which to sound alerts. In recent experience, sources of initial alerts have ranged from the country desk officer to the under secretary of state for political affairs. The complete alerting process could take place in as little as five minutes or, if interrupted by a judgment to collect more information, could result in the secretary not receiving word until much later, perhaps during his next regular review of intelligence and other cable reports.

In contrast to the Joint Chiefs of Staff and CIA, there is no crisis management separation between planning and operations at the State Department. The regional bureaus are small, not exclusively oriented toward operational matters, and may be somewhat overtaxed when called upon to devote total activity to crisis functions—political analysis, development of alternative courses of action, writing of situation reports, preparation of press guidance, interdepartmental coordination, and periodic meetings on a twenty-four-hour basis. The State crisis system operates on an ad hoc basis as specific needs are perceived. Crisis-action teams are not organized on a permanent basis, and thus the crisis system does not enjoy the kind of staff support available to the Joint Chiefs of Staff, where planners, operators, intelligence analysts, and supervisory personnel are task-organized in sufficient numbers to permit sustained operations across the full range of anticipated crisis actions.

Within the State Department, the formal determination that a crisis exists is made by the secretary. However, no special organization or procedures are automatically invoked. The secretary may direct that a task force be established, but, historically, even then, its makeup and duties have been determined ad hoc according to the preference of the task force director, normally the assistant secretary for the region concerned. If the crisis is not sufficiently threatening to warrant a task force, a working group may be formed with somewhat less formality (e.g., no required situation reports).

The task force is located in the Operations Center in spaces specifically designed for that purpose. Thus, it has immediate access to communications facilities for messages both to and from the field, as well as some secure voice and telecopying capabilities for coordinating written matter with other departments and the White House. The task force is normally composed of the assistant secretary, at least one deputy assistant secretary, and as many other professionals—usually about ten—as are required or can be mustered from the ranks of the country directors and desk officers. This team is supported by the administrative staff from the regional bureau. Thus, as confirmed by interviews, the gearing up which takes place during times of crisis is perceived as disruptive to the lives of the State Department participants. Officers must leave their desks, their files, and their normal ways of doing business and establish themselves in a new environment under great pressure.

This is not to say that Defense Department professionals seek or enjoy crisis while State Department officers do not. It does appear that the Defense Department is better manned and attuned to accommodate the special demands of crisis. One could perhaps study this contrast for root causes. Is the fundamental nature of military service—eternal training toward proficiency one may never use—conducive to a mentality which welcomes crisis? For a Foreign Service officer, does the very acknowledgment of crisis represent a failure and thus stand as a threshold one seeks to avoid crossing? These are rhetorical and rather flaccid questions which are not closely tied to our primary purpose and unfortunately cannot be addressed in detail.

Once formed, the responsibilities of the task force have included preparation of situation reports at least twice daily, analysis of events for the secretary, development of alternative political and diplomatic courses of action to support the secretary's participation in interdepartmental meetings (NSC or WSAG), representing the department in interdepartmental working group meetings, and preparation of directive cables associated with implementation of a presidential decision.

Usually, the State Department task force will include representatives from other departments (Defense, CIA) and in some cases the department will send an officer to represent it on other agencies' task forces. These officers have performed more in the role of consultants on technical issues, e.g., military response times, than contributors in a policy sense.[4]

From the foregoing discussions, it might be concluded that the president and all government agencies have a road map to keep them on track in a crisis. This is an overstatement. As stressed earlier, each president, upon assuming office, has modified the structure he inherited to match his own management concept. Similarly, each head of a federal department or agency and each military commander executes his responsibility as he sees fit within his established guidelines. For this reason, organization and procedures alone will never suffice to resolve a crisis. Individuals breathe life into organizational procedures, and the structure of their belief systems is an important component of any study of decision making. We will now review the principal actors who participated in the *Mayaguez* and Korean DMZ decisions.

KEY POLICY MAKERS DURING THE PERIOD 1975-76

The President

At the time of the *Mayaguez* crisis, President Gerald Ford had been in office approximately nine months. In the area of national security matters, he had in that period travelled to Vladivostok, where he negotiated a tentative framework for a SALT II agreement, and to Japan and elsewhere in East Asia. These had been successful trips in terms of enhancing the public view of the president as a capable leader in the international community. More recent than these successes, however, and more important as a conditioning element prior to the *Mayaguez* crisis, were the calamitous collapse of South Vietnamese forces and the subsequent humiliating evacuation of U.S. forces from Southeast Asia after an exhaustive and domestically divisive ten-year struggle. Within the White House and in the nation as a whole, there was a consensus that in terms of international prestige, the United States had suffered a clear loss. Although there was undoubtedly a subconscious recognition among Americans that President Ford had not been responsible for this defeat, he obviously suffered guilt by association as the presiding chief executive. Clearly, President Ford understood the depth of disillusionment which prevailed among Americans and foreigners. Morale was low. Allies were uncertain of our ability to recover and to lead once more. The president sensed the international exigencies very keenly, and entered the crisis determined that he would not preside over another humiliation. American interests would be protected and it would be clear that America would continue to play a positive role in international affairs.

Gerald Ford's ascendancy to the presidency is unique in our history. Throughout his term in office, there were constant examples of his recognition of—even preoccupation with—the nature and requirements of his situation. Even had he been elected to succeed President Nixon, his task, to restore confidence in the presidency at home and abroad, would have been enormous. Without such a mandate, it was doubly so, requiring as it did the utmost care to gain popular understanding and backing for the countless decisions to be made. President Ford felt deeply that only through very careful deliberation and consultation with representatives from all sectors could he expect to restore credibility and pride among Americans in their president. From that conviction he adopted a fairly standard approach to all the issues he faced.

First, well before the issue required a decision, he wanted to read into it thoroughly. Perhaps a month before, he would ask for material on the subject, be it energy, reorganization of the intelligence community, or SALT. While many of these were new to him, he easily absorbed the complexities and frequently raised issues not considered before by experts. With a command of the substance, the president would then meet with interest groups to discuss the competing demands at issue. Later, he would meet with congressional leaders and personal advisors. This process might stretch out over a period of six weeks for a domestic issue, punctuated by trial balloons from the press office to stimulate public comment. Finally, with high confidence that he understood both the issue and how Americans felt about it, he would make a decision.

One step in the above description which deserves amplification concerns the domestic political element. President Ford had been a politician for most of his adult life. He obviously would not have succeeded through thirteen terms in the House without considerable political acuity. Here again the unique circumstances surrounding his accession to the presidency—or perhaps the axiom according to which all presidents "get religion" once in office—had the effect of removing politics entirely from the discussion of virtually every major issue which came before him. One case stands out in particular.

In early 1976, as the political primaries were unfolding and the character of the opposition was taking shape, political stability in southern Africa was eroding. Angola had fallen to the control of a minority Soviet- and Cuban-backed regime. Nationalist groups in Rhodesia took heart and each day became more threatening to the Salisbury regime. With or without outside help, a civil war would have meant enormous loss of life and bloodshed. President Ford saw the potential violence at hand and believed that the United States had an opportunity and a responsibility to try to prevent it. One mission by Secretary Kissinger had established a relationship of mutual confidence with the parties, and an attempt to bring the parties together seemed possible. The issue came to a head at a cabinet meeting (which was normal before deciding to launch any major initiative) in late March. It was just before the Texas primary. By this time, Ronald Reagan's candidacy, revived by his showing in North Carolina, was in high gear, and Texas promised to be an important indicator of each candidate's strength. The meeting got quickly past pleasantries and the summary of the foreign policy substance of the issue, and Kissinger's trip came under very severe attack by the president's political advisors. A bitter argument ensued, with those concerned with the president's nomination becoming extremely emotional over the political damage that the president would suffer in Texas if the African initiative were pursued. Throughout the meeting, as tempers and voices rose, the president said very little. He sat back calmly in the center, puffing on his pipe, making an occasional note, asking one or two questions. After almost two hours, both sides had tired and lapsed into an uneasy silence. The president leaned forward, put his pipe down, and delivered a very short but moving closing to the meeting. Typically, he thanked each person around the table directly; then, noting the thoughtfulness and wisdom of their remarks, he said, "I cannot judge what the political impact may be, good or bad, but we must do this because it is the right thing to do."

The Vice-president

Vice-president Nelson A. Rockefeller came to the *Mayaguez* crisis with extensive experience in international affairs spanning the administrations of six presidents and including extensive service within the Department of State and as a presidential advisor. While he was often characterized within Republican circles as a liberal, such a label was clearly inappropriate in the context of national security matters, where he had always championed a strong national defense and vigorous U.S. leadership within the international community. This strong belief in firmness under challenge was reflected throughout crisis periods in all of his contributions at NSC meetings. Although, like the president, he was not elected to his office, there is no evidence to suggest he felt any inhibitions toward asserting views which he believed represented American values and which were required to fulfill his responsibilities as a statutory member of the NSC.

Secretary of State

At the time of the *Mayaguez* crisis, Secretary Henry A. Kissinger was serving as both the secretary of state and assistant to the president for national security affairs. His participation in the NSC deliberations brought to that forum a set of qualities which were virtually unique among members during the postwar period. He had come to government from the academic community, where he had studied crisis management as a social scientist. In addition, he was an historian with a sense of the imperative of U.S. leadership of the free world almost equivalent to "manifest destiny." Although his policy proposals during his previous six years in the White House had been attacked by some as reflecting a Spenglerian pessimism toward the ability of the West to preserve itself and continue on a course of positive social development, these allegations clash with the facts, particularly as reflected by his actions during times of crisis.

Since 1969, Secretary Kissinger had been personally engaged in, and largely responsible for, U.S. actions directed toward the resolution of the Jordan crisis, in September 1970; the Middle East war, in October 1973; and the Cyprus crisis, in July 1974. While it is undoubtedly true that he was extremely conscious of the setback to U.S. interests and prestige represented in the collapse in Indochina, it is the authors' view that this impelled him all the more toward assuring that the U.S. response when next challenged would be firm and effective. Secretary Kissinger is a man of enormous self-confidence. This confidence was based upon an uncommon breadth of knowledge as an historian and strategic analyst with a specialty in the use of military force. He had been among the foremost contributors to the postwar development of the discipline of strategic studies within the United States. These contributions reflected exhaustive knowledge of capabilities and limitations of various weapons systems, both strategic and tactical.

At the same time, Secretary Kissinger was a diplomat of substantial accomplishment. While he was keenly sensitive to the limitations imposed on the ability of the United States to act in certain circumstances, such as the Cyprus crisis, during the preresignation days of 1974, this sense by no means represented any fundamental pessimism toward the long-term imperative of, or capability for, U.S. leadership in the world.

It is true that two elements of Dr. Kissinger's character—his supreme self-confidence and his belief in assuring bureaucratic consensus—might have led him in opposite directions.

That is to say, he might have been biased toward circumventing a normal deliberative process so as to minimize opposition or dissent and maximize the likelihood that his solution would prevail. In reviewing the secretary's writings on this subject, however, as well as his performance in previous crises, such a charge is difficult to document. The purpose of the NSC system, as enunciated by the secretary in 1969, was to elicit the fullest possible range of information and policy alternatives. This system had been pursued through more than one hundred major policy studies. It facilitated the rapid aggregation of a broad spectrum of views throughout the national security community for presentation to the president, whether on a long-term policy issue or within the context of crisis resolution. During that time, there were frequent examples of decisions taken that did not conform precisely to the secretary's preference.

In discussions with Dr. Kissinger and several of his close associates, it became apparent that his approach to crisis management was an extension of his grand strategic framework of "geopolitics." The following components of his belief system concerning crisis decision making can be outlined:

Opportunity. Crisis is a period which heightens a nation's political consciousness and presents opportunities for action that are not present during normal times.

Executive authority. Dr. Kissinger advocates executive authority, as opposed to congressional or interest-group authority.

Crisis management. He has a belief in the viability of crisis management, that crises can be managed in consonance with an overall strategic plan.

Symbolic effect. An important value of diplomatic or military instruments derives from their symbolic effect on adversaries and third parties, which should not be neglected.

Firmness. The image, prestige, and ultimately the ability of the United States to influence world events can be affected by the firmness of U.S. resolve. In a crisis, response to a provocation should be used if necessary to demonstrate the point.

Deterrent effect. The security of the United States depends both on an active defense and on psychological deterrence. There is a value in being even brutal in local crises to signal to superpowers and regional adversaries about U.S. intentions.

The use of sufficient force. If you have to use force with all its attendant moral risks, do it well; act with great force. Avoid gradualism. If a key policy maker advocates an action that will be criticized, conducting the action incompetently does not remove the moral criticisms from it. Excess moderation in a crisis situation can bring about the very escalation one is trying to avoid. The secretary was often quoted as admonishing his aides with the observation, "We will get no plaudits for losing with moderation."

Force as an instrument of diplomacy. The use of force is only a method of implementing foreign policy, even in a crisis. Force can be a valuable device for signaling during tacit bargaining situations, but negotiations are the logical end of the bargaining process. Force, through its deterrent, defensive, and compulsive roles, and diplomacy have to be used together to accomplish the objectives of the nation.

The U.S. role in the world. The strategic responsibility of the United States is to make clear by military strength and determination that expansions of Soviet influence will be met at all points. The United States should maximize its pivotal role in any particular situation. The nations of the world should be convinced that the United States holds the key power and the Soviets do not.

Domestic consensus. The "national will" is an important component of a state's power, but in crisis situations public opinion will follow a strong leader. "Initiative creates its own consensus."[5]

The Secretary of Defense

Dr. James R. Schlesinger had been secretary of defense for nearly two years at the time of the *Mayaguez* crisis. He brought to the office enormous intelligence, experience, and knowledge in defense matters. He had been an undergraduate classmate of Henry Kissinger at Harvard, where both received their formative academic training on the role of force in international politics. Since that time, he had become an acknowledged expert in military matters—involving both strategic and general purpose forces—through writings while at the Rand Corporation and during subsequent periods of service in government within the Office of Management and Budget (associate director for international security programs), as director of the Atomic Energy Commission, and as the director of the Central Intelligence Agency. In addition, he had successfully managed Defense Department operations during an extremely difficult and turbulent period, including the evacuation of U.S. personnel and local supporters from Saigon and Phnom Penh. He was also a man of enormous self-confidence, and was particularly sensitive about the prerogative of the secretary of defense to manage the implementation of operational military matters. In the wake of the successful evacuations from Saigon and Phnom Penh, he was entirely confident of his ability to handle the *Mayaguez* crisis.

The Deputy Assistant to the President for National Security Affairs

Lieutenant General Brent Scowcroft, USAF, had served as deputy assistant to the president for national security affairs since January 1973. Prior to that time he had been the military assistant to the president. Before coming to the White House in January 1972, he had established a distinguished record as a military strategist, writer, and scholar, including assignments in DOD (International Security Affairs), with the JCS, at the Department of Social Science at West Point, and as the head of the Department of Political Science at the Air Force Academy. His relationship with President Ford began shortly after the latter was sworn in as vice-president in December 1973. At that time General Scowcroft began a series of biweekly meetings with Vice President Ford for the purpose of discussing international issues of current importance. Over the course of the several months during which these meetings took place, a close relationship of mutual respect and confidence developed. When Vice President Ford became President, this relationship endured and deepened to one of particular trust and reliance. As with Secretary Kissinger, General Scowcroft had been tested and had performed extremely well during participation in NSC meetings associated with the Yom Kippur War and the Cyprus crisis as well as the evacuations from Saigon and Phnom Penh. His relationship with Secretary Kissinger was warm and was characterized by strong mutual trust.

It would be difficult to overstate Brent Scowcroft's contribution to both the substance and process of United States national security policy during his four years in the White House. It is ironic, although perhaps understandable, that his brilliance and effectiveness have received relatively little credit. Some might say that anyone working in the same community with Dr. Kissinger, a man of enormous charisma, would receive relatively little attention. The authors believe, however, that even without Kissinger, Scowcroft would have remained obscure. He simply is not given to self-promotion, but possesses precisely those qualities which were essential to an effective complementary relationship with Henry Kissinger, and to assuring the sound management of the vast and complex policy process. Kissinger's style is to take the offense even when discussing a course of action on which his mind may still be open. His forcefulness would sometimes intimidate even the most self-assured staff officers. While there is no doubt that he sought a rigorous dialectic, his actions sometimes had the opposite effect, where individuals were ill-prepared or lacked total conviction. Although his purpose was to challenge and encourage argument, the effect was occasionally the reverse.

Scowcroft and perhaps one or two others—Larry Eagleburger, Alexander Haig—had the perceptiveness and sense of timing to know when argument was unnecessary as well as when it was possible or vital. On countless occasions when Kissinger was concerned over a policy issue—perhaps following an argument with the president, a cabinet officer, or foreign counterpart—Scowcroft could sense the degree of rhetorical pedagogy and substantive conviction on both sides and serve as an incredibly effective foil not only to Kissinger but to his interlocutors as well.

Such a talent would have been sufficient; however, Scowcroft's substantive contributions to the resolution of countless extremely complex issues reflected extraordinary intellect and wisdom not only in regard to international political issues but economic issues as well. For example, it was through General Scowcroft's efforts that the United States was able to play a vital and extremely delicate role between the International Monetary Fund and the British government in resolving the potentially catastrophic British financial crisis during the fall of 1976. It was only through Scowcroft's efforts, and against Kissinger's strong misgivings, that a comprehensive study of United States nuclear policy (energy, reprocessing, proliferation) was conducted in 1976.

It is sometimes asserted that Secretary Kissinger designed the NSC system to place policy initiative in the White House at the beginning of the Nixon administration, but that once the new directions were charted, the locus of decision making went with him to the State Department in September 1973. The authors disagree. While there is no doubt that the secretary believed strongly in "institutionalizing" his methodology toward the analysis and resolution of international political issues within the Foreign Service, this did not require, nor did the secretary seek, the subversion of the NSC system. Because of his charismatic appeal, it was to be expected that the media limelight would follow him, but there can be no question that the center of the interdepartmental policy-development process remained in the White House under President Ford and Brent Scowcroft. Their handling of such issues as SALT, arms sales, economic development assistance, and of crises bears witness to this fact.

General Scowcroft exemplifies a level of character and ability that is very uncommon in government. Like most cabinet-level officials, he is confident of his knowledge and analytical abilities. Unlike most of his peers, however, he is not argumentative, bombastic, or aggressive in debate. At meetings of the cabinet or the NSC, being usually two or three steps ahead of the protagonists, he was normally content to wait until called upon and then deliver a rather terse statement of the core of the issue in terms of the national interest (e.g., during *Mayaguez,* "Our objectives must be the recovery of the crew and ship in such a fashion as to make clear that the United States will not tolerate violence to its interests and remains able to act decisively as a free world leader"). Though patient to a fault, he would occasionally interject a rhetorical question or comment that would advance the debate quickly.

In general, he agreed philosophically with the main lines of Secretary Kissinger's concepts concerning the U.S. role in the world and how our interests should be advanced. He never hesitated, however, to state his opposition—again, with an uncanny feel for optimal timing—whenever he disagreed on a fundamental premise or possible course of action.

In his personal relations and even in staff management he was kind to a fault, often accepting unsatisfactory work, which he would then rewrite. He worked constantly while at the White House, usually leaving home at 6:30 a.m. and never returning before 11:00 p.m. (except on Sundays, when he usually left the White House by 6:00 p.m.). In 1973, he worked 364 days and within two or three of that number in his other years in the west wing. He was not a "workaholic"—devoted to the act of working regardless of the subject. In other jobs he had worked normal hours. In the White House, however, he devoted his total energies to doing every possible act within his authority that might contribute to furthering American interests and security. General Scowcroft is a patriot, and in the authors' judgment his contributions to U.S. policy and world stability were immense.

Counselor to the President for Legislative Affairs

John Marsh served as an advisor to President Ford with cabinet rank from the time Ford assumed office, in August 1974. Immediately prior to that time he had been Vice-President Ford's advisor for national security affairs. This association derived from their earlier service together in Congress, where Counselor Marsh, a Democrat, had represented a district in southern Virginia. In addition, he had served as assistant secretary of defense for legislative affairs, where he had gained close familiarity not only with the organization of the department, but with the capabilities of military forces as well. Thus, he was knowledgeable about the substance of the issues and alternative military contributions to their resolution. More importantly, he was particularly sensitive to the importance of congressional involvement. He had handled the consultation with the Congress associated with the War Powers Resolution during the evacuation of Saigon and Phnom Penh, and thus was keenly aware of the congressional sense of its prerogatives in crisis situations. Counselor Marsh, who had served in the army and had maintained a close affiliation with civilian/military organizations, was conservative by philosophy and strongly inclined toward firm U.S. action to defend its interests at whatever level. His foremost concern in the *Mayaguez* context, however, was for fulfillment of his own responsibilities to the president as an advisor on congressional matters. While he did not seek to influence NSC deliberations toward a particular course of action, he was very firm in assuring that congressional considerations and prerogatives were kept in mind throughout the crisis period.

In addition to these key policy makers during *Mayaguez*, the Joint Chiefs of Staff were represented by the acting chairman, General David C. Jones, USAF, and the CIA was represented by Director William E. Colby. Other counselors to the president and an NSC staff member were also present at some of the meetings. As can be seen, the policy makers coming to the NSC during the *Mayaguez* crisis brought with them a substantial degree of expertise in national security matters generally and in crisis resolution specifically.

KEY POLICY MAKERS DURING THE KOREAN DMZ INCIDENT

By the time the Korean crisis took place, some of the high-level policy makers had changed. While Secretary Kissinger remained secretary of state, he had passed his responsibilities as assistant to the president for national security affairs to General Scowcroft. The latter and President Ford were in Kansas City for the Republican National Convention throughout the crisis. They did, however, remain in close communication with the Washington Special Actions Group through the chairman (Secretary Kissinger) during its deliberations. At the Defense Department, Secretary Schlesinger had relinquished his responsibilities to Donald Rumsfeld, formerly assistant to the president, and formerly U.S. ambassador to NATO. During most of the crisis, however, Secretary Rumsfeld was ill and away from the city; his responsibilities were exercised by the acting secretary, William B. Clements. George Bush had become the director of the Central Intelligence Agency. Also in attendance at WSAG meetings was Deputy Assistant to the President for National Security Affairs William G. Hyland. The chairman of the Joint Chiefs, General Brown, was out of the country, and the acting chairman for this crisis was Admiral James L. Holloway III.

THE ROLE OF THE CONGRESS

The War Powers Resolution, Public Law 93-148 (see Appendix C), requires consultation by the president with Congress prior to and after use of U.S. armed forces in hostilities or in situations where imminent involvement in hostilities is clearly indicated.[6] In either of these events, the resolution requires the president to make a written report within forty-eight hours of such use of U.S. armed forces to the speaker of the House and the president of the Senate setting forth the relevant circumstances, authority, and estimated scope and duration of the hostilities or involvement. The resolution further provides that within sixty days thereafter the president shall terminate any use of forces to which such a report relates, unless the Congress has declared war, has enacted a specific authorization for such use, or has extended by law the sixty-day period. The sixty-day period can be extended for another thirty days if the president determines and certifies that unavoidable military necessity requires the continued use of such armed forces in the act of withdrawal. A presidential report is also required within forty-eight hours of the introduction or substantial enlargement of U.S. forces into foreign areas, except for deployment which relates solely to supply, replacement, repair, or training of such forces. In addition, reports to Congress are required at six-month intervals while U.S. forces are deployed abroad in hostilities or when involvement in hostilities is imminent.

During the *Mayaguez* crisis, the president directed that the spirit and letter of the War Powers Resolution be observed de facto without recognition of de jure responsibility to do so. The president informed congressional members on three different occasions of actions taken, and provided them with an after-action report at the conclusion of combat operations. In the Korean tree incident no report was ever submitted to the Congress, because the incident was considered by the administration as outside the realm of its reporting requirements. These interpretations were hotly debated during congressional hearings on the incidents.

THE CARTER ADMINISTRATION

The focus of this book is on the Ford administration's handling of two international crises. In January 1977, President Jimmy Carter redesigned the NSC system and announced that he was going to emphasize the role of cabinet officers in both departmental and interdepartmental policy making, with only general guidance from the White House. While it is too early for hard conclusions on the effectiveness of the Carter reforms, it does appear that he is drawing away from the White House–centered system for national security policy development practiced over the past eight years. As of this writing, the National Security Council staff has not been reduced—indeed, it has increased—but it has been subjected to a certain amount of internal reorganization that appears to make it somewhat less able to control the policy-planning community. The seven major groupings under the National Security Council have been reduced to two.

The two new committees are the Policy Review Committee, chaired either by the secretary of state, defense, or treasury, depending on the question under consideration, and the Special Coordination Committee, which is chaired by the assistant to the president for national security affairs. This reorganization is consistent with President Carter's stated intention to reduce White House management of national security policy development, and to decentralize government generally. Regardless of any future changes in U.S. crisis management organization, it is the authors' view that the critical decisions will continue to be made by the president and his principal advisors. It is unrealistic to expect that the president would delegate responsibility for U.S. actions during an international crisis to subordinates. Even to give the public impression of doing so would be dysfunctional and possibly very harmful.

In all phases of a crisis situation, people and organizations must depend upon the available communications systems. In the next chapter, we will examine in more detail the roles of command, control, and communications in crisis management.

Crisis Command, Control, and Communications

Secretary of the Air Force Thomas Reed, in a 1976 speech, stated:

> The very beginning of our American Revolution was marked not by a birth or a death, nor the completion of a monument, nor the fall of a fortress. It was marked and is now remembered by an information processing event—"one if by land, two if by sea"—a rather low data-rate system, with a rather primitive ground station in the old north church. For its time, though, it was good enough. Based on that signal, Paul Revere rode into history and the fight was on.[1]

Command, control, and communications (C^3) systems are visualized by many as a series of black boxes linked by satellite to all points of the globe for the control of military forces. As will be discussed in this chapter, effective C^3, while it may in some cases have this capability, must encompass the hardware, software, and manpower necessary to ensure the president's ability to instantaneously communicate with, command, and control U.S. military forces operating worldwide as he discharges his responsibility as commander in chief of these forces.

To a great degree, the United States' requirement for reliable C^3 has been dictated by technology, the evolution of geopolitical relationships, and the diminished resources available to deal with far-flung interests and potential crises. The reduction in U.S. forces stationed overseas, increases in the number of crises occurring in widely separated geographic areas, the need for faster and more precise warning systems, and the growing military power of the Soviet Union have all helped to focus more critically the need for a truly outstanding C^3 capability. This chapter will identify in broadest terms those C^3 systems currently available to decision makers and describe them in sufficient detail to make them understandable to those not technically oriented.

THE WORLDWIDE MILITARY COMMAND AND CONTROL SYSTEM

A major technological achievement developed to satisfy U.S. C^3 requirements is the Worldwide Military Command and Control System, commonly called the WWMCCS. The WWMCCS is the system that provides the means for operational direction and technical administrative support involved in the function of command and control of U.S. military forces.

While WWMCCS is classed as a military system, it is *the* command and control system used, either directly or indirectly, by all departments of government during a crisis. The system can be summarized as consisting of five basic elements designed to enable the commander in chief, the Joint Chiefs of Staff, and commanders at appropriate subordinate levels to plan, direct, coordinate, and control the operations of U.S. military forces. These five basic elements are: (1) designated command and control facilities; (2) data collection and information networks; (3) selected special communications capabilities; (4) selected warning systems; and (5) executive aids.

Several systems will be discussed in this chapter that are not part of WWMCCS, but that are internal systems developed by a particular agency for its own needs. While these systems were not designed primarily for the command and control of forces worldwide, they do have the capability of interacting with the WWMCCS, and do so as the situation dictates.

At this point it might be well to define the WWMCCS system. Webster defines "system" as "a regularly interacting or interdependent group of items forming a unified whole." Within the context of WWMCCS, this definition would imply that WWMCCS is a single entity designed to perform its designated mission of C^3. This is not really the case. The WWMCCS consists of *independent* C^3 systems, including those developed by unified commands and the individual services. Service and unified/specified command C^3 systems that fall under the WWMCCS umbrella must be capable of providing some support to the national-level command system if required. The various systems and their relationships to each other will be discussed later in this chapter.

Three general groups of systems fall within the context of the WWMCCS:

1. *WWMCCS unique:* those systems providing direct support to the national command authority, the unified and specified commands, and their service components
2. *WWMCCS-related support:* those systems that belong to the service headquarters and DOD agencies but which meet WWMCCS standards and interact with the WWMCCS unique systems
3. *non-WWMCCS:* systems external to WWMCCS but capable of information exchange.

WWMCCS Development

When the unified and specified commands were organized as directed in the National Security Act Amendment of 1958, officials perceived that the existing service communications systems would not provide the measure of effectiveness necessary to command and control these forces under the new organization. A method for integrating the existing systems and developing others to meet the changing requirement was needed. However, proceeding from concept to reality proved to be a lengthy process. It was October 1962 before a concept called the Worldwide Military Command System was established as a DOD requirement.

By 1969, the WWMCCS had grown to a conglomerate of command and communications centers that were fixed, airborne, and seaborne. The command posts were linked by a vast collection of communications assets located around the world. Supporters of WWMCCS were sure that there would never be another communications failure such as that experienced by military forces at Pearl Harbor in 1941, when the message from the War Department that war with Japan was imminent was not received until after the attack started. Despite the WWMCCS advocates' assurance, there was ample evidence to the contrary. While the communications failures that occurred over the next several years did not have the grave international consequences of those during World War II, the ever-present threat of nuclear war made the requirement for reliable command and control facilities absolutely imperative. The WWMCCS of the late 1960s, however, was not measuring up to expectations, as several events dramatically pointed out:

1. On June 8, 1967, the U.S.S. *Liberty* was attacked by Israeli air and naval forces in the eastern Mediterranean, with a resultant thirty-four killed and seventy-five wounded. Four messages from the U.S. warning the ship to move were not received in time. The first message was released for transmission some thirteen hours and the last some three and a half hours before the attack. Two messages were misrouted to the Pacific Command. One of those was redirected to the Pentagon, but was received instead at Fort Meade. The other was not placed on Fleet Broadcast until nine hours after the attack. One copy was lost in a relay station and never sent.

2. On January 23, 1968, the U.S.S. *Pueblo*, while on an intelligence collection mission off the coast of North Korea, was boarded and captured by Korean forces, with the death of one sailor, the loss of the ship, and the imprisonment of the remaining crew for eleven months. Two messages sent from the *Pueblo* with a "Pinnacle" designation—denoting a message of major significance requiring immediate delivery to national command authorities—required two and a half and one and a half hours, respectively, before they reached the National Military Command Center in Washington, D.C.

3. On April 14, 1969, an EC-121 aircraft, while on a reconnaissance mission off the coast of North Korea, disappeared from friendly radar screens after being tracked for several hours and then intercepted by North Korean aircraft. It was later confirmed that the aircraft had been shot down, with the loss of all crew members. Three messages reporting that the aircraft

was being tracked and was in imminent danger were sent from South Korea; they took three hours; one hour, forty-five minutes; and one-half hour, respectively, for transmission to Washington.[2]

The House Armed Services Investigating Subcommittee of the Ninety-second Congress, in their report of May 10, 1971, delivered a blistering indictment of DOD communications management and operations. Key portions of the congressional report are extracted below:

> Communications systems are only as good as those who operate and use them in the command and decisionmaking process. The fragmented and overlapping responsibility for communications within the Department of Defense has resulted in inefficient and ineffective management of that essential defense support function. . . .
>
> The time required for processing of messages, before and after their electronic transmission, has prevented any significant improvement in "writer-to-reader" time, despite installation of automatic switch equipment. *Statistics reflect that an average of 70 minutes is required for processing a "flash" message, whereas the average time for electronic transmission of such a message is only 5 minutes.* [Italics added.]
>
> Unresponsive communications systems of the Department of Defense delayed the execution of command decisions and retarded the transmission of information to command officials in critical international situations. . . .
>
> The lack of effective secure voice communications systems was identified as the most serious deficiency in Department of Defense communications.[3]

While this report may have been excessively critical of the WWMCCS effort to that date, it did point out some severe shortcomings that required immediate attention.

The fault was not entirely one of ineffective management, but stemmed more from attempting to force a relationship between separately developed and technically incompatible systems that defied all attempts at integration. The diverse interests of the various organizations and services, with their many conflicting views, contributed to this failure.

After considering the allegations made by the House Armed

Services Investigation Subcommittee, the Department of Defense revised the prime management document dealing with WWMCCS. This document focused the developmental effort on the National Military Command System. Key provisions of this directive were:

- o a definition of the National Command Authorities (NCA) as consisting of the president and the secretary of defense or their duly deputized alternates or successors
- o identification of the channel of communications for execution of strategic nuclear plans and other time-sensitive operations
- o definition of the primary mission of the WWMCCS as "to support the NCA." The directive designated as a secondary goal WWMCCS support of the unified and specified commands and of the WWMCCS-related management information systems of other DOD components.
- o designation of the chairman, JCS, as responsible for the overall operation of the NMCS
- o designation of the chairman, JCS, as responsible for developing and validating requirements of the NMCS and for validating WWMCCS requirements of the unified/specified commands. The chairman was also identified as responsible for overseeing all WWMCCS programs and capabilities and for developing an overall WWMCCS objectives plan.
- o identification of the assistant to the secretary of defense (telecommunications) [later changed to the assistant secretary of defense for command, control, communications, and intelligence] as having the primary staff responsibility in the office of the secretary of defense (OSD) for WWMCCS, NMCS, and WWMCCS-related systems
- o establishment of a WWMCCS council
- o identification in broad terms of the command and control systems that constitute the WWMCCS.

The WWMCCS council was established as the focal point for all major programs and for evaluating the effectiveness of the

WWMCCS. The council, as organized by the secretary of defense, consisted of the deputy secretary of defense as chairman; the director, telecommunications and command and control; and the chairman, Joint Chiefs of Staff. The council is supported by representatives from each of the member offices who provide administrative support to the principal. This group, called the WWMCCS Council Support Group, assists in developing key issues and options for the council to consider.

In 1973, it became apparent that the complexity of WWMCCS was such that detailed guidance was required to coordinate the elements—the engineers and services—for an indefinite period. Consequently, that December, the IBM Corporation was commissioned to design an "architecture" that would guide the development of the WWMCCS for an indefinite period.

Mr. Irving Luckom, manager of the WWMCCS architecture for IBM, reported the progress of his efforts before the Signal Officers' Association in June 1976.

> Two years ago when we undertook an effort to define the WWMCCS architecture, there were two major uncertainties to face. First, what is WWMCCS? And, second, what is meant by architecture? Depending on whose definition you use, WWMCCS could very from a relatively limited system involving the NMCS [National Military Command System] and the CINCs [Commanders, Unified and Specified Commands], to a system including almost everything but the forces. There was an equally broad range of answers for architecture. For example, there were those who hoped that an architect would not only identify all of the problems, but would also solve them or at least be the advocate for a particular solution.[4]

The IBM study, while not constituting a cure-all for WWMCCS' problems, did offer substantial recommendations for improvement and constitutes a major milestone in the progress of managing the WWMCCS.

In commenting on this, Secretary of Defense James R. Schlesinger, in his report to the Congress on budget and defense programs on February 5, 1975, reported:

> Our present C^3 resources have not been systematically designed to accommodate today's complex C^3 requirements. In general,

they were introduced in response to specific changes in the threat or to take advantage of a particular technology. As a result the overall C^3 system is not as thoroughly integrated as it should be. Although there will always be a need for specialized subsystems to serve certain unique functions, such as the command and control of our strategic forces in a nuclear war, our basic C^3 system should be planned within an overall system framework to serve all of the needs of the Defense establishment, ranging from a response to a crisis situation to all-out nuclear war.[5]

WWMCCS Description

As described earlier, the WWMCCS consists of capabilities designed to allow the national command authorities to exercise command and control through the Joint Chiefs of Staff and appropriate commanders, services, and agencies at subordinate levels. In review, the five basic elements of the WWMCCS are:

○ designated command and control facilities
○ automatic data collection and information processing networks
○ selected special communications capabilities
○ selected warning systems
○ executive aids

In order to understand the relationship between command and control, and information systems at the national and subordinate levels, a discussion of Figure 5 should prove helpful. Consider, first, that there are three levels to this system, represented by the three columns. The five basic elements of the WWMCCS shown at the bottom of the chart are present to some degree in all. The Defense Communications System (DCS), as shown at the base of the chart, ties all the components together and supports a number of DOD users during both noncrisis and crisis periods.

WWMCCS unique systems. The WWMCCS unique systems provide direct support to the command structure. The National Military Command System is the most critical component of WWMCCS; it provides the president, the secretary of defense, and the Joint Chiefs of Staff with the capability to direct and

FIGURE 5

COMMAND, CONTROL AND COMMUNICATIONS (C³)
SYSTEMS TO SUPPORT PLANNING
AND EXECUTION DURING CRISIS

WWMCCS UNIQUE	WWMCCS RELATED (SUPPORT)	NON WWMCCS
National Command Authorities	DOD Agencies C¹	Tactical C¹
National Military Command System	Management Information Systems of Service Headquarters	
Unified and Specified Commands C¹	DOD Information System	
Service Component Commands C¹		

The Defense Communications System (DCS) (Facilities, Communications, Executive Aids, Warning Systems and Automatic Data Processing Systems)

Other Communications Systems That Can Interact with the DCS

Presidential Communications
Non-DOD Systems
    Department of State
    Central Intelligence Agency
    US Intelligence Board
    UN Military Mission
    US Coast Guard
    Federal Aviation Administration
    Federal Protective Agency

control military forces in a crisis.

Represented in Column 1 are the command and control systems of the Joint Chiefs of Staff, the unified and specified commands, and the service component commands. At the top are the national command authorities—the president and secretary of defense—who exercise direction of deployed forces through the chairman, Joint Chiefs of Staff. The NCA is supported by the JCS and the JCS staff as well as by other agencies. Directly supporting the NCA is the National Military Command System (NMCS). Its facilities have the ability to receive, evaluate, and display information for NCA decisions. They provide for the direction and control of forces in the execution of national decisions. Shown next in Column 1 are the C³ systems of the unified and specified commands and their component commands. These systems provide the means through which field commanders receive information and exercise operational control of assigned forces.

WWMCCS-related systems. Column 2 represents the management and information systems that support the headquarters of the military departments, services, and DOD agencies. These systems consist of the facilities, equipment, communications, procedures, and personnel that provide the means through which the headquarters of the military departments, services, and DOD agencies carry out their assigned functions in support of WWMCCS.

Non-WWMCCS systems. The third column of the WWMCCS system represents the non-WWMCCS subsystems. These are command and control systems that provide support and interface with the WWMCCS but do not belong to the WWMCCS.

Other systems. At the bottom of Figure 5 are the command, control, and communications systems of other government departments and agencies that can interact with WWMCCS during periods of crisis.

WWMCCS Information Processing

This element of the WWMCCS involves the collection and handling of the tremendous volumes of data associated with sophisticated military forces and associated current weapons systems belonging to the United States. The levels of information processing generally correspond to the three functional levels of the WWMCCS discussed previously.

The various information-processing systems were developed independently by the services and agencies within the DOD and it was not until the early 1970s that an attempt was made to integrate these programs under the WWMCCS and provide access to other agencies by means of an effective management program. In 1970, the DOD decided to procure a standard computer system for the WWMCCS users. In competitive procurement, Honeywell Information Systems was awarded a contract for thirty-five standard systems to be installed under the supervision of a WWMCCS automatic data processing program manager from the Joint Chiefs of Staff.

The transition from the several separate systems to the Honeywell system has not been an easy one. The system improvement envisaged by the project manager is now overcoming some major hurdles and great effort is currently being made to upgrade the system through a systematic improvement program.

WWMCCS in Operation During Crisis

During day-to-day operations, there are three primary means of transferring information rapidly between commands and agencies: message communications, which transmit most of the operational information required; data communications, generally used to transfer great volumes of administrative and logistical information; and voice communications, used for the immediate off-the-record transfer of information between individuals. When a crisis occurs, the same three means of communication are employed, but with a major shift in utilization.

Message communications. A review of past crises reveals that an overwhelming amount of information is collected and disseminated utilizing the worldwide Defense Communications System. Despite this increase in traffic there was no backlog in the JCS Message Center.

Voice communications. While difficult to quantify, estimates indicate that a large percentage of the information requirements during crises is met utilizing direct telephone or radio voice communications. Experience indicates that existing estimates may be conservative, particularly during the latter stages of crisis action, when rapid response and direct following of the situation may be required.

Data communications. Numerous attempts have been made during exercises to utilize computer-based information systems to meet some of the information requirements, particularly as they relate to forces and deployment planning. These have met with some degree of success.

In theory, there is no command, control, communications, or information-processing problem that cannot be solved during a crisis within the present WWMCCS configuration. This, of course, presumes that all systems are functioning properly and that the people operating the systems are fully qualified to use them. Such is rarely the case.

In many crises this man-machine problem is amplified by the sheer volume of message traffic or information search generated by the crisis. As the intensity of the crisis increases, the stress on the human element rises correspondingly.

Studies conducted by the Defense Communications Agency (DCA) show that under WWMCCS the communication capability of the Defense Communications System has never been exceeded during a crisis. Breakdowns have occurred, however, with the human element at either end of the communications line. The Defense Communications Agency has established many procedures to minimize this communications problem. These procedures—entitled "MINIMIZE"—were established to restrict the communications traffic in specific areas of the world during periods of emergency. During recent tests, the DCA experienced a substantial decrease in message traffic entering its automatic switching centers from user-access lines when MINIMIZE was imposed.

The DCA went further and analyzed the character of the message traffic during periods of MINIMIZE. The principal conclusions of the DCA study were:

- There was no drastic increase in total traffic during periods of crisis. The imposition of MINIMIZE more than allowed for the accommodation of traffic associated with the crisis.
- Speed of service at the communications terminals improved during MINIMIZE.
- Message originators tended to assign a higher precedence and classification to messages during MINIMIZE.
- MINIMIZE did significantly reduce the message traffic of large administrative and logistical installations, since only urgent administrative traffic was permitted.

While the DCA study indicated that there were no significant problems in message handling when the entire system was considered, it did consider the effect at the two ends of crisis communications lines. The volume of communications focused on these two extremities is high and the command centers in both Washington and in the area of the crisis become overloaded very quickly. Some of the most prevalent causes for communications overload at the command centers were found to be:

○ More people ask questions in shorter periods of time than in noncrisis periods.
○ A crisis brings about a restructuring of the day-to-day communications network. Agencies are providing information and asking questions to players who are different than during noncrisis conditions.
○ Rapid changes occur in the situation at the crisis location.
○ Redundant questioning by all agencies is common.
○ Additional people are introduced into the process to help handle the crisis, e.g., crisis task forces and watch teams.
○ Cross-agency coordination of messages is required.
○ Hierarchy of message traffic often precludes the direct transmission of information between agencies because of restrictions imposed by parent agencies.
○ Attempts are made to confirm one's own analysis or conclusions. This is most apparent in the intelligence community.

The net effect of this communications increase is a potential reduction in providing timely estimates and options to the decision makers. It also, in part, accounts for the possible loss of key pieces of information that can take place during most crises.

The two case studies described in Chapters 5 and 6 provide the contrasts in C^3 that the WWMCCS is able to accommodate. During the Korean tree incident, traditional command lines existed and communications lines were well established. As a result, when the crisis occurred, little had to be done with the communications system to conduct the operation. On the other hand, when the S.S. *Mayaguez* was captured, the United States had some residual communications equipment in the area left from the Vietnam evacuation, but not as much as might have been desired. As a result, when it was recognized that a crisis situation existed, a new communications routing was required on very short notice. By utilizing an airborne command post from Thailand, the WWMCCS established the link from the NMCC to the operating forces off Cambodia.

Automated Assistance for Decision Makers

A brief discussion of some of the more important automated capabilities currently available to assist in crisis planning may help in understanding what is available to decision makers. The information processing program under the jurisdiction of the Joint Chiefs of Staff is charged with the task of providing users with timely and accurate data. This system currently consists of numerous medium to large Honeywell computers located throughout the world.

The JCS planning procedures were designed specifically to assist in the process of planning force deployment during both normal and crisis conditions. Under crisis conditions, through the use of common applications programs and data bases, the system is used to develop movement data for the deployment of forces to the crisis area. Basically, the system consists of three major subprograms, each contributing a portion of the data for the movement of forces being considered. The "force requirements generator" either puts together a force for an assigned mission or draws on a force already created and prepares the movement data required. This can be done by a planner sitting at a computer console located in the Command Center. The information is passed to the second major program, the "movement requirements generator," which computes the material support required to sustain the force for a determined period of time. This new data is passed to the "transportation feasibility estimator." Here, all of the previous data is tested against transportation needs in order to provide the user with optimal aircraft or ship transportation schedules in line with movement parameters he has established.

The Joint Operations Planning System is not without its problems. It is clear, however, that great advances have been made in recent years in the technological support of decision makers. The president of the United States can talk directly to commanders or leaders on the scene of a crisis through satellite communications. He can influence the local situation directly, sometimes at the expense of intervening echelons. Technology, however, will never be able to replace the human element; in the final analysis, it is the human who must make the decision.

The *Mayaguez* Crisis: Piracy on the High Seas

On May 12, 1975, an incident occurred at a remote location involving an obscure vessel of U.S. registry known as the S.S. *Mayaguez*. At 2:18 p.m. local time, Mr. John Neal of the Delta Exploration Company in Jakarta, Indonesia, received a mayday radio call from the U.S. merchant vessel *Mayaguez* stating that she had been fired upon and boarded by Cambodian naval forces and was being towed to an unknown Cambodian port.

The *Mayaguez*, which belonged to Sea-Land Services, Inc., had been en route from Hong Kong to Sattahip, Thailand, with a containerized cargo of commercial items including food, clothing, medical supplies, mail, and other products. The incident occurred in the vicinity of Poulo Wai Island, approximately sixty miles southwest of the Cambodian port of Kompong Som. During the next three and one-half days, the United States mounted a major military operation against Cambodian Communist forces on another offshore island claimed by Cambodia, Koh Tang, attacked the Cambodian mainland directly, and secured the release of both the crew and the ship. This chapter is a study of this major international crisis and the decision-making process that led to the use of U.S. military forces in its resolution.

The style of this chapter and the next will be primarily narrative, reserving analysis, comparisons, and conclusions for the final chapter. For a detailed listing of the events in this incident, see Appendix A: Chronology of the *Mayaguez* Crisis.

BACKGROUND TO CRISIS

International Context

The seizure of the *Mayaguez* came at a time in U.S. foreign relations when the prestige of the United States in Asia was at low ebb. After more than ten years of a controversial war in Southeast Asia, the United States had suffered a demoralizing military and political setback with overtones concerning its continued reliability as an ally which went far beyond the Asian context. Phnom Penh had fallen on April 17, and Saigon had fallen on April 30, signaling the end of the U.S. presence in Indochina. In the Middle East, Secretary Kissinger's efforts toward an agreement for a second disengagement of forces between Egypt and Israel in the Sinai were rebuffed by the Israeli government in March. The effects of the oil price rise of 1974 continued to push most economies into a serious recession. The world was in general political disarray and the apparent decline of the United States—as exemplified by its fortunes in Indochina—was raising serious questions in capitals throughout the world as to its ability to continue to play a positive role in international affairs.

In addition, only nine months had passed since the Nixon resignation. For the first time in history, a U.S. president had resigned under public and congressional pressure. President Ford, as the first appointed president, was obviously well aware that he did not have a political mandate from the people. Nevertheless, it was eminently clear that Americans, and indeed the free world, desperately needed leadership. It is in this context that the interaction of people, agencies, nations, and armed forces will be examined to determine what lessons can be learned for the benefit of future decision makers.

Cambodian Context

After thirty years of fighting in Southeast Asia, the Indochinese Communists had toppled the last of a series of non-Communist governments in Cambodia and the Republic of Vietnam. Their war of liberation was concluded and ten years of combat with the United States had ended, with the Communist forces victorious. In the aftermath of this tragic war, the authorities in Phnom Penh pursued several initiatives, all designed to establish their nationalist credentials and legitimacy. Members of the defeated regime were systematically executed. It has been estimated that as many as six hundred thousand Cambodians were killed or died during the first months after the Lon Nol government fell—from a population estimated at 7 million in 1973. The same ratio applied to the United States would mean the loss of 22 million Americans! The Khmer Rouge were intent on destroying millenniums of Cambodian history and the professionals and intellectuals who kept this history alive.[1]

As a separate manifestation of nationalism, the Phnom Penh authorities decided to extend their territorial waters to ninety miles from shore, which included several of the islands located in the Gulf of Thailand, islands to which Cambodia had historically laid claim.[2] These new limits included the islands of Paulo Wai, Tang, and the surrounding waters, which had historically been used as major trade routes to and from Asian ports. The government reportedly planned to seize any foreign vessels violating the new ninety-mile limit.

By the time of the *Mayaguez* capture on May 12, 1975, four incidents had occurred which signaled the seriousness of Cambodian intentions:

o   the seizure by Cambodian forces, and subsequent release, of several Thai fishing boats ten days previously
o   the firing upon a South Korean ship and an attempt to board her eight days earlier
o   the seizure of several South Vietnamese small craft six days before
o   the detention of a Panamanian ship for thirty-six hours five days previously

The Ship

This, then, was the setting into which the *Mayaguez* sailed on the morning of May 12, 1975. As ships go, the *Mayaguez* wasn't much. She was thirty-one years old, and had borne such unremarkable names as the *White Falcon, Sea,* and *Santa Eliana.* Although her engine room remained essentially the same as when she was built in 1944, the hull had been cut, broadened, stretched, and then welded back together to allow her to carry more cargo.[3]

In 1960, the *Mayaguez,* then known as the *Santa Eliana,* had been rebuilt by the Grace Lines to become the first fully containerized ship in the United States. On her maiden voyage to Venezuela, which began a much heralded "new era in transportation," she became involved in an international incident when Venezuelan stevedores refused to unload her because they thought containerization threatened their livelihood. For twenty-two days, the ship lay idle in the water awaiting unloading. Finally, the Venezuelan dock workers unloaded the ship by hand and let her return to Baltimore, where she sat idle for two years.

When the Southeast Asian war broke out, the *Mayaguez* was put into operation by Sea-Land Services, Inc., transporting general containerized cargo under government contract. Her ability to load and unload the 274 containers she carried, by using the two large cranes on board, made her especially valuable in operating from Asian ports.

THE CRISIS EVENT

The *Mayaguez* and her forty-man crew had sailed from Hong Kong on the morning of May 7, 1975, for the port of Sattahip, Thailand. She was carrying 274 thirty-foot containers of general cargo. Steaming at 12.5 knots, she had rounded the southern tip of Vietnam on Sunday, May 11, staying well away from the coastline. By early Monday afternoon, May 12, the *Mayaguez* was located abeam of the small island of Poulo Wai, an island whose ownership had been contested by several countries for a number of years (see Figure 6). Shortly after 3:00 a.m. (all time will be Washington time unless stated otherwise), the *Mayaguez* was fired upon by Cambodian-manned gunboats of U.S. manufacture that had been captured when Cambodia fell to the Communists on April 17, 1975. Upon hearing the Cambodian warning shots, the captain of the *Mayaguez,* Charles T.

FIGURE 6

LOCATION OF MAYAGUEZ AND CREW
May 12-15, 1975

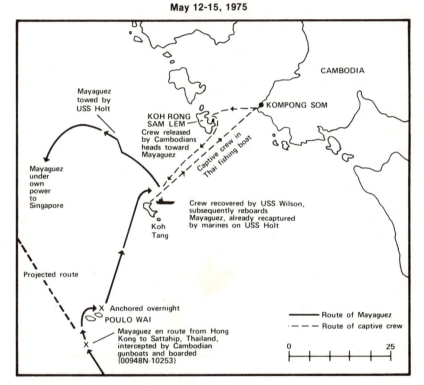

CAMBODIA

Mayaguez towed by USS Holt

KOH RONG SAM LEM
Crew released by Cambodians heads toward Mayaguez

● KOMPONG SOM

Captive crew in Thai fishing boat

Mayaguez under own power to Singapore

Crew recovered by USS Wilson, subsequently reboards Mayaguez, already recaptured by marines on USS Holt

Koh Tang

Projected route

X Anchored overnight
POULO WAI

Mayaguez en route from Hong Kong to Sattahip, Thailand, intercepted by Cambodian gunboats and boarded (00948N-10253)

—————— Route of Mayaguez
‑ ‑ ‑ ‑ ‑ ‑ Route of captive crew

0   25

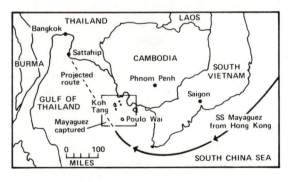

THAILAND   LAOS
Bangkok

Sattahip   CAMBODIA
                                SOUTH
Projected   Phnom Penh   VIETNAM
route
GULF OF   Saigon
THAILAND Koh
          Tang
          ○ Poulo Wai
Mayaguez   SS Mayaguez
captured   from Hong Kong

0   100
MILES   SOUTH CHINA SEA

BURMA

*Seizure of the Mayaguez Part IV. Reports of the Comptroller General of the United States submitted to the Subcommittee on International Political and Military Affairs, Committee on International Relations. October 4, 1976.

Miller, brought his engines to idle and instructed the radio operator to send an immediate distress signal to any station listening. Captain Miller had no means to resist the armed Cambodian force, but took every opportunity to delay compliance with Cambodian instructions in an attempt to provide time for a rescue force to respond. Delay was not difficult because none of the young Cambodians could speak or write English, and he had difficulty understanding their instructions.[4]

John Neal, of the Delta Exploration Company in Jakarta, was on duty at his company's office early on the morning of May 12. At approximately 2:18 p.m. local time (3:18 a.m. Washington time) he was startled to hear a call on his radio from a ship identifying herself as the *Mayaguez* stating: "Have been fired upon and boarded by Cambodian armed forces at 9°48′N and 102°52′E. Ship is being towed to an unknown Cambodian port."[5] During the next two hours, Neal had several conversations with the ship but lost all communications before 5:00 a.m. At about that time he notified the U.S. embassy in Jakarta of the incident. The officials there notified key agencies in Washington by a series of messages dispatched at about 4:54 a.m. For the next two hours, agencies in Washington and the Pacific were searching for any information available and were discussing possible courses of action.

NOTIFICATION AND INITIAL ACTIONS

The initial report from the embassy arrived in Washington at the National Military Command Center (NMCC) at 5:12 a.m., Monday, May 12, and it was followed by a series of messages in the next two hours.[6] The initial actions of the military duty officers were to notify their superiors in the Joint Staff and to obtain more information. Specifically, their immediate reaction was to launch reconnaissance aircraft.[7] NMCC officials conferred with officers in the U.S. Pacific Command in Hawaii at 5:34 a.m. and again at 6:20 a.m. and discussed both the *Mayaguez* seizure and the possibility of sending a military aircraft to conduct reconnaissance. At 6:46 a.m., NMCC personnel notified General David C. Jones (USAF), the acting chairman of the Joint Chiefs of Staff. (General George S. Brown, the chairman, was in Europe on official business.)

The commander in chief, Pacific (CINCPAC), was ordered shortly after 7:00 a.m. to get a reconnaissance crew ready to launch, and the actual order to take off was transmitted by the JCS at 7:30.[8]

Meanwhile, the White House Situation Room had also received the initial messages and notified Lieutenant General Brent Scowcroft, the President's deputy assistant for national security affairs upon his arrival at the White House at about 7:00 a.m. President Ford received his first information on the seizure of the *Mayaguez* at his regular morning intelligence briefing with General Scowcroft at about 7:30.[9] The exact location of the vessel was unknown, but it was believed to be headed for the Cambodian port of Kompong Som.[10] According to President Ford, "My feeling was that seizure of a U.S. vessel and crew, especially by a country which had so recently humiliated us, was a very serious matter."[11] President Ford asked General Scowcroft to keep him informed.

The secretary of state was not notified until his morning staff meeting at 8:00 a.m. At the State Department, the director of the Bureau of Intelligence and Research, Mr. William G. Hyland, was reading through the incoming cables at about 7:30 a.m. when he noticed that one of them mentioned something about a U.S. ship being detained in Southeast Asia. He read the message more closely and then mentioned it to Secretary of State Kissinger at the opening of the secretary's eight o'clock staff meeting. Dr. Kissinger reportedly became extremely concerned and called the president at once. At 9:23, Kissinger arrived in the Oval Office to discuss the matter with the president and General Scowcroft. After the discussion, the president called for a meeting of the National Security Council at noon.

In Hawaii, the Pacific Fleet headquarters ordered the nearest surface craft to proceed to the scene at 9:37 a.m. By this time, the *Mayaguez* had been escorted to the island of Poulo Wai and had been anchored for several hours. This fact, of course, was not known in Hawaii or in Washington, where the assumption remained—until after the first NSC meeting—that the ship was en route to Kompong Som.[12]

Commander J. A. Messagee, the squadron commander of

Navy Patrol Squadron Four, had a P-3 reconnaissance aircraft airborne from his detachment at Utapao, Thailand, at 9:57 a.m. Washington time, a second P-3 airborne from Cubi Naval Air Station, Philippines, at 10:05 a.m., and a third P-3 shortly thereafter. The navy reconnaissance crews were told to assume that the *Mayaguez* was on her way toward Kompong Som, and they were ordered to begin their search patterns over Poulo Wai.[13]

The first P-3 (from Utapao) arrived on station over Poulo Wai at 10:28 a.m. (9:28 p.m. Cambodian time) and immediately discovered several vessels, large and small, within sixty miles of the island. Two of the ships appeared to be large enough to be the *Mayaguez,* and several others were similar. The most likely ship was lying dead in the water seven miles off Poulo Wai. Since the Asian night cast a black pall over the sea, the P-3 crews dropped parachute illumination flares in an attempt to identify the ships. Positive identification was not possible, however.

THE DECISION-MAKING PROCESS

Monday, May 12, 1975

The first formal step in the decision-making process was the National Security Council meeting at noon on May 12 (nine hours after the seizure). There were several reasons President Ford decided on an NSC meeting as opposed to starting the process at a somewhat lower level, with the WSAG. First, he believed that time was of the essence and that the goal of securing the release of the crew and ship could rest on the speed and efficiency of rescue operations. The history of the U.S.S. *Pueblo,* captured by North Korea in 1968, had vividly pointed out that any possibility of rescuing the crew and ship had been reduced to near zero when that ship reached the North Korean harbor. The similarity of the two situations was obvious to the president. There was no time for a slow "bubbling-up" of analysis through the many layers of the bureaucracy.

Second, the president wanted to handle the crisis himself. Contextual factors undoubtedly influenced the president's thinking. American confidence in the presidency had been severely shaken only nine months before. Allies and adversaries were looking on in amazement as the Congress intervened repeatedly to seize the initiative in foreign policy (e.g., the Jackson-Vanik amendment, which led to a treaty abrogation, the cutoff of aid to Turkey, a NATO ally, and the intensive congressional investigation of the U.S. intelligence community). To a very real extent, the future role of the executive branch as the creative, dominant voice in foreign policy was in question.

When asked in a later interview why he personally took charge of the *Mayaguez* situation, President Ford stated unequivocally:

> First, I think it is the responsibility of the president. The American people expect their president to act—particularly during crises—to restore matters to normal and protect U.S. interests. Perhaps it was also a carryover from the evacuations of Saigon and Phnom Penh. Certainly in the environment we were in, it was essential for the president to be directly involved.[14]

Present at the first NSC meeting were the president; the vice-president, Nelson Rockefeller; the secretary of state, Henry A. Kissinger;[15] the secretary of defense, James R. Schlesinger; the director of central intelligence, William E. Colby; the deputy secretary of state, Robert S. Ingersoll; the deputy secretary of defense, William P. Clements, Jr.; the acting chairman of the Joint Chiefs of Staff, General David C. Jones, USAF; Assistant to the President Donald H. Rumsfeld; Deputy Assistant for National Security Affairs, Lieut. Gen. Brent Scowcroft; and senior NSC staff officer for East Asia, Richard Smyser. The format for the meeting followed very closely that of NSC meetings over the previous six years. This format, as described in Chapter 3, was basically designed to: determine the facts; attempt to determine the motives of the other party and its objectives; define U.S. interests and objectives; assess the possible interests and objectives of third parties (particularly those of great powers—the Soviet Union and China); and discuss alternative means of securing U.S. interests, including diplomatic, military, and economic initiatives. Finally, possible reactions by the adversary to alternative U.S. actions were to be discussed.

This first meeting was no exception to the conventional NSC pattern. It opened with a briefing by Director Colby to present the *facts*. At that time it was believed that the *Mayaguez* was moving toward the Cambodian mainland port of Kompong Som. Secretary Kissinger argued strongly that the issues at stake went far beyond the seizure of a U.S. civilian ship to the question of international perceptions of power and national will.

The president followed with several questions about the location of the crew and the availability of U.S. resources to respond to the situation. Some NSC members perceived a problem with using the closest U.S. forces—those in Thailand— because of possible adverse reaction by the Thai government. The instruction given to the military leaders at first was that Thailand-based U.S. forces were not to be used, but as the crisis developed and it became clear that Thai-based fixed-wing aircraft and helicopters would be essential, this posture shifted to permit more use of these units.[16]

The participants quickly agreed on the two foremost U.S. objectives: to recover the ship and its crew; and to do so in such a way as to demonstrate firmly to the international community that the United States could and would act with firmness to protect its interests, in this case its right of passage in international waters. The discussions centered on the efficacy of alternative actions in achieving these objectives. During these discussions it became apparent that the objectives were similar, but not identical; some participants pointed out that they were even contradictory when used to evaluate certain policy proposals.

In a later interview, President Ford commented on the style he established at this NSC meeting and his preference for hearing open discussion.

> I don't know what style President Nixon used, although I believe he liked to digest written reports before making decisions. But I like to hear a verbal presentation and to hear the different viewpoints expressed. I was always at ease in NSC meetings. I liked to hear the discussions on the various points of view. I don't mind contention. At some meetings the discussion got very frank.[17]

When asked if he thought his presence at the NSC inhibited any discussion, he said:

> I don't believe so, at least not in the way I ran the meetings. We had pretty freewheeling discussions. I don't think anyone was inhibited because I was there. You know, we had some pretty strong personalities there. I did have occasion to act in an arbitration role, but I believe this is a proper role for the commander in chief. [18]

~ The president directed that a strong diplomatic protest note be delivered to the Cambodian authorities via the PRC; that the U.S.S. *Coral Sea* be turned around on its voyage to Australia and ordered to the area of seizure; that an amphibious task force be assembled in the Philippines; that continuous photo reconnaissance be maintained over the area; and finally, that a public statement be issued (designed to reach Phnom Penh) reporting the facts and noting the U.S. demand for the immediate return of the vessel and its crew. (The latter statement was released by the White House at 1:50 p.m.)

It was agreed that the meeting should adjourn and efforts be made to gather more information and to initiate the planning of alternative courses of action—both diplomatic and military. At this point the expectations of the participants apparently diverged. The NSC staff and General Scowcroft were under the impression that the JCS was asked to develop written military options and to present them to the White House later that afternoon (Monday). The JCS staff and General Jones operated under the assumption that the request for military alternatives was only a generalized one with no specific White House deadline.

The perception of the Joint Chiefs was that the location and status of the *Mayaguez* were highly uncertain and that the entire crisis situation was changing rapidly. In addition, the military planning problem for the Joint Staff was complicated by many factors: the exact location of the *Mayaguez* was still not known; there were no U.S. ships in the Gulf of Siam; the nearest land-based air forces were in Thailand and diplomatic problems might preclude their use; the closest ground forces were the marines in Okinawa; and the intentions of the adversary force were unknown. General Jones was reluctant to offer premature options that would inevitably be based on "soft" or inadequate information. The result was that the JCS did not present an options paper to the White House on Monday afternoon.

The State Department prepared a note for the Cambodians to be transmitted to the Chinese Liaison Office in Washington. At 4:30 p.m., Ambassador Huang Chen, chief of the P.R.C. Liaison Office, was called to the State Department and presented with this note. He refused to accept it.

Tuesday, May 13, 1975

After a long night of attempting to identify the many ships below them, the crews of the navy P-3 reconnaissance aircraft over Poulo Wai were glad to see the dawn. At 8:16 a.m (9:16 p.m. Washington time), one of the three P-3s made a low pass and read the name *Mayaguez* on both the stern and bow of one of the ships anchored near Poulo Wai.[19] During this pass, the aircraft was fired on by Cambodian boats near the *Mayaguez* and one .50 caliber projectile hit the P-3's tail. The pilot checked the aircraft for controlability, radioed a report of the incident, and decided to remain on station for his assigned patrol period. His report reached General Scowcroft within twenty minutes. The general notified the president immediately and after discussing contingency measures with him departed for his quarters. Almost immediately upon his arrival at home (10:15 p.m.) the general was called by his assistant, Marine Major Bud McFarlane, with word that the *Mayaguez* had weighed anchor and was reportedly en route to Kompong Som. Based on the ship's speed and direction, the P-3 crew estimated that the *Mayaguez* would arrive at the mainland port in six hours. After the crisis was over, it was learned that the *Mayaguez* was only at half speed, due to the stalling tactics of the ship's captain, Charles T. Miller.[20] The general returned to the White House immediately and notified the president. Scowcroft remained in his office throughout the night.

Motivated by his great concern over the much more difficult situation that would be created if the Cambodians succeeded in getting the *Mayaguez* to the mainland and hiding the crew (as had happened in the *Pueblo* incident), the general's first action was to call the Pentagon and speak to Major General John A. Wickham, USA, military assistant to the secretary, to ask for a prompt assessment of whether aircraft could intercept the *Mayaguez* and prevent its reaching the mainland. At approximately 1:00 a.m., May 13, General Wickham called back to report affirmatively that Thai-based F-4 fighters could reach the ship and attempt to turn it using strafing runs. The necessary aircraft were already being loaded. General Scowcroft told him to launch the aircraft so that they would arrive in time if their use were approved. He immediately went to the White House, where he sought and received the president's authority for the interdiction effort. Upon his return from the president's quarters to his office at approximately 2:30 a.m., word was received that the *Mayaguez* had anchored off Koh Tang. General Scowcroft notified the president, who was relieved but, as might be expected, uneasy at the rapid succession of contradictory reports.

The nature of the reports received thus far—and the apparent uncertainty as to the ship's movements—were of serious concern to the president. Specifically, on Monday morning the president had been told that the *Mayaguez* was en route to Kompong Som (when it was actually anchored off Poulo Wai). That evening at 9:30 p.m., he was informed that a P-3 had sighted the vessel and that it was anchored off Poulo Wai. Approximately one and one-half hours later at 11:00 p.m., reports conveyed to the president stated that the vessel was again en route to Kompong Som. By 2:30 a.m., only four hours later, reports fixed the vessel as anchored off Koh Tang.[21] These reports created some doubts in the White House as to the reliability of intelligence monitoring of events and raised questions in the mind of the president concerning the validity of the information he was receiving.[22]

The second NSC meeting was held on Tuesday, May 13, 1975, 10:30–11:30 a.m. (thirty-one hours after the seizure). Attendance was essentially the same as at the first meeting, with the addition of counsellors to the president Robert T. Hartmann and John O. Marsh (the latter to handle reporting to the Congress). In addition, due to Secretary Kissinger and Deputy Secretary Ingersoll's absence for travel to Kansas City, the State Department was represented by Under Secretary Joseph J. Sisco.

William Colby, director of the Central Intelligence Agency, opened with an intelligence briefing. Colby stated that after her capture, the *Mayaguez* had moved under gunboat escort to Koh Tang, where she presently lay anchored dead in the water. He further reported that there had been considerable movement of small craft around the *Mayaguez* and between the *Mayaguez* and Koh Tang, and that the crew had probably been moved to Koh Tang.

Following this briefing, there was a general discussion concerning the status of events ordered at the first NSC meeting. In the diplomatic area, it was reported that no response had been received from the note of protest sent to the Cambodians through the Foreign Office in Peking. It was also reported that the Chinese Liaison Office in Washington had refused to accept the protest note directed at the Cambodian government.

One potentially disturbing situation arose. The chargé d'affaires in Thailand had reported to the State Department that the prime minister of Thailand would not permit the use of its bases for U.S. action or retaliation against Cambodia. The chargé d'affaires had further promised the Thai government that U.S. planes based in Thailand would not be used without prior clearance from them.

The NSC was moving toward a discussion of firm military and diplomatic options, but they were never stated together in any single package or presented in rank order. The following proposals were discussed at one or another NSC meeting:

o   Use diplomacy with the People's Republic of China, the Cambodian government and (later) the United Nations in an attempt to have the ship and crew returned.
o   Conduct a military show of force.
o   Seize a Cambodian island in retaliation.
o   Authorize a helicopter landing on the *Mayaguez.*
o   Order a landing on the U.S.S. *Holt,* with a subsequent seaborne approach to the *Mayaguez.*

○   Assault Koh Tang with marines.
○   Attack the port of Kompong Som with navy tactical aircraft.
○   Authorize B-52 bombing of Kompong Som.

Because the situation was changing rapidly, President Ford was not ready to make a final decision on the major alternatives. He was convinced, however, of the urgency of deploying appropriate military forces to the scene to provide the capability for concerted U.S. action should military force become necessary. Accordingly, he ordered the U.S.S. *Hancock,* a second aircraft carrier, to embark with a marine amphibious assault unit from the Philippines to the area of operations as soon as possible. He further directed that the *Mayaguez* and Koh Tang be isolated from the mainland by the use of Thailand-based air force F-4, F-111, and A-7 tactical aircraft. "We told the aircraft," said the president, "that they should use whatever means they could to head off either ships going to the mainland or from the mainland to Koh Tang. During the day, I was to be given periodic reports on whether there was any movement."[23] Other orders concerned the movement of a marine battalion from Okinawa to Utapao, Thailand, to provide the capability for a heliborne assault by Wednesday night (May 14 Washington time). In closing the fifty-six-minute meeting, President Ford directed that a plan for dealing with the War Powers Resolution be prepared.

During the course of the *Mayaguez* crisis, President Ford consulted with members of Congress on four occasions. Consultation was in acknowledgement of Section 3 of the War Powers Resolution, and consisted of both formal and informal briefings by President Ford, members of his staff, and representatives from the departments of Defense and State. The first of the four consultations began on May 13 at about 5:30 p.m. At the direction of the president, John Marsh and other White House staff officers contacted ten House and eleven Senate members. They related the military measures that the president had directed to prevent the *Mayaguez* and its crew from being transferred to the Cambodian mainland and to prevent Cambodian reinforcement of Koh Tang.

During the day of May 13 in Cambodian waters, the P-3 and C-130 reconnaissance aircraft were reinforced by Thai-based F-111 and RF-4 aircraft and established a more sophisticated surveillance pattern over the ship and Koh Tang. The search for the crew continued and concentrated on several Cambodian gunboats and fishing craft located in coves on the island. On each occasion that the aircraft came close to these craft, they received small arms and antiaircraft fire from the island.

Early on the morning of the 13th, the crew of the *Mayaguez* had been observed apparently being transferred from the ship to the island by fishing boat. In the early evening (Washington time), a group of possible Caucasians were observed on a boat between Koh Tang and the mainland. Efforts by air force A-7 fighters from Thailand to halt the movement by firing in front of the boats proved unsuccessful. Some reports indicated that a part of the crew was on Koh Tang, and others indicated that the crew was en route to the mainland. All these reports were based on the tentative sighting of *possible* Caucasians. There had been no positive reporting of any crew member en route to the mainland.

At approximately 12:10 a.m. on May 13, the U.S. Liaison Office in Peking delivered two messages reiterating the demands contained in the first note which Ambassador Huang Chen had refused in Washington on Monday. One message was delivered to the Foreign Ministry of the People's Republic of China. On May 14, the Chinese returned their copy of the message, and the Cambodian Embassy returned theirs through the mail. Notwithstanding this formal diplomatic charade of rejecting the note, there is little doubt that the message reached authorities in Phnom Penh.[24]

The third meeting of the NSC was at 10:40 p.m. on May 13, and those in attendance, as in the morning meeting, included Dr. Kissinger. The meeting proceeded in the same general format as the first two. The briefing by CIA Director Colby included the information that several *possible* Caucasions—"possibly" crew members—had been sighted en route to the mainland.

The NSC was briefed on the refusal of the Cambodian embassy to receive the U.S. note of protest and that Chinese

Communists officials in Paris had stated that China would not do anything to assist in securing the ship and crew if the United States used military force.

The operational reports covered a number of incidents ranging from the crash of an air force helicopter near Nakhon Phanom, Thailand, killing all twenty-three military policemen on board, to the continued efforts of the tactical aircraft to isolate the ship and Koh Tang. Progress reports were also given on the location and speed of movement of combat forces converging on the crisis area.

General Jones described five military options in general outline. They included proposals to board the *Mayaguez,* to land marines on the island, to bomb the mainland with tactical aircraft, to bomb the mainland with B-52s from Guam, and other military measures. These options prompted a lively discussion, as described in a later account.

Kissinger was emphatic on the use of force. He felt it was important for the American action to have impact on President Kim Il-sung and the North Koreans. The *Pueblo* seizure was on everybody's mind, and so were the most recent North Korean provocations, particularly the tunneling under the thirty-eighth parallel, the border between the North and South. Kissinger wanted whatever action was taken to be read clearly by the North Koreans as well as by the Cambodians. He argued that if Cambodia used the *Mayaguez* crew the way North Korea had used the *Pueblo* crew, it could radically deteriorate the American position in the rest of Asia. Secretary James Schlesinger, on the other hand, stressed the need to recover the ship and punish the Cambodians, but was less eager to use the *Mayaguez* incident as an example for Asia and the world.[25] *1) NY Times May 16, 1975*

During the final part of the NSC meeting, the president, after all discussion was over, directed that additional measures be taken to prepare for the recapture of the ship and that detailed plans for this operation be developed. Later, the president reflected on his motivations.

Subjectively, I was having thoughts like this: if I had done nothing, the consequences would be very, very bad, not only in failing

to meet that problem, but the implications on a broader international scale. Something was required. I felt it would be best to
try diplomacy first and, if that failed, to take strong, decisive
action—as opposed to the incremental use of force—even though
the odds might be against us. It was far better than doing nothing. [26]

The president gave the following specific orders:

o   The State Department would deliver a letter to the U.N.
    secretary general seeking help in securing the release of
    the ship and crew.
o   The JCS would plan to attack Tang Island on Wednes-
    day night, May 14, Washington time (the earliest possible
    time after essential forces had arrived). The attack
    would include simultaneously landings by marines on
    Koh Tang, the recapture of the ship by marines from
    the U.S.S. *Holt,* and naval air attacks against mainland
    targets to prevent Cambodian reinforcement of the island
    or ship.
o   B-52 bombers in Guam would be alerted for deployment
    against the Cambodian mainland if required (although
    the president thought that very unlikely and unde-
    sirable). "To have used B-52s would have been overkill."
o   Small vessels would not be permitted transit between
    Koh Tang and Kompong Som.

Thus, the basic concept of an armed assault had been approved by the president at this midnight meeting. The question
of timing then became the primary consideration. Secretary
Kissinger pressed for the earliest possible commitment of forces
to recapture the ship and prevent the movement of the crew to
the mainland. The JCS was asked if the military could mount
the operation one day earlier (which would have moved it from
the morning of May 15 to the afternoon of May 14, Cambodian
time). General Jones considered the proposal briefly, but replied
to the White House that the JCS could not recommend such
action. There were simply too many ships, aircraft, and ground
forces to coordinate in such a short time, and most of them
were still out of range of the target area. [27]

Wednesday, May 14, 1975

Diplomatic efforts to obtain the release of the crew and simultaneously to inform U.S. allies of possible military operations were conducted by the State Department. At approximately 2:00 p.m., a letter from Ambassador John Scali, United States representative to the United Nations, was delivered to the secretary general of the United Nations, Kurt Waldheim. In the letter, Ambassador Scali pointed out the gravity of the seizure, told of diplomatic efforts to reach a satisfactory solution, and reserved the right to take whatever measures were appropriate to protect American lives and property. The letter went further and requested Secretary General Waldheim's assistance in securing the release of the ship and crew.

Throughout the day of May 14, air force, navy, and marine forces were moving into position to execute the decisions of the president. By this time, the air over that small sector of the Gulf of Thailand was extremely active, with many types of aircraft conducting reconnaissance and interdiction missions. Other military forces continued to converge on the scene of the crisis. The operation involved air force and navy aircraft from Thailand and the Philippines; aircraft carriers *Coral Sea* and *Hancock;* marine units from Okinawa and the Philippines; and other naval combat ships from the South China Sea and the Philippines.

The president was in overall command of the military forces, but his orders were expected to be communicated through the secretary of defense and the Joint Chiefs of Staff.[28] From Washington the orders went to CINCPAC, which had unified command of the navy's Seventh Fleet and Pacific Fleet Marine Forces, the Pacific Air Forces, and the U.S. Support Activities Group (USSAG) Seventh Air Force (the residual USAF command in Thailand, which had conducted the air operations over North Vietnam and Laos).[29]

The *Mayaguez* operations plan was developed by JCS planners with the assistance of Admiral Noel Gayler, the commander in chief of the Pacific Command (who had been in Washington when the crisis erupted). The plan to recapture the *Mayaguez* and release the crew called for landing marines on the U.S.S. *Holt,* moving alongside the *Mayaguez,* and taking the ship with a boarding party. A helicopter combat assault would be launched against Koh Tang using two landing zones as shown in Figure 7. It was estimated that 175 marines would participate in this initial assault. Air strikes would be conducted concurrently on two target complexes on the Cambodian main-land, the Ream airfield and naval base complex, and the port installations at Kompong Som.[30]

Throughout the operation, air force fighters were to fly cover for the marines and provide air strikes as needed. Rein-forcements for the first marine wave were not immediately available. The plan did call, however, for a second wave of marines transported in ten CH- and HH-53s to arrive at Koh Tang as soon as they could be refilled. This would place about 450 marines on the island with additional reinforcements avail-able on the same round-trip basis.

The intelligence estimate concerning the threat of Cambodian forces on Tang Island proved to be one of the most critical areas of the operation plan. Estimates ranged from a low of eighteen to twenty irregulars and their families on the island to as high as two hundred Khmer Rouge soldiers armed with auto-matic weapons, mortars, and recoilless rifles. This latter esti-mate, prepared by the Defense Intelligence Agency on May 12, proved to be very accurate. Field reports estimated a maximum force of ninety to one hundred with some heavy weapons. The most serious aspect of these wide variations in enemy estimates was that they were never reconciled, nor were the factors that led to the variations ever considered by all intelligence analysts. Based on the estimate of ninety to one hundred enemy troops on the island, limiting the first wave to 175 marines was con-sidered an acceptable risk. Based on the estimate of twenty to thirty given to the marine landing force, the 175-man assault was considered more than adequate.[31]

Between the third and fourth NSC meetings, the JCS met in the Pentagon to consider the military feasibility of the pro-posed operations plan. The most critical aspect to them was the question of whether the diverse and widely separated forces would come together in time to conduct an effective combined arms operation. It is always a problem to guarantee the arrival

FIGURE 7

KOH TANG RESCUE OPERATION

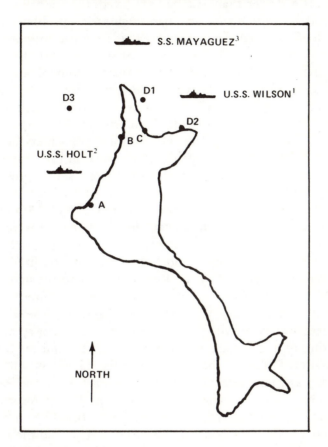

A   LANDING SITE OF MARINE COMMAND GROUP OF 29 PERSONNEL

B   LANDING SITE OF GROUP OF 60 PERSONNEL

C   LANDING SITE OF GROUP OF 20 PERSONNEL

D1   D2   D3   DOWNED HELICOPTERS

1   THE DESTROYER U.S.S. WILSON PROVIDED GUNFIRE
     DURING THE MARINE ASSAULT

2   THE POSITION OF THE DESTROYER U.S.S. HOLT
     AFTER MAYAGUEZ CREW HAD BEEN RESCUED

3   THE POSITION OF THE S.S. MAYAGUEZ WHEN THE
     MARINE ASSAULT BEGAN

time of widely scattered ships, and in this case the ships had been a little slower than JCS had expected. (At least one of the ships had to refuel and one had engineering problems.) The Joint Chiefs reached a consensus that if they had an extra day they could have a higher assurance of success; that the forces would then be in place and that command, control, and communications arrangements would be satisfactory. The feeling was that for a number of reasons—most importantly, the recovery of the crew prior to their imprisonment on the mainland—this would be too late. On balance, the Chiefs decided that the degree of risk in going as planned on the fourteenth was acceptable and that the urgency of recovery should govern.[32]

Meanwhile, the White House attempted to keep congressional members informed of the situation. At 11:15 a.m. on May 14, eleven House and eleven Senate members were contacted by John Marsh and informed that three Cambodian patrol craft had been sunk and four others immobilized in an effort to prevent removal of the *Mayaguez* crew to the mainland. At 2:00 p.m. there was a briefing of the House International Relations Committee by Morton Abramowitz, the deputy assistant secretary of defense for international security affairs. A briefing of the Senate Foreign Relations Committee by the legal advisor, Office of the Chairman, Joint Chiefs of Staff, and the acting assistant secretary of state for East Asian and Pacific affairs was conducted later in the day. The House Appropriations Defense Subcommittee was briefed by the (CIA) national intelligence officer for South and Southeast Asia, and the House Committee on Armed Services was briefed by Deputy Assistant Secretary Abramowitz.

The fourth NSC meeting was held on Wednesday, May 14, from 3:52 p.m. to 5:40 p.m. (sixty hours after the seizure). Those attending were the same as on Monday plus Admiral James Holloway, chief of naval operations, and Philip Buchen, counsel to the president. The purpose of this fourth NSC meeting was to review the diplomatic state of play, and consider the details of the landing plan. Director Colby once again summarized the situation in the area. He confirmed that the ship was still anchored off the north side of Koh Tang and that it was possible that part of the crew had been moved to the mainland. The presumption remained that at least part of the crew was on Koh Tang. General Jones reported that the destroyer U.S.S. *Holt* was on the scene near the *Mayaguez* and that a second destroyer, the U.S.S. *Wilson,* was only three hours away. Jones further stated that the aircraft carrier U.S.S. *Coral Sea* was within striking distance of the Cambodian mainland and Tang Island.

General Jones presented in detail the Joint Chiefs of Staff recommendation for a military operation to achieve the national objectives as they were articulated in the first NSC meeting. The briefing covered military action in three areas:

o   a marine boarding party on the *Holt* to seize the *Mayaguez*
o   a concurrent helicopter combat assault by marine forces on Koh Tang
o   carrier-based air strikes on mainland military targets

General Jones also noted the advantages of delaying twenty-four hours and noted that to meet the scheduled take-off times for a Thursday morning landing, a decision to go ahead would be required within the hour. A story in the *Washington Post* quoted an NSC participant's description of the reactions of the president to General Jones' briefing.

> "He was very calm and deliberate. . . . For some reason, he gave me the impression of being a general himself. The impression I got was of a man who had been in the military, and the members of the NSC were obviously impressed with his knowledge of the military.
> "He was the one who pressed all the questions. He wasn't going to be rushed into something that would fall on his head."

The story continued,

> In the discussion of the various options, according to another administration source, . . . there was essential agreement about the use of military force once those at the table were convinced diplomatic overtures were getting nowhere.
> "We're criticized for examining options and for not examining options," this source said. "Well, they were examined."[33]

124

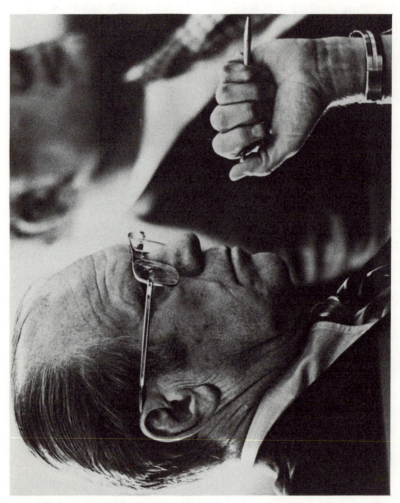

President Ford during NSC meeting, May 14, 1975. (Official White House photo by David Hume Kennerly)

Vice-president Rockefeller during NSC meeting, May 14, 1975. (Official White House photo by David Hume Kennerly)

126

Secretary of State Kissinger during NSC meeting, May 14, 1975. (Official White House photo by David Hume Kennerly)

Secretary of Defense Schlesinger during NSC meeting, May 14, 1975. (Official White House photo by David Hume Kennerly)

128

Director of Central Intelligence Colby during NSC meeting, May 14, 1975. (Official White House photo by David Hume Kennerly)

The National Security Council meeting, May 14, 1975. (Official White House photo by David Hume Kennerly)

130

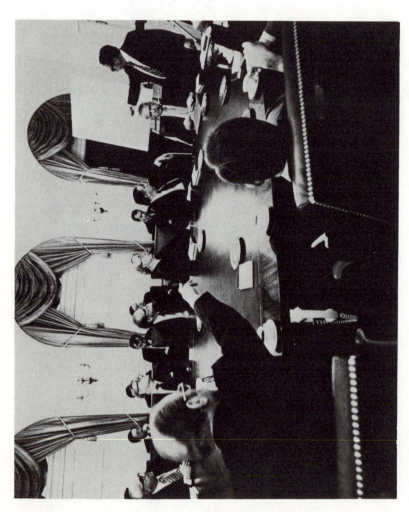

Briefing of congressional leaders in the Cabinet Room, May 14, 1975. (Official White House photo by David Hume Kennerly)

After all the discussion had been completed, President Ford approved the plan at about 4:45 p.m. and ordered it executed. Admiral Holloway left the meeting to communicate the execution order from the White House Situation Room to the NMCC. At 4:52 p.m., the JCS verbally ordered CINCPAC to execute the combined operation.

After the NSC meeting, President Ford used the same room to brief the leaders of the Congress personally on his specific orders for the recapture of the ship and the release of the crew. When interviewed the same day, however, Senate Democratic Majority Leader Mike Mansfield, said, "I was not consulted. I was notified after the fact about what the administration had already decided to do."[34] Between 5:55 p.m. and 8:20 p.m., John Marsh and the White House staff contacted many of the senators who had not been able to attend the president's personal briefing. According to one White House staff member, about one-half merely "acknowledged" the information. Press Secretary Ron Nessen characterized the response of the congressional leaders as "a strong consensus of support and no objections."[35]

OPERATIONAL IMPLEMENTATION[36]

The critical logistical factor in the implementation of the president's decision was the number of helicopters that could be flown to Utapao. Originally, arrangements had been made for twelve USAF helicopters,[37] but one had crashed on take-off on May 13 at Nakhon Phanom. Of the remaining eleven, three were assigned to ferry personnel to the U.S.S. *Holt,* for boarding the *Mayaguez.* The other eight rescue helicopters were to carry the initial assault force into two landing zones, on the east and west sides of the island. Five helicopters were to approach the island shortly after 7:00 a.m. The other three were to make their landings one hour later. The uncertainties of the situation included the location and status of the *Mayaguez* crew and the degree of enemy opposition on Koh Tang. The strong possibility that at least some of the *Mayaguez* crew might be on the island ruled out any preparation of the landing zones by a preassault bombardment. The rate of reinforcement, if it was needed, would be slow.

The first USAF/marine assault force of five helicopters approached the island just after dawn on May 15 (6:09 a.m. Cambodian time; 7:09 p.m. May 14 in Washington), only ninety minutes after the final NSC meeting. No enemy fire was received as the helicopters approached the beach and attained a hover position. Just as the first aircraft touched down and assumed a stationary position, the Cambodian defenders opened with a withering fire of rockets, mortars, small arms, and automatic weapons.

Two helicopters were immediately shot down on the eastern beach, which was the most heavily defended area of the island. On the western beach, a third helicopter was hit several times and ditched a mile off shore; a fourth suffered extensive battle damage (over seventy-five shell holes) but returned to Utapao; the fifth was hit repeatedly, developed an acute fuel leak, and barely made it to an emergency landing on the mainland. At the end of the first hour, only fifty-four Americans had been landed on the island. Fourteen others were dead. Further, one of the first helicopters shot down had carried all of the radios of the marine command and fire support group.

One hour later three helicopters attempted to land, but were faced with the same withering ground fire. Two successfully landed their marines, but were severely damaged in the process and had to withdraw to Utapao. The third made three attempts to get into the western landing zone, but was repulsed each time. Still with a full load of marines, the pilot headed for the tanker aircraft and refueled.

Meanwhile, the three helicopters that had flown to the U.S.S. *Holt* had delivered their boarding party and air refueled also. Two of the aircraft headed back for Utapao to pick up the second wave of marines, while the third made an attempt to rescue the downed USAF crew members and stranded marines on the eastern beach. Heavy ground fire greeted them, and the aircraft absorbed punishing hits from heavy automatic weapons. When fires were ignited in the flare box and auxiliary fuel tank of the helicopter, the pilot reluctantly withdrew to Thailand. The aircraft had severe rotor damage; was leaking fuel, oil, and hydraulic fluid; and had sustained thirty-five hits.

The first assault wave was now on Koh Tang. A total of

131 marines and 5 USAF crew members were on the island, but 15 Americans had been killed in action. The cost in aircraft had been high also. Eight of the nine helicopters that had participated in the first phase had either been shot down, ditched, or damaged so severely that they were out of action.[38]

As mentioned earlier, the boarding party had been landed on the U.S.S. *Holt* at the time of the first Koh Tang landings. About an hour later, the *Holt* pulled alongside the *Mayaguez,* and USAF aircraft dropped riot-control agents.

When the marine force boarded the vessel, at about 7:25 a.m. Cambodian time, 8:25 p.m. Washington time, no one was found and the ship was declared secure.

Unknown to all these men in the Gulf of Thailand and officials in Washington, the Cambodian government had finally decided to communicate with the United States. At 6:07 a.m. in Phnom Penh (7:07 p.m. in Washington) the Cambodian minister of information and propaganda began a local radio broadcast on the subject of the *Mayaguez.* Two paragraphs from the end of the nineteen-minute speech, he stated that his government was prepared to release the ship if it would depart Cambodian territorial waters and perform no further acts of espionage or other provocations.[39]

The message was monitored by overseas stations of the Foreign Broadcast Information Service, where it was translated and relayed to Washington immediately. General Scowcroft received a summary of the long message at about 8:15 p.m., while he was preparing for the state dinner to be held in honor of Dutch Prime Minister den Uyl. He immediately called the president, who was also preparing to attend the dinner. President Ford received the information at 8:29 p.m., while the marine assault was in full progress. The president noted the Cambodian offer to release the ship, but as he later stated, "I made the point that they made no mention of the crew, and thus I decided that the operation should proceed as planned since we had received no indication assuring the safety of the crew. Nor was it clear that this local broadcast had any official standing in Phnom Penh."[40] He instructed the White House Press Office to acknowledge receipt of the message by issuing a statement for immediate national broadcast. Press Secretary

The U.S.S. *Holt.* (U.S. Navy photo)

The S.S. *Mayaguez* on May 15, 1975. (USAF photo)

136

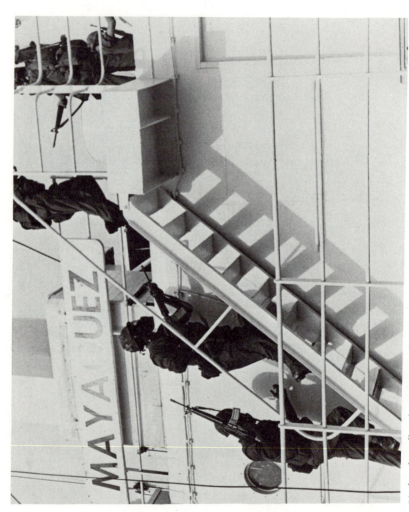

Marines boarding the *Mayaguez*. (U.S. Navy photo)

Marines raising U.S. flag on *Mayaguez.* (U.S. Navy photo)

Ron Nessen issued the following statement at 9:15 p.m.:

> We have heard radio broadcast that you are prepared to re-
> lease the S.S. *Mayaguez*. We welcome this development, if true.
>   As you know, we have seized the ship. As soon as you issue
> a statement that you are prepared to release the crew members
> you hold unconditionally and immediately, we will promptly
> cease military operations.[41]

Nessen went on to stress that the president had the constitutional authority to protect the lives and property of Americans.[42]

The president had also approved strike operations from the
U.S.S. *Coral Sea* against the Cambodian mainland. The first
time over target—7:45 a.m.—coincided with the estimated recovery of the *Mayaguez*, but not with the assault on Koh Tang
which had started about an hour and a half earlier.

From 7:05 a.m. to 10:30 a.m., three aircraft attack waves
departed from the U.S.S. *Coral Sea* to strike targets on the
mainland. The first wave was ordered by the White House to
withhold its ordnance when the information about the Cambodian government broadcast became known. After the message was evaluated by the president—a period of about twenty
minutes—instructions were issued to strike as planned.

The second cycle of navy attack aircraft struck Ream
airfield about 9:57 a.m., cratered the runway, damaged the
hangars, and destroyed numerous aircraft. An hour later, the
third wave hit the Ream naval base and the Kompong Som
naval facilities, damaging a fuel storage area, two warehouses,
and the railroad marshalling yard.

By 11:00 a.m., the strikes were complete. The primary
tactical mission of the naval air forces was considered accomplished because no Cambodian reinforcements attempted to
interfere with the operations on Koh Tang.

Although it was unknown at that time, the *Mayaguez* crew
had been released from Rong Som Lem Island in Kompong
Som Harbor at approximately 6:20 a.m., and were returned to
their ship with several Thai fishermen in a Thai fishing boat.
They were given long bamboo poles on which to tie articles of
clothing to wave at the U.S. planes. At 9:49 a.m. (10:49 p.m.

The presidential party upon hearing that the *Mayaguez* crew had been released, May 15, 1975. (*New York Times* front page photo taken in Oval Office)

in Washington), the crew of the *Mayaguez* was recovered by the destroyer U.S.S. *Wilson.*

The information that the crew had been recovered was relayed to Washington by both the captain of the U.S.S. *Wilson* and the airborne command and control aircraft. The news was greeted with elation in the White House, although President Ford remained concerned over the safety of the marines on Koh Tang. He directed that all offensive operations cease, but ordered that all ships and aircraft remain alert to support the withdrawal of the marines. Shortly after midnight, the president read the following statement to the American public and the world:

> At my direction the United States forces tonight boarded the American merchant ship *Mayaguez* and landed at the island of Koh Tang for the purpose of rescuing the crew and the ship, which had been illegally seized by Cambodian forces. They also conducted supporting strikes against nearby military installations. I have now received information that the vessel has been recovered intact and the entire crew has been rescued. The forces that have successfully accomplished this mission are still under hostile fire, but are preparing to disengage. I wish to express my deep appreciation and that of the entire nation to the units and the men for their valor and their sacrifice.[43]

The disengagement of the marine landing force was to be a very hazardous affair, however. Just after noon on May 15, the landing of reinforcements was completed, bringing the total on the island to 222 Americans. Although the marines remained under periodic heavy fire from mortars and automatic weapons, at 12:08 p.m. the marine commander Lieutenant Colonel Austin reported that his troops were prepared for the extraction.

During the next five hours, the remaining four helicopters attempted desperately to fight their way through the intense ground fire to the two landing zones. Two separate attempts to extract personnel from the eastern beach were made in mid-afternoon. The first attempt was repulsed by heavy automatic weapons fire which ruptured a fuel line, causing a massive leak. Leaving the island on one engine, the aircraft returned to the *Coral Sea.* The second helicopter made it to the eastern beach despite the ground fire and picked up the entire contingent of twenty-five marines and airmen who had been stranded there. Although the second helicopter was not hit severely, the one providing covering fire for the extraction suffered damage to the tail rotor section, hydraulic lines, fuel tanks, and rotor blades.

The 213 marines and USAF crew members on the western beach were not picked up until well after sunset. In an all-out effort, the three remaining helicopters made repeated landings on the beach while fire support was provided by the helicopters themselves, small boats from the U.S.S. *Holt* and *Wilson*, an airborne forward air controller, USAF fighters, and a gunship.

By 8:15 p.m. (9:15 a.m. in Washington) on May 15, all of the marine landing force had been removed from Koh Tang, and military operations ceased. The four days of the *Mayaguez* crisis were over. The immediate results included the recovery of the ship and the crew, but the losses had been high. All but one of the eleven USAF helicopters had suffered battle damage. The U.S. had fifteen men killed in action, three missing in action, and fifty wounded by hostile fire. Although the marines had spent some fourteen hours on Koh Tang, all fifteen men killed were hit in the first ninety minutes.[44] An additional twenty-three were killed when their Air Force CH-53 crashed en route to Utapao during the deployment phase of the crisis.

AFTERMATH AND OUTCOMES

The domestic reaction to the president's actions was immediate and indicated overwhelming approval. A front page story in the *New York Times* called the incident a "domestic and foreign triumph," noting that the *Mayaguez* was the visible symbol of United States resolve.[45]

Although the release of the crew was greeted with universal relief in the United States, the congressional reaction was influenced by partisan political objectives and the broader struggle for power between the executive and legislative branches of government. The latter theme had been strongly influenced by the War Powers Resolution (see Appendix C).

President Ford and Secretary Kissinger were acutely aware of the potential compromise to timely U.S. actions during a crisis inherent in the War Powers requirements. To them, the issue was no less than fulfillment of the commander in chief's responsibilities for crisis management. From the beginning of the *Mayaguez* crisis, the president was adamant that War Powers reporting requirements be observed without acknowledging the constitutionality of the law and without prejudice to an ultimate challenge to that constitutionality. To these ends, he insured that congressional leaders were periodically informed of crisis developments.

Within two hours after the *Mayaguez* crew had been returned, President Ford submitted his report to the Congress in the form of a letter advising that body of actions taken during the crisis.

Dear Mr. Speaker (President Pro Tem): On 12 May 1975 I was advised that the S.S. *Mayaguez,* a merchant vessel of United States registry en route from Hong Kong to Thailand with a U.S. citizen crew, was fired upon, stopped, boarded, and seized by Cambodian naval patrol boats of the Armed Forces of Cambodia in international waters in the vicinity of Paulo Wai Island. The seized vessel was then forced to proceed to Koh Tang Island where it was required to anchor. This hostile act was in clear violation of international law.

In view of this illegal and dangerous act, I ordered, as you have been previously advised, United States military forces to conduct the necessary reconnaissance and to be ready to respond if diplomatic efforts to secure the return of the vessel and its personnel were not successful. Two United States reconnaissance aircraft in the course of locating the *Mayaguez* sustained minimal damage from small firearms. Appropriate demands for the return of the *Mayaguez* and its crew were made, both publicly and privately, without success.

In accordance with my desire that the Congress be informed on this matter and taking note of Section 4(a)(1) of the War Powers Resolution, I wish to report to you that at about 6:20 a.m., 13 May, pursuant to my instructions to prevent the movement of the *Mayaguez* into a mainland port, U.S. aircraft fired warning shots across the bow of the ship and gave visual signals to small craft approaching the ship. Subsequently, in order to stabilize the situation and in an attempt to preclude removal of the American crew of the *Mayaguez* to the mainland, where

their rescue would be more difficult, I directed the United States
Armed Forces to isolate the island and interdict any movement of
the ship itself, while still taking all possible care to prevent loss
of life or injury to the U.S. captives. During the evening of 13
May, a Cambodian patrol boat attempting to leave the island dis-
regarded aircraft warnings and was sunk. Thereafter, two other
Cambodian patrol craft were destroyed and four others were
damaged and immobilized. One boat, suspected of having some
U.S. captives aboard, succeeded in reaching Kompong Som after
efforts to turn it around without injury to the passengers failed.

Our continued objective in this operation was the rescue of
the captured American crew along with the retaking of the ship
Mayaguez. For that purpose, I ordered late this afternoon an
assault by United States Marines on the island of Koh Tang to
search out and rescue such Americans as might still be held there,
and I ordered retaking of the *Mayaguez* by other marines boarding from the destroyer escort *Holt.* In addition to continued
fighter and gunship coverage of the Koh Tang area, these marine
activities were supported by tactical aircraft from the *Coral Sea,*
striking the military airfield at Ream and other military targets
in the area of Kompong Som in order to prevent reinforcement or
support from the mainland of the Cambodian forces detaining the
American vessel and crew.

At approximately 9:00 p.m. EDT on 14 May, the *Mayaguez*
was retaken by United States forces. At approximately 11:30
p.m., the entire crew of the *Mayaguez* was taken abroad [sic] the
Wilson. U.S. forces have begun the process of disengagement and
withdrawal.

This operation was ordered and conducted pursuant to the
President's constitutional Executive power and his authority as
Commander-in-Chief of the United States Armed Forces.

Sincerely,

Gerald R. Ford[46]

In the eyes of many members of Congress the four "consultations" were merely efforts to inform the Congress rather
than consult with it. House Resolutions 536 and 537 bear this
out. In these two documents, the Congress directed the secretary of state to provide specific information on the *Mayaguez*
crisis and actions that were taken to resolve the situation short

of the use of troops. In his reply to these resolutions, Robert J. McCloskey, the assistant secretary of state for congressional relations, responded that actions taken by the White House and the State and Defense Departments were considered sufficient to satisfy the requirements of the War Powers Resolution. Some members of Congress interpreted these actions differently, and at least three appeared before hearings held by the House International Political and Military Affairs Subcommittee of the House International Relations Committee (chaired by Congressman Dante B. Fascell, Florida), soundly condemning both the military action and the lack of consultation with the Congress.[47] (Appearing were Representatives John Burton, California; Elizabeth Holtzman, New York; and Patricia Schroeder, Colorado.)

Two days earlier, on June 23, 1975, Congressman Fascell had written to Mr. Elmer B. Staats, the comptroller general of the United States, asking him to have the General Accounting Office review all aspects of the *Mayaguez* crisis management operations and to submit a report. The GAO study was completed and made public in early October 1976.[48] This report has an important part in the aftermath of the *Mayaguez* case because the GAO: criticized the administration's substantive handling of the crisis; criticized the executive decision-making process; and itself became a subject of controversy.

The GAO report criticized President Ford's handling of the crisis and particularly the decision to use force. The GAO's International Division pointed out several other alternatives to military force that were not used. These included:

○   contacting Cambodians in Phnom Penh directly
○   contacting Cambodian representatives in Paris and Moscow
○   enlisting the diplomatic assistance of governments other than the Chinese

To most of the policy makers in the administration, the near total diplomatic isolation of Cambodia and its apparent lack of the means, or willingness, to communicate with anyone effectively precluded all of the options listed by the GAO within the time constraints of the situation. Nor were such attempts necessary, since there is little doubt that Cambodian authorities received the U.S. protest through their embassy in Peking. In the entire report, which is characterized by retrospective misconceptions and interpretations, their conclusions on diplomatic lost opportunities are most flagrantly misguided. As Lawrence S. Eagleburger, deputy under-secretary of state, stated in his letter of March 15, 1976, to the comptroller general:

> The drafters of this report had a special responsibility to attempt to understand the realities of the diplomatic environment at the time of the *Mayaguez* seizure. They did not meet this responsibility. Instead, they went out of their way to develop wholly fictional diplomatic scenarios which bore no resemblance to fact or reality, and then criticized the Administration for its "failure" to pursue their fantasies.[49]

There is ample reason to assume that the Cambodian government knew fully what was taking place off their coast. In addition to the communications attempts made by the United States directly, the Voice of America beamed stories on the *Mayaguez* situation into Cambodia on nine different occasions. Since the Cambodians chose a public radio broadcast to announce their terms for release of the ship on May 14, there is little credibility to the theory that they were unversed in this form of strategic bargaining. There is also no evidence to refute the thesis that the Cambodian leaders were playing the *Mayaguez* seizure for all it was worth, believing the United States had lost its national will to react swiftly and effectively in Southeast Asia.

The General Accounting Office report asserted strongly that the assault on Koh Tang was unnecessary, since the crew of the *Mayaguez* had already been released.[50] This judgment, made in the calm aftermath of battle, ignores the fact that the crew's release was not known (nor had it been promised) until four hours after the assault began. The president's offer to cease all military operations if the Cambodians released the crew was met with stony silence.

Beyond the substantive arguments of the GAO, the report's release came under considerable criticism, especially among

Republicans who viewed it as a partisan political attempt by the Democratic leadership of the Congress to criticize the president during an election year. This belief was generated by the apparent timing of the release, only one day before the second debate—a debate on foreign policy—between President Ford and Governor Carter. Comptroller General Staats attempted to defend the integrity of his agency and was quick to point out that the timing of the release was beyond the control of the GAO.

The Republican counter to the release was written by Lewis Perdue and published in *Congress Today.*

> A democratic political effort to use an independent investigatory agency to bias the Ford-Carter foreign policy debate seems to have backfired on its instigator, Rep. Dante Fascell, a Florida Democrat. Fascell rushed into print a study that mildly criticized the Ford Administration's handling of the *Mayaguez* incident and released it on Oct. 5, the day before the debates, accompanied by a news release that alleged "extensive" criticism by the study. Fascell is Chairman of the House Subcommittee on International, Political and Military affairs of the International Relations committee.[51]

In the estimation of most international observers, the retaking of the *Mayaguez* caused few repercussions except within the Communist community. The comments by Communist government organs were predictably critical of U.S. actions.

The single exception to acceptance of U.S. actions by non-Communist nations was in the case of Thailand. The Thai government formally protested the use of its territory to stage military action without prior notification and approval. The United States, in a formal note, expressed regret over the misunderstanding that had arisen between the two governments and this apparently resolved the problem.

No specific polls were taken concerning how the American public perceived President Ford's performance. Gallup polls were taken, however, to determine the American public's perception of Ford's performance in general terms. Responses to this poll yielded the statistical summary in Table 1.

Table 1. President Ford's Popularity: February 28–June 2, 1975*

Time Period of Poll	Approve	Disapprove	No Opinion
February 28–March 23: Before *Mayaguez;* before fall of Phnom Penh	39%	45%	16%
April 18–21: Before *Mayaguez;* after fall of Phnom Penh	39%	46%	15%
May 30–June 2: After *Mayaguez*	51%	33%	16%

* Question: "Do you approve or disapprove of the way President Ford is handling his job as President?"

Source: *Gallup Opinion Index—Political, Social and Economic Trends*, Report no. 120, June 1975 (Princeton, N.J.: American Institute of Public Opinion, 1975).

The May 30 poll was the first poll conducted after the *Mayaguez* crisis. The increase in popularity of 12 percent following an international crisis is characteristic of past crises in other recent administrations.[52] At the same time, it must be acknowledged that these polls reflect perceptions colored by many other events and presidential decisions. The responses were not focused solely on the president's performance in recovering the *Mayaguez,* but on the totality of his performance. As a result of our inability to extract the effect of other events, only tentative conclusions may be drawn. At least his *Mayaguez* performance did not hurt the president's popularity, and there is a good chance that it increased it significantly.

In summary, the *Mayaguez* crisis generated a complex set of outcomes that continued to be controversial for at least a year and a half after the event. The domestic political discussions tended to focus on the issue of executive-legislative relations and to obscure the military and foreign policy outcomes. There was, however, an undeniable consensus across the country that at last, after so many setbacks, we had done something right.

On the strategic/international outcome, the *Mayaguez* crisis must be called conclusive. The crew was returned, and the vessel was recovered. The United States did not have to negotiate with the Cambodians for the next year to get the crew back. The means of crisis resolution included elements of diplomacy, but the dominant method was the use of military force. For the first time in several years, the utility of force was demonstrated in a successful U.S. military operation. That success generated a moral uplift for the American people, restored a belief in American credibility, and demonstrated a strategic resolve worthy of a great power.

6
The Korean Tree Crisis: Murder on the DMZ

On August 18, 1976, while supervising the pruning of a giant poplar tree in the Joint Security Area of the Korean Demilitarized Zone, two American Army officers were murdered by North Korean soldiers. This incident—brutal and criminal in its own right—triggered an extensive series of diplomatic and military actions in Korea, in Hawaii, in the departments of State and Defense, and in the White House. Before it was over, it would involve a presidential decision and a military reaction that would send strategic signals around the world. The objectives of this case study are to examine both military and political aspects of the crisis, the U.S. organizational arrangements for crisis management, and the command and control of the military forces involved; and to provide data for further analysis of crisis behavior.[1]

BACKGROUND: THE CONTEXT OF THE CRISIS

From a political point of view, a leading factor in the background to the Korean tree incident was undoubtedly the *Mayaguez* crisis. In that situation, the United States had responded quickly with large military forces, attacked Koh Tang and the Cambodian mainland, and achieved the swift release of the ship's crew. Despite the public criticism of the high cost in casualties, the speed and overwhelming nature of the military and political response undoubtedly sent a clear signal to U.S.

For a detailed listing of the events relating to this incident, see Appendix B: Chronology of the Korean DMZ Crisis.

allies and adversaries alike.

United States interests in the Korean peninsula extend primarily from the Korean War (1950-1953), and have revolved around two fundamental foreign policy objectives: (1) preservation of peace and stability in the region; and (2) maintenance of the independence and viability of the Republic of Korea. One might also add a third objective of U.S. policy, so often asserted by former Secretary of State Henry Kissinger: blocking the expansion of Soviet influence. Stability on the peninsula has been considered critical to the defense of Japan as was publicly reaffirmed by President Ford on December 7, 1975, when he announced a Pacific doctrine, stating, "Partnership with Japan is a pillar of our strategy." He went on to say, "Since the Japanese consider the security of South Korea to be intimately related to their own security, U.S. support to South Korea is essential to stability in Northeast Asia."[2] The U.S. commitment is specifically formalized by the Mutual Defense Treaty of 1954 with the Republic of Korea.

Since the end of the Korean War in 1953, the United States has maintained military forces in South Korea under U.S. command. However, the U.S. commander also exercises operational control of the Republic of Korea forces in his capacity as commander in chief, United Nations Command (CINCUNC), the position originally held by General Douglas MacArthur. In 1973, the combined position of CINCUNC; commander, U.S. forces; and commander, Eighth Army was assumed by General Richard G. Stilwell. General Stilwell, a 38-year veteran, had previously been deputy chief of staff for military operations, U.S. Army Headquarters, and was widely respected throughout the army and in Washington as a tough soldier.

In 1976, General Stilwell's command consisted of approximately 42,000 U.S. troops. The principal military units were the Second Infantry Division, the Thirty-eighth Air Defense Artillery Brigade, the Fourth Missile Command, the Nineteenth Support Brigade, the Eighth Tactical Fighter Wing, the Fifty-first Composite [Tactical Fighter] Wing, and smaller support units.[3] The purposes of these military forces were to: (1) provide tangible evidence of U.S. support for South Korea; (2) deter an attack by North Korea; and (3) dissuade the P.R.C.

or the USSR from condoning such an attack.[4]

Far from signaling a true peace, the cessation of armed hostilities in 1953 only transformed the nature and scale of the conflict into less dramatic, lower-order events. The formal political conference that was to provide the peace never took place. Since the armistice, 49 Americans, 1,000 South Koreans, and over 600 North Koreans have been killed along the Demilitarized Zone (DMZ)—the 4-kilometer band that separates the two Koreas. In the period 1967-73 alone, the United States, the United Nations, and South Korea submitted nearly 2,000 formal complaints of incidents of harassment and violence on the DMZ. A large number of these were in the Joint Security Area (JSA)—the 800-meter diameter circle within the DMZ that houses the Military Armistice Commission (MAC) Headquarters, intended as a neutral zone where both sides can travel freely and conduct meetings in an open environment.

A particularly serious incident in the Joint Security Area took place on June 30, 1975, when a U.S. Army major was seriously injured in an attack precipitated by a North Korean newsman while a MAC meeting was in progress. Without provocation, the officer was attacked by North Korean guards and suffered a serious throat injury requiring emergency surgery and evacuation to the United States. Although physical injury has been rare, the daily level of hostility, provocation, and verbal abuse in the Joint Security Area has been extremely high. The North Korean guards are powerful and aggressive, and most of them have been on duty in the JSA for the majority of their military careers. To operate effectively in this difficult atmosphere, the U.S. Army has routinely applied special requirements to men assigned to JSA duty. They are selected for their height, physical fitness, and even temperament. After selection, U.S. personnel undergo special training to prepare them to cope with a steady stream of insults and harassment. These low-level incidents and the hostility they represent are symptomatic of the continuing tension between the two Koreas.

Congressional interest in Korea has centered around three primary concerns. The first is the perennial question of whether the United States is overextended in its foreign policy commitments. This question has two variants, "Has the need for U.S.

forces in Korea declined?" and "Is the economic burden of maintaining forces in Korea too great?" The second concern, and one that became a part of the 1976 presidential campaign, is that of human rights and the degree of repression in the regime of Korean President Park Chung-hee. That the South Korean government has established and maintained an authoritarian rule is generally accepted, especially since a new Korean constitution came into being in October 1972. Recent concern had been heightened by the number of political arrests for alleged violations of emergency ordinances which President Park maintained were required in the interests of Korean national security. The third, and politically most explosive, concern is the extent of South Korean attempts to interfere with the U.S. political process. Beginning in 1975 and accelerating in 1976, Washington headlines had reported allegations of illegal Korean Central Intelligence Agency activities, centering on improper influence peddling, gifts, and payments to U.S. congressmen. Congressional concern was manifested in efforts, particularly in the House, to enact legislation cutting off U.S. assistance to Korea until fundamental human rights were restored.[5] Thus, in the summer of 1976, U.S.-Korean relations had become a contentious domestic political issue in the United States, and proposals had been made to withdraw U.S. forces from the peninsula.

The two Koreas had always presented volatile international political problems, since they were aligned as client-states of the superpowers. The Democratic People's Republic of Korea (D.P.R.K.) had been established in 1948 with the full support of the Russian army of occupation. Relations with the People's Republic of China were formalized in 1949 with the signing of a little-known bilateral defense treaty in Moscow.[6] The Republic of Korea (R.O.K.) had been established with U.S. support, which had included a large military advisory group until the North Korean invasion of June 1950 and since then had been reinforced with a varying number of regular military units.

By 1976 the D.P.R.K., with its centrally controlled and highly inefficient economy, was on the economic defensive. It had a poor international reputation for defaulting on debts and had extreme difficulty obtaining credit for imports. Time, substantial U.S. economic assistance, and the much higher growth rate of their flourishing economy, tended to work in favor of the South Koreans, and provided incentive for the North Koreans to push for unification before South Korea got too strong.

North Korea's ruler, Kim Il-sung, who had led the North since its formal inception in 1948, reportedly had three main concerns: his succession, unification of the country, and his control over the people of North Korea. The degree of control he exercised has been described in the following terms:

> The political system of the DPRK (North Korea) is one of the most monolithic, exacting, and centralized systems of control ever instituted over a large human group. It is proud of and, for a socialist system, outstandingly insistent on its own independence. It is also one of the most isolated of all polities; North Korean citizens are perhaps more sedulously sealed from foreign contact than any other major educated people on earth.[7]

Kim's foreign policy strategy had apparently been to maintain the delicate balance between Chinese and Russian friendship, to take the diplomatic offensive through the nonaligned countries, and to persuade the U.N. General Assembly to *order* U.S. forces out of Korea. With the accomplishment of the last objective, many analysts argued, the armistice would collapse, and the way would be open for Kim to reunify the country by force.[8] The Thirtieth U.N. General Assembly in November 1975 was faced with two conflicting resolutions on Korea. The U.S.-backed resolution was on the agenda first and called for both Koreas to continue their dialogue, expressed the hope that both parties would negotiate new arrangements to replace the armistice agreement, and proposed talks which might permit the dissolution of the U.N. Command (UNC) concurrently with other arrangements for maintaining the armistice. The pro-North Korean resolution advocated the immediate dissolution of the UNC, the negotiation of a peace treaty between the United States and North Korea (neglecting South Korea), and the withdrawal of all foreign forces. Despite their contradictory implications, both resolutions passed the General Assembly.[9]

In mid-1976, Kim's political position was strengthened by a message of congratulations and support from Chairman Mao Tse-tung and Premier Hua Kuo-feng, on July 10, the fifteenth anniversary of the China-Korea Treaty of Friendship, Cooperation, and Mutual Assistance. The P.R.C. leaders stressed the "great unity of our two peoples cemented with bloodshed in their protracted fight against common enemies." Further,

> The Chinese people firmly support the Korean people in their just struggle for the independent and peaceful reunification of their fatherland and resolutely condemn all schemes aimed at creating "two Koreas." We are sure that the heroic Korean people will remove interference by any outside forces and accomplish the great cause of opposing U.S. imperialist aggression and realizing the independent and peaceful reunification of their fatherland.[10]

In addition to the personal message, the P.R.C. communicated to North Korea what may have been interpreted as a more specific signal in a *People's Daily* editorial on the same day. It charged the United States had

> shipped into South Korea big quantities of modern weapons, and repeatedly staged military exercises to aggravate tension on the Korean peninsula. The United States must dissolve the "U.N. Command" and withdraw all its troops from South Korea in accordance with the resolution of the 30th session of the U.N. General Assembly.[11]

Although there is no public intelligence available as to the North Korean interpretation of these messages, they may well have strengthened Kim's resolve and given added support to a specific intention or a generalized desire for a renewed political offensive. (It is worth noting that these messages were sent to North Korea while the "radical" elements in Chinese domestic politics were in authority, just before the death of Mao.)

The Mao/Hua message was followed by the publication by the North Korean government of a special White Paper attacking the United States and its forces in Korea with terms that had never been used before. On August 5 the North Korean News Agency in Pyongyang broadcast the following excerpt from the White Paper:

The long-standing tensions in Korea have now reached an acute state as never before and the Korean people are faced with the critical situation in which war may break out at any moment. The United States and the South Korean authorities, who have been stepping up pre-preparations for war to invade the Northern half of the Democratic People's Republic of Korea, *have now finished war preparations* and are going over to the adventurous machination to directly ignite the fuse of war. . . . All this is an act that the imperialists can commit on the eve of the provocation of an aggressive war and reminds one of the situation in 1950 when the United States provoked the Korean War. The U.S. imperialists have long pushed ahead with adventurous war preparations against the Korean People. Particularly after it had been ignominiously defeated in and driven out of Indochina, the United States directed the spearhead of its Asian aggression to Korea and openly declared South Korea its "forward defense zone."[12] (Italics added.)

Although this broadcast and the accompanying White Paper were dismissed by the U.N. Command as normal ideological rhetoric, they were considered especially strident in Washington. According to U.S. Defense and State Department analysts, the unusual features about this broadcast were the claim that the United States and South Korea had actually *completed* war preparations, and second, that it was a *government* statement. Such formal statements had only been issued on two previous occasions, to protest U.S. actions after the 1968 seizure of the *Pueblo* and the 1969 loss of the EC-121 aircraft. Although attacks on the U.S. presence and posture in South Korea were common, these two unusual features led several lower-ranking U.S. officials to attempt to get a warning message sent to U.S. forces in Korea. This attempt was apparently unsuccessful for two reasons: first, the signal, if it was one, was deemed too ambiguous; and second, the only logical request would have been to "be watchful" to men and organizations who were expected to do that routinely, and further, had been living under the continued high tension of the Korean situation for an extended period.

The next day, August 6, in the Joint Security Area of the DMZ, six South Korean Service Corps workers and four U.N. Command (U.S. Army) guards approached a large poplar tree with the intent of felling it. The tree had long been a problem for U.N. guards because it grew so fully it obstructed the view from U.N. Observation Post Five to the general area around U.N. Guard Post Three. This kind of activity, the trimming of trees and cutting and clearing of brush, had been carried on for years in the Joint Security Area without serious incident, although like almost all activity there, it had been the source of many disagreements and disputes.

The Korean People's Army (KPA) and the Military Armistice Commission joint duty officer had been informed on July 28 that up to 150 U.N. personnel would be in the Joint Security Area during the month of August for the purposes of construction, beautification, and routine maintenance. On July 29, that number was increased to 200 personnel. On August 2, this particular tree had been surveyed, and it had been determined that felling the tree would be required. Now, on August 6, when the work crew attempted to cut it down, a Korean People's Army guard reportedly questioned them and told them to leave the tree alone. Not wishing to cause an incident, in line with their strict operating instructions, the crew withdrew and reported the impasse to the JSA commander. The North Korean guard did not make an official protest, and apparently neither did the U.N. forces. The incident was routine in the Joint Security Area, and did not appear to differ from any of hundreds of such instances in the day-to-day tension of living in proximity to potentially hostile forces. As it was not reported to U.N. Command headquarters, the incident was certainly not reported to Washington. It was, however, noted by the JSA commander that any further maintenance on this tree might require special precautions.

Meanwhile, official Washington was increasingly concerned with campaign politics and the upcoming Republican convention. Candidate Carter had won the Democratic nomination on the first ballot and was leading President Ford in national polls by a wide margin. The major campaign issues were the economy and unemployment. The Democratic candidate was advocating a more activist government role in reducing inflation, cutting taxes, and providing jobs. On foreign and defense policy, the Democratic candidate was advocating a $5-7 billion cut in defense spending and, specifically, a withdrawal of U.S. ground forces from Korea.[13] President Ford, on August 13, declared that foreign policy could become a major issue in the campaign, and he strongly criticized Mr. Carter's apparent willingness to have the United States "withdraw from world responsibilities."[14]

President Ford was also being criticized by his Republican competitor for the nomination, California ex-Governor Ronald Reagan. Mr. Reagan had steadily gained in political strength over the preceding year, largely on the basis of an unusually strong attack on the administration's foreign policy and the architect of détente, Secretary of State Henry Kissinger. Reagan, in a surprise move, had named liberal Pennsylvania Senator Richard S. Schweiker to be his intended vice-presidential nominee, and he challenged President Ford to name his running mate. This was one of the first crucial issues at the Republican Convention, as the Rules Committee was given a Reagan-backed resolution that would have required all presidential contenders to name their vice-presidential choices before the convention balloting.

On August 15, President Ford's supporters prevailed on the Rules Committee, and that body rejected the Reagan proposal. That afternoon, President Ford and his national security advisor, Lieutenant General Brent Scowcroft, flew to Kansas City. Governor Reagan insisted, however, that the issue be taken to the floor of the convention and proposed there. Two days later, in the early morning hours of August 18, the president obtained enough committed delegates to defeat the Reagan-backed rules change and presumably to win the nomination on the floor of the convention. (The vote was 1,180 to 1,069.) The defeat was not conclusive, however, in that a number of uncommitted delegates who had supported the president did so with ambivalence. They remained open to opportunities to cast a deciding vote during consideration of the platform. Sensing this possibility, the president's supporters acceded to a modification of the platform proposed by Governor Reagan's supporters that included a strong reaffirmation of the U.S. intention to honor its commitments worldwide. While this specific provision did not depart from President Ford's oft-stated pledges of fidelity to allies, the convention debate cast Mr. Reagan as the hawk and left the impression, however unwarranted, of relatively less commitment on the part of the president. The result was to create an atmosphere in which the president could have been expected not to shirk an opportunity to demonstrate U.S. constancy and firmness.

At the same time as the Republican National Convention, August 17, North Korea launched a two-pronged political attack on the United States. At the United Nations, a group of twenty-one Communist and developing nations submitted a draft resolution to be considered by the Thirty-first General Assembly demanding: (1) that all new types of military equipment and arms, including nuclear weapons, be removed from South Korea; (2) an end to all acts of aggression against North Korea; and (3) the termination of all provocative actions such as military maneuvers and exercises. The sponsoring nations included the USSR, Bulgaria, Poland, Algeria, Iraq, and Laos.[15] However, by August 18, the resolution had only twenty-three cosponsors as compared to forty-three the previous year.

The second phase of the attack was aimed at gaining international support at the Nonaligned Nations Conference in Sri Lanka. Kim Il-sung had planned to attend this conference and lead his country's diplomatic effort, but he apparently changed his mind. On August 15, according to Belgrade radio, Kim wired President Tito that he would not be attending the conference because of a "deteriorating situation on the Korean border." When the conference began on August 16, more than eighty nations were in attendance. Sri Lankan Prime Minister Sirimavo Bandaranaike opened with a strong attack on U.S. plans to expand the air and naval facilities on the Indian Ocean island of Diego Garcia. The next day, August 17, North Korean Premier Pak Song Chul made a fiery plenary speech against the United States—arguing for withdrawal of all nuclear weapons from South Korea, withdrawal of all foreign troops, abolishment of all foreign military bases, replacement of the Korean armistice with a peace agreement, and reunification of Korea. His was a virtual repeat of the virulent August 5 statement, but this time he added that any attack on a nonaligned member should be considered an attack on all, requiring the severence of political and economic relations with the aggressor. He further proposed a lengthy resolution to condemn "imperialist maneuvers to provoke a war in Korea."[16]

The next day, August 18, had been selected by the JSA commander to trim the poplar tree.

THE CRISIS EVENT

Lieutenant Colonel Victor S. Vierra was the U.S. commander of the U.N. Command Joint Security Area. His mission was to maintain a system of observation posts, checkpoints, and command posts in order to support CINCUNC in discharge of his armistice responsibilities. At the same time, he was charged with providing security for his men in the face of continual North Korean harassment and the threat of assault. His resources included 135 men, a mixture of enlisted men and officers, U.S. and Korean, organized basically into three platoons. He operated under the strict constraints of the 1953 armistice agreement, which permitted each side to maintain a security force of only five officers and thirty service members inside the Joint Security Area (JSA) at any one time. (Additional nonsecurity personnel were permitted within the JSA upon notification.) Normally, Colonel Vierra's force was disposed as follows. One unit, the duty platoon, was to be in the area manning guard posts, protecting the U.N. negotiating team or visitors, and accompanying work details; members of the duty platoon not on one of these tasks were habitually assembled at U.N. Checkpoint Four (see Figure 8), about 660 yards by road from the tree. The second platoon was the Quick Reaction Force and was normally stationed during daytime hours 80 yards south of U.N. Checkpoint Two, about 680 yards from the tree. The third platoon was normally off duty. In addition, one rifle company from the Second U.S. Infantry Division was routinely kept on sixty-minute alert as a reinforcement unit, at the JSA advance camp outside the DMZ and almost two miles from the JSA.

The armistice agreement permitted the arming of both Korean People's Army (KPA) and U.N. Command security personnel with either sidearms or nonautomatic rifles, and it guaranteed their freedom of movement within the JSA. This agreement notwithstanding, the North Koreans in 1965 had

160

FIGURE 8

THE JOINT SECURITY AREA IN THE KOREAN DEMILITARIZED ZONE

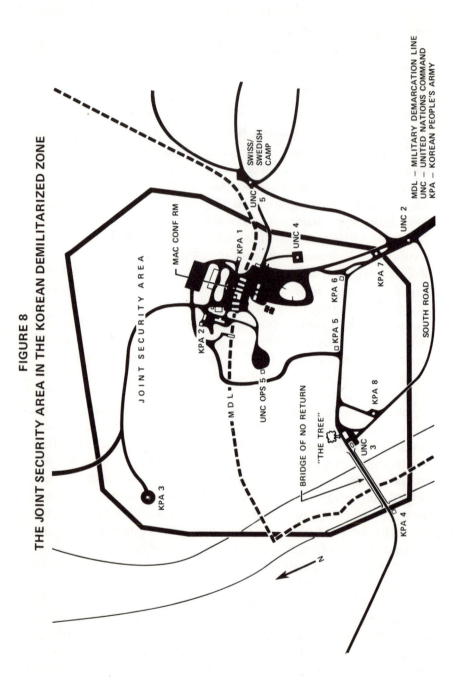

MDL — MILITARY DEMARCATION LINE
UNC — UNITED NATIONS COMMAND
KPA — KOREAN PEOPLE'S ARMY

erected four control points with two drop gates on the south half of the JSA. (Although the control points were technically not violations of the agreement, the drop gates were periodically used to restrict movement and were therefore illegal. The UNC had no similar posts on the north side of the JSA.) When asked to remove the barriers, the North Koreans repeatedly denied their existence. The relevance of the illegal road barriers in August 1976 was that they were between the Quick Reaction Force location at Checkpoint Two (UNC 2) and the offending tree.

Lieutenant Colonel Vierra was well aware of the hostile situation in the JSA. He had been assigned there for nearly a year, and, since February 1976, had noted an increase in the number and intensity of North Korean provoked incidents. He received weekly intelligence summaries from the U.S. Second Infantry Division and Foreign Broadcast Information Summaries daily. Specifically, he was aware of the Mao/Hua letter, and he understood the aggressive North Korean broadcast on August 5 as being part of the preparation for the Nonaligned Nations Conference. However, he received no intelligence warnings of an impending incident.

In planning the tree-trimming detail, Lieutenant Colonel Vierra knew of the North Korean interest in this particular tree expressed on August 6, but the harassment seemed to be no more than usual. In fact, a meeting of the KPA and UNC security officers on August 16 had seemed unusually friendly. But, in the JSA, Vierra took nothing for granted, and he prepared for the worst. He therefore selected a reinforced work detail of fifteen men. A South Korean foreman was assigned to the five-man labor force. The security force of ten included two U.S. Army officers (Captain Arthur G. Bonifas and First Lieutenant Mark T. Barrett), three enlisted men, and four South Korean enlisted guards. A South Korean Army captain was included to act as an interpreter.

Several other standard operating procedures were selected or modified for the situation. First, Lieutenant Colonel Vierra decided to station the rest of the duty platoon at their habitual location, in UNC 4, a distance of 660 yards from the tree. They were to monitor the progress by telephone and radio.

Second, he added one guard to the two already at UNC 3, only 55 yards from the tree. Third, he instructed the Quick Reaction Force (backup platoon) of thirty men to monitor the operation from their normal position about 80 yards south of UNC 2. Fourth, he instructed the U.S. Army Support Group operations officer to monitor the operation from the advance camp outside the DMZ and to report any problems to higher headquarters. On their own volition, the joint duty officer, the supply officer, and Captain Bonifas' replacement (Bonifas was due to return to the United States in one week) decided to observe the operation from UNC 5. Bonifas, as the commander of the detail, placed several cameras at OP 5 and UNC 3 to record any unusual events. He also ordered the placement of pick handles in the back of the work detail's two-and-a-half-ton truck.[17]

This plan for the availability of potentially deadly weapons in what some might consider a work detail only slightly out of the ordinary may merit some comment. The decision to have the clubs nearby, like the other precautions taken, tends to confirm the concern with which this operation was viewed. Tactically, the clubs may also be considered a type of conventional arms control. Arms were to be present, but there seemed to be a tacit understanding that the presence of clubs made the use of firearms less likely. The clubs were potentially deadly weapons, but they were perceived as less deadly and less likely to provoke escalation than conventional arms. Firearms had never been used in the twenty-three-year history of the JSA, but clubs had been introduced some years before and had become an accepted weapon on both sides. Although the clubs were not deployed on every occasion, UNC personnel believed them to be an effective deterrent to higher levels of violence.

Finally, Lieutenant Colonel Vierra carefully briefed Captain Bonifas, telling him that if the North Koreans confronted him with the usual harassment, he should continue the work; but if a real confrontation developed, he was to disengage and withdraw. The difference was really left up to Captain Bonifas' judgment.

It would be difficult for the casual observer to believe that all these steps were routine, but to the men of the JSA they were just normal precautions in the presence of an unpredictable adversary. The routine nature of the tree-trimming detail tends to be verified by the fact that the JSA command continued to conduct tours from its special services organization on the morning of August 18.

This small force of five workers and the ten-man security detail entered the Joint Security Area about 10:25 on the morning of Wednesday, August 18. They drove to the deserted tree in a two-and-one-half ton truck and Captain Bonifas' radio-equipped jeep, arriving there at 10:30. Within a minute, two North Korean Army officers and nine guards arrived in a similar truck. One of the North Korean officers was later identified as Lieutenant Pak Chul, an intense and vitriolic seven-to-eight-year JSA veteran, who as a sergeant had been one of the attackers of the army major injured in the last serious JSA incident (June 1975).

Captain Kim, the South Korean Army officer, informed the KPA of the purpose of the detail. When told that their intent was only to trim and not to fell the large tree, Lieutenant Pak reportedly replied, "Good." The North Koreans then began an almost friendly commentary on methods of trimming the tree. During the next fifteen minutes, additional North Korean guards began to congregate in the vicinity of the tree. Lieutenant Colonel Vierra, from his duties at the JSA advance camp, called to OP 5 at 10:45 and was told the work was progressing normally.

At approximately 10:50, when the work was nearly complete, Lieutenant Pak instructed Captain Bonifas to stop. A short discussion followed in which Lieutenant Pak told the South Korean captain, "If you cut more branches, there will be a big problem (trouble)." Captain Kim translated this from Korean to English for Captain Bonifas, who directed the work to continue. Lieutenant Pak then dispatched a runner to get more North Korean guards, another traditional tactic in the JSA. About 11:00, a second North Korean Army truck arrived with another eight to ten guards, and more guards continued drifting in from the North Korean side of the so-called Bridge of No Return. The total number of North Korean guards now on the scene was twenty-eight to thirty, and photographs show that they virtually surrounded the outnumbered U.N. forces.

(Being outnumbered and surrounded are tactical disadvantages UNC personnel have been forced to concede to the North Koreans in almost every JSA incident since 1953. The basic reason behind this enduring disadvantage has been the U.N. and U.S. Army insistence on scrupulous adherence to the legal interpretation of the armistice agreement on limiting personnel in the JSA.)

Lieutenant Pak again directed that the work stop, and told Captain Kim, "The branches that are cut will be of no use, just as you will be after you die." This more violent threat was typical of North Korean tactics in the past, after the arrival of reinforcements. Captain Bonifas indicated to Captain Kim in return that he believed the North Koreans were just threatening, as they had done so many times in the past, and did not intend to act. He directed a continuation. One of the North Korean guards was then heard to say, "If you cut more branches, you are going to die."

Lieutenant Colonel Vierra, still mindful about the tree detail, called OP 5 again at 11:05 and learned that the KPA was reinforcing and the work had stopped. He immediately called UNC 3, near the tree, and instructed his men there to tell Captain Bonifas to cease work and call for a security officers' meeting on the spot.

At the same time as this order was given, Lieutenant Pak reportedly removed his watch, wrapped it in a handkerchief, and placed it in his pocket. The second KPA officer rolled up his sleeves. These movements were not seen by Captain Bonifas, who was apparently trying to cope with the North Korean harassment by ignoring the KPA guards. One U.N. soldier's attempts to get his attention were too late.

Lieutenant Pak yelled the single word "kill" in Korean (which translated as a military order means "kill them all"), and kicked Captain Bonifas in the groin. Immediately, several North Korean guards jumped on Captain Bonifas and beat him, while all the remaining guards attacked the U.N. Security Force with fists and feet. Within seconds, the North Koreans produced clubs from the back of their own truck, and the fighting escalated. Lieutenant Barrett ran to the aid of a U.N. guard and was attacked by four North Korean soldiers with axe handles and

U.N. Command work detail arrives at the tree in the Korean Joint Security Area. (U.N. Command photo)

After twenty minutes, North Korean lieutenant orders the workers to stop trimming the tree. Note the number of branches that have been cut and the North Korean reinforcements. (U.N. Command photo)

The fight begins—North Korean soldiers attack. (U.N. Command photo)

The fight ends—Captain Arthur G. Bonifas lies dead on the road. (U.N. Command photo)

iron pipes. He was beaten severely and thrown over a low wall near the tree. The U.N. guards attempted to put up a group defense, but several were isolated and beaten badly, while the South Korean workers were left unmolested. Several pictures show clubs, axe handles and axes themselves being swung in the immediate vicinity of Captain Bonifas, as he lay on the ground. Only the two officers were knocked to the ground, although all the guards were attacked. One Korean enlisted man was beaten by six to eight North Koreans but never went down. About 11:07, one of the South Korean workers got into the security force's truck, drove it around the body of Captain Bonifas, picked up the rest of the Korean workers, and left the area via the south road. Captain Kim and the U.S. driver then jumped in Captain Bonifas' jeep, which had been parked nearby, picked up his body, and followed the Security Force truck. At the same time another U.S. guard got into the UNC 3 truck, drove it *into* the assembled North Koreans, dispersed them, picked up the remaining U.N. guards, and attempted to leave the area past the North Korean checkpoint (KPA 5) when he saw the illegal drop gate in the down position. He immediately backed up, turned around and departed down the south road at 11:10. Meanwhile, the remainder of the duty platoon, which had been stationed 660 yards away at UNC 4, attempted to reinforce the U.N. contingent, but their truck was blocked by the same North Korean drop gate at KPA 5. The U.S. guards got out, raised the gate, and drove to the vicinity of the tree. Finding the fight had already ended, these men then proceeded to a blocking position at the east end of the Bridge of No Return, where more of the North Koreans had reassembled. These U.N. guards left the area in their truck at 11:10. The Quick Reaction Platoon had been alerted about 11:06, and had moved to UNC 2 by 11:10, when they saw the two trucks and the jeep retreating from the tree. Within five or ten minutes, it was determined that Lieutenant Barrett was missing; the Quick Reaction Platoon then proceeded to the tree, found Lieutenant Barrett amid scrub brush behind the wall, and brought him out. Captain Bonifas, Lieutenant Barrett, and the most severely injured South Korean guard were immediately evacuated to a Seoul hospital, but the two U.S. officers were pronounced dead on arrival. The results on the U.N. side were two U.S. officers killed, one wounded, four enlisted men wounded, and four South Korean guards wounded. North Korea claimed at a subsequent Military Armistice Commission meeting that five of their guards had been injured. The entire fight had lasted only minutes, and not a shot had been fired!

NOTIFICATION AND INITIAL ACTIONS

Immediately after the incident, the U.S. Army/United Nations Command staff in the forward operations center at Yongson, in Seoul, South Korea, formed a crisis-action team under the supervision of the chief of the Current Operations Branch. This team began integrating the reports coming out of the Joint Security Area and started actively thinking about possible U.S. responses. Meanwhile, the chief of staff notified the U.N. commander in chief, General Stilwell. The telephone call reached General Stilwell in Kyoto, Japan, where he was touring as the official guest of the chief of staff of the Japanese Ground Self-Defense Force. He immediately flew back to Tokyo, obtained further transportation, and landed in Korea about 8:00 p.m. that evening, local time.

The Operations Center also sent out a message within minutes of the killings, directly to the Joint Chiefs of Staff in Washington, with information copies directed to the U.S. embassy in Seoul and the Pacific Command headquarters in Hawaii.

Within an hour, the National Military Command Center (NMCC), the crisis communications hub of the Department of Defense, had received the message and activated its own notification procedures. At 11:20 p.m. Washington time, the NMCC duty officer activated the Watch Officers' Net which linked the operations centers of the Defense Department (including the National Security Agency and the Defense Intelligence Agency) with the State Department, Central Intelligence Agency, and the White House Situation Room. This net permitted the NMCC to inform the other agencies of the U.N. Command message reporting the two murders in the Joint Security Area. Ninety minutes later, at 12:53 a.m. Wednesday morning, the NMCC initiated another call based on a follow-up message from Korea indicating that no firearms had been used in the incident, only tools and axes.

The State Department Operations Center duty officer called the senior Korean desk officer shortly after receiving the first call at 11:20 and relayed the news of the incident. The Korean desk officer also received a telephone call from a Foreign Service colleague in the political/military section of the U.S. embassy in Seoul at about the same time. The telephone message from the embassy was that there had been a fight, that one person had been killed in the JSA, but that the details were still sketchy. The embassy official and the desk officer were generally aware of the forty-nine U.S. deaths near the DMZ since the 1953 armistice, but they were not aware that this incident was the first one in which a killing had occurred in the Joint Security Area.

The Korean desk officer then called the deputy assistant secretary for East Asia and relayed all he knew about the situation. The deputy, in turn, called the assistant secretary of state for East Asia and Pacific affairs. When the assistant secretary received the message, after midnight, he understood it to mean that an incident had occurred, but the details were far from clear. With this understanding, it was deemed that the incident was not time-sensitive, did not require notification of any other officials, and could be handled the next day.

Early Wednesday morning, August 18, in Washington, news of the incident spread rapidly through both official and public means. Duty officers in the NMCC, at the State Department, CIA, and other agencies were briefed as they came on duty and began to gather further information for the normal morning intelligence briefings. Radio news broadcasts provided the first information on the incident to the majority of the staff members of the Joint Chiefs of Staff, State Department, CIA, and the National Security Council.

Secretary Kissinger was informed at about 6:00 a.m., when he was called by his personal assistant, Lawrence S. Eagleburger, deputy under-secretary for management. (This was a daily practice in which Eagleburger, after familiarizing himself with Operations Center message traffic and other indications of worldwide events during the night, would call the secretary at home and provide him with summaries.) Kissinger's immediate reaction was one of outrage, and his initial action, upon arriving at the State Department, was to confer with the assistant secretary for East Asian and Pacific affairs, Arthur W. Hummel, Jr., and Under-Secretary for Political Affairs Philip Habib. As a result of these discussions, two decisions were made: to inform General Scowcroft and the president; and to call a meeting of the Washington Special Actions Group for 3:30 p.m.[18]

General Scowcroft, the president's assistant for national security affairs, was alerted by cable traffic on the morning of August 18. Shortly after he read of the incident, he received a telephone call from Secretary Kissinger about 8:45 a.m. in Kansas City. General Scowcroft informed President Ford in his morning intelligence briefing at 9:00 a.m. (10:00 a.m. EDT). The president was extremely upset by the brutal and apparently unprovoked killings, but he noted that the passage of time was not as critical to a successful response as it had been in the *Mayaguez* crisis. Although he had been under attack from the conservative wing of the Republican party—which would probably have endorsed strong retaliatory action—the president considered the matter to be apart from partisan (and convention) politics. His instructions to General Scowcroft, to be relayed to Washington, were: that the WSAG be convened; that options be developed for a U.S. response; and that he be kept informed. The president directed White House Press Secretary Ron Nessen to work with General Scowcroft in developing a statement for release to the media.[19] The presidential party in Kansas City had full communications capabilities, and General Scowcroft received all important diplomatic and military cables within minutes of their arrival in Washington.

The initial news, and especially the notification by the NSC staff that a WSAG meeting would convene at 3:30 p.m., put the Washington national security agencies in high gear. The morning briefings, which occurred all over Washington between 7:30 and 8:30 a.m., had brought together what little operations and intelligence information was available, but had generated more questions than answers. Dozens of staff officers began by attempting to obtain more current information on the crisis event in the Joint Security Area, but they also began to plan for possible U.S. responses.

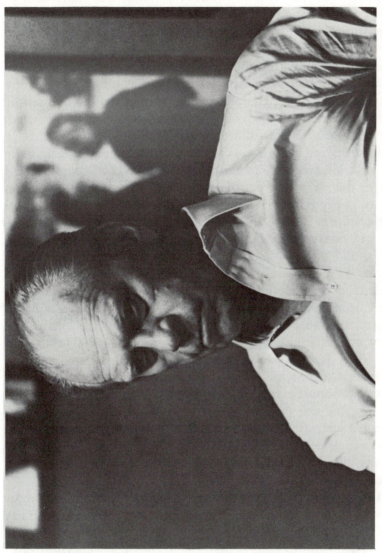

President Ford immediately after being informed of the murders. (Official White House photo by David Hume Kennerly)

173

In the Defense Department, two primary agencies were involved, each with a specialized mission. One was the Joint Chiefs of Staff, where the Current Operations Branch was permanently organized to handle the day-to-day movement of military forces and fast-breaking crisis operations. "Current Operations" in any military unit tends to be a crisis-oriented organization, and in the JCS it rapidly became the focal point for coordination within the Operations Directorate.

Although many activities were going on, they can generally be categorized under three headings: information search on the specific incident; information search on the crisis background; and preliminary course of action development.

Information search was generally conducted through the National Military Command Center, and was directed toward finding out exactly what had happened in Korea. The officers sought background information largely from within the JCS staff on the geography and procedures within the JSA, the location and military capabilities of U.S./R.O.K. and North Korean forces, and the political situation. The Mao/Hua letter, Kim's August 5 speech, the U.N. General Assembly resolution on Korea, and the Colombo conference were *not* well known within the Joint Staff, but JCS members were rapidly brought up to date. Course of action development was carried on concurrently and attempted to survey the broadest possible alternatives. The Joint Staff used several military plans already in existence to form the basis for some of the alternatives. The attitude within the JCS staff was one of anger and resentment, remembering the *Pueblo* seizure, the loss of an EC-121 reconnaissance aircraft, and previous U.S. casualties near the DMZ, all of which were attributed to North Korea. Many of the JCS officers had personally served in Korea and felt a sense of shared danger with the men in the field.

The second Defense Department agency that was directly involved in the crisis was the International Security Affairs Directorate in the Office of the Secretary of Defense (OSD/ISA). There, the Korean office was in the midst of a transition, with one of the army officers having been assigned only three days previously and one taking over the two-man office on the morning of August 18. Both worked with Deputy Assistant

Secretary of Defense Morton I. Abramowitz, chief of ISA's Bureau of East Asia and Pacific Affairs. He was an experienced Foreign Service officer, spoke Chinese, and was the coauthor of *Remaking U.S. China Policy.*[20] He had served in the Department of State in several positions in Taiwan and Hong Kong and had directed the ISA East Asia bureau since 1974.

Being removed from the communications of the NMCC, the military planning of the JCS, and the diplomatic efforts of the State Department, the ISA officers had difficulty in obtaining a clear picture of the event. The Joint Staff (particularly J-3) and ISA staff were, however, charged with the responsibility of providing the Secretary of Defense with complete briefings as a basis for his participation in the WSAG as well as the department's execution of decisions.[21] The ISA directorate was aware of the various political initiatives North Korea had attempted, especially the hostile August 5 speech, but its officers were not aware of the specific warnings about the tree twelve days earlier. No one in Washington was. (The August 6 warnings had not been communicated to General Stilwell at the U.N. Command at the time, and they were not mentioned in the initial messages from the U.N. Command to Washington on August 18.)

In the State Department Operations Center, starting at 7:00 a.m. the morning of the eighteenth, notifications and briefings were being conducted by the senior watch officer and the (JCS) military representatives on duty. Under-Secretary for Political Affairs Habib, and the deputy assistant secretary for East Asian and Pacific affairs, Oscar V. Armstrong, were briefed by the military representatives on background events and the current situation. It was determined that representatives from the Defense Department, OSD/ISA, and the Joint Staff, and experts in East Asian affairs would be needed to formulate decisions in joint political-military activity. In addition, both military and embassy field reports were being sent directly to the Korean bureau and to Secretary Kissinger's office in an effort to keep all parties appraised of the ongoing situation.

In the Korean bureau, the senior desk officer put a call through to the embassy in Seoul to obtain more information to send up to Secretary Kissinger and Under-Secretary Habib. Then he continued to work on a formal press release that the department would have to make that afternoon. The State Department was just as interested as the Joint Staff and ISA in the total range of potential political and military responses the United States could make to this provocation. But the Korean desk officers were also driven by shorter term objectives— the need to write and internally coordinate public releases for the State Department and to coordinate press releases by the Defense Department and the White House. In addition, State Department desk officers had the direct responsibility of writing instructions for the U.S. embassy in Seoul and coordinating statements of the U.S. representative to the Military Armistice Commission, Rear Admiral Mark P. Frudden. This flurry of diplomatic activity tended to occupy the full attention of the Korean desk officers and left little actual time to reflect on and consider the full range of possible political and military responses.

About midday on the eighteenth, Edward Hurwitz, who had previously been selected to be the country director for Korea, was moved from his other duties on a terrorism task force into the Korean office. Continuing with the proposed press release, Hurwitz, the other Korean desk officers, and Assistant Secretary Hummel carefully worded the department's views.

In Seoul, the South Korean Ministry of Culture and Information held a press conference and accused the North Koreans of "premeditated, atrocious provocation" and noted that the South Korean government was "enraged by the unimaginably barbarous and inhumane act of murder."[22]

The State Department news conference was held at 1:45 p.m., Wednesday, August 18. Frederick Z. Brown briefed for the department and opened by reading a statement which said in part,

> On the morning of August 18, Korean time, North Korean military personnel made an unprovoked attack on the United Nations Command personnel in the Joint Security Area in the Demilitarized Zone, brutally murdering two American officers and injuring four Americans and five Republic of Korea military personnel.

The details regarding this act of aggression are contained in a statement issued by the United Nations Command, which I will now read to you:

"Two United Nations Command Officers were murdered in an unprovoked assault by North Korean guards this morning at the Joint Security Area, Panmunjom.

"The two army officers, both Americans, died from massive head injuries and stab wounds inflicted by an estimated thirty North Korean guards who attacked a small United Nations Command work party with axes, metal pikes and axe handles, about 10:45 a.m. . . .

"The U.N. Command has called for the 379th Military Armistice Commission Meeting to convene at 11:00 a.m., Thursday, August 19. North Korea has not yet replied.

"The three U.N. Command officers and the enlisted guards were escorting five Korean Service Corps workers who were routinely trimming branches from a tree some 35 to 40 yards from a U.N. Command Checkpoint Number 3, at the south side of the Bridge of No Return . . ."

The North Koreans have falsely charged that the personnel of the United Nations Command first assaulted North Korean guards. This is a lie and a flagrant attempt to deceive. We find it significant that the North Korean account does not claim that any North Koreans were wounded or that reinforcements from the U.N. Command side were sent into the Joint Security Area.

This brutal behavior by the North Korean regime tells us something of its true nature, and demonstrates the hollowness of North Korea's alleged desire for a peaceful resolution of the differences that exist between it and South Korea.

The United States Government considers these cowardly acts of murder a serious violation of the Armistice Agreement. The North Koreans have committed violent acts in the Joint Security Area before, but these murders are the first such deaths that have occurred in that area since the signing of the Armistice Agreement twenty-three years ago.

The United States views this brutal and unprovoked assault with gravity and concern, and warns the North Koreans that such violent and belligerent actions cannot be tolerated. North Korea must bear full responsibility for all the consequences of its brutal action.[23]

Mr. Brown then answered a variety of questions about the availability of sidearms, the possibility of this incident being staged for the benefit of the Nonaligned Conference in Sri Lanka or the upcoming U.N. debate, and the probability of the tree trimming being used as a pretext by North Korea. When asked specifically, "What is your response to the question of whether the United States is contemplating any retaliatory action?" Mr. Brown replied, "I am saying that in this briefing I am not going to go into any possible consequences of this act." [24]

At the same time as the State Department briefing in Washington, Ron Nessen of the White House Press Office made the following statement at the daily news briefing in Kansas City:

> The President condemns the vicious and unprovoked murder of two American officers last night in the demilitarized zone near Panmunjon [sic] in Korea.
>
> These officers were peacefully supervising a work detail in the neutral zone when they were subjected to a brutal and cowardly attack totally without warning.
>
> Total responsibility for the consequences of these murders rests with the North Korean Government. [25]

The Defense and State departments were at this time considering a wide range of possible responses to the North Korean incident. The major national security officials in Washington and the president's party in Kansas City had already been engaged in many urgent consultations. But the Washington officials would meet to discuss the matter formally for the first time at the WSAG meeting.

The intelligence community had organized earlier in the day to integrate the efforts of the CIA, Defense Intelligence Agency, National Security Agency, and the intelligence agencies of the military services. These agencies were attempting what had been requested by every president since Truman—an integrated, consolidated, intelligence community analysis of adversary intentions in a crisis.

Before discussing the WSAG meeting, it may be helpful to review the situation as it was perceived by the staffs of the State Department, JCS, and ISA. Briefly, they held various views of the national interest that led them to believe that the United States should fulfill most of these objectives:

- o counter the North Korean actions
- o defend against North Korea doing anything worse
- o deter future hostile actions
- o punish North Korea
- o avoid provocation and thus incentives to escalate
- o get out of the crisis

Not all of the objectives were advocated by each policy maker, but later interviews indicated an unusually high degree of unanimity on the need "to take a strong hand," "to mount a strong reaction to avoid giving Kim Il-sung the wrong signal," and "to take enough military action to show we were serious." At the same time, there was also a shared perception that the situation was dangerous and could easily escalate into a major military confrontation.

As the policy makers saw it, the range of possible alternatives included:

- o do nothing
- o stage a show of force with the units in Korea
- o deploy forces from other Pacific units to Korea
- o deploy a squadron of fighters from the United States to Korea
- o deploy an aircraft carrier to Korean waters
- o increase the readiness posture of U.N. forces
- o conduct a retaliatory response

THE DECISION-MAKING PROCESS

The First WSAG Meeting, Wednesday Afternoon, August 18

The participants at the Wednesday WSAG meeting were familiar with one another. The WSAG had been created in 1969 by President Nixon for crisis decision making, and chaired by then Presidential Assistant for National Security Affairs Henry Kissinger. By 1976 it was almost a routine meeting of men who had worked on many issues and had weathered many crises together. The Wednesday meeting was chaired by Dr. Kissinger in the White House Situation Room. In attendance from the Defense Department were William Clements, Jr., deputy secretary of defense, and Deputy Assistant Secretary Morton Abramowitz. The State Department was represented by Philip Habib, under-secretary for political affairs, who had previously served as both U.S. ambassador to the Republic of Korea and assistant secretary for East Asia and Pacific affairs. Since General George Brown was out of the country, the JCS was represented by Admiral James Holloway. The deputy assistant to the president for national security affairs, William G. Hyland, was also present. The intelligence community was represented by George Bush and a CIA briefing officer. The total attendance was twelve.

The purposes of this first WSAG meeting were: to review the situation; to receive an intelligence briefing on the background and possible intentions of the North Koreans; to receive a military briefing on the location and capability of various military forces; to discuss a range of military and diplomatic options and to give departments and agencies the task of further developing these options.

The WSAG meeting began with an intelligence briefing from George Bush on the latest information on the situation.[26] According to the *New York Times,* a participant commented afterward that there was no evidence of any North Korean offensive movement toward the DMZ. "Lacking such information, the session became more a discussion group, . . . without a sense of imminent conflict."[27] On the subject of intentions there was some speculation. On the one hand, the murders seemed deliberate and premeditated, the product of an unusually isolated and harsh regime. On the other, the motivation for the assault seemed obscure. What did North Korea hope to achieve by such action?[28]

In a review of military capabilities, the North's overall superiority on the ground did not appear significant, although the balance in the immediate area of the zone substantially favored the North, particularly in artillery. North Korea had a decided numerical advantage in air forces, with over 588 combat aircraft to South Korea's 216.[29] Even the U.S. contribution of 60–70 fighter aircraft based in South Korea did not appear to be enough to create an even military balance.

The WSAG members reviewed the location of other U.S. forces in the Pacific and the availability of stateside units to deploy to Korea. Of special concern was the fact that the only aircraft carrier in the area—the *Midway*—was in its Japanese port for normal repairs and would not be available to sail for several days. If any deployments were to be directed, they would have to be initiated quickly for the forces to arrive in time to contribute to any contemplated U.S. response. Other actions that were discussed included increasing the alert status of U.N. forces, and various retaliatory actions involving air, naval, or ground forces, or a combination of these.

At this point in the meeting, there was no consensus on a precise course of action. Secretary Kissinger's position was one of outrage at the actions of North Korea. The others were less inclined to support offensive action, but his forceful appeal, keyed to the essentialness of redressing a premeditated act of such brutality, was persuasive and successful in bringing them to a consensus. They then agreed on the need to deploy aircraft and ships to the area and to increase the readiness level of U.S. forces in Korea.

Given the status of the United States as a great power and the implications of U.S. actions beyond the immediate context, the WSAG members were all concerned about the indirect impact of any U.S. action on the international community, in general, and on the Soviet Union and the People's Republic of China, in particular. The members agreed that Secretary Kissinger should contact representatives of the USSR and the P.R.C. to indicate U.S. outrage and to make clear our intention to carry out strong measures in reply. The State Department was to insure consultation with the Japanese on military deployments, coordination with the South Korean government on the increase in readiness level, notification of NATO allies of the impending Korean alert, and communication to the U.S. representatives at United Nations headquarters in New York. The Joint Chiefs of Staff were to coordinate with General Stilwell and to continue to develop plans for possible offensive actions. The WSAG members agreed that an outbreak of hostilities seemed unlikely, but that the U.S. should be prepared for any contingency. They agreed in their views of U.S. objectives, and their recommendations seemed less influenced by their departmental position than by their personal appraisal of the situation.

The WSAG meeting adjourned shortly after 5:00 p.m. with instructions to State and Defense to continue with preparation of options for consideration at a second meeting to be held at 8:00 a.m. the next morning. Immediately after the meeting, Secretary Kissinger called General Scowcroft and the president in Kansas City and discussed the WSAG proceedings and its members' recommendations. With General Scowcroft's endorsement, President Ford approved each of the WSAG recommendations and authorized Kissinger to order the following list of diplomatic and military actions:[30]

- ○ deployment of one F-4 fighter squadron from Okinawa to Korea
- ○ an increase in the alert status of U.S. forces in Korea
- ○ preparation for deployment of one F-111 squadron from the U.S. to Korea
- ○ preparation for the use of B-52s on training missions from Guam to Korea
- ○ preparation for deployment of the aircraft carrier *Midway* from its port in Japan to Korean waters
- ○ notification of U.N. delegates and the Security Council of the North Korean assault

Although U.S. congressional and public opinion were factors considered in the WSAG deliberations, the specific provisions of the War Powers Resolution were reportedly not discussed. The subject of executive reporting responsibilities to the Congress was handled by John Marsh and others of the presidential party in Kansas City, as collateral to the main discussion of appropriate U.S. actions.

While the WSAG was in session, messages continued to arrive at the NMCC and the State Department on the crisis. One of these messages was a United Nations Command summary which included valuable background information on the previous North Korean warnings in the Joint Security Area. (Many State Department personnel stated the opinion that the U.N.

Command had been remiss in not including this information in the original notification message, but the U.N. Command headquarters, itself, was not aware of the full background at this time. Knowledge of the August 6 warnings did, however, change most policy-making officials' view that the attack had been a surprise.)

General Stilwell had arrived at his headquarters at 10:00 a.m. Washington time and immediately consulted with his staff. In a later interview he described his initial actions:

> I arrived at my office about 2100 [9:00 p.m.]. In the following three hours we put together three messages:
>
> 1. A proposed text for Admiral Frudden's remarks (to be given to North Korea at the 379th MAC meeting scheduled for the next day);
>
> 2. A proposed text of a letter from me to Kim Il-sung as my opposite number in the North Korean armed forces; and
>
> 3. The initial concept of an operations plan to remove the tree.
>
> I felt the minimum we had to do was to reassert our rights in the Joint Security Area and cut down the tree.[31]

General Stilwell's concept of operations was dictated to his secretary, typed, and then sent to the Joint Chiefs of Staff by message at 4:35 p.m. EDT. The message emphasized that the field commander in Korea had an inherent responsibility for the defense of his forces, and that the U.N. Command must maintain its legitimate rights in the Demilitarized Zone. General Stilwell made the point clear. "Thus, although it is only a damn tree, it involves a major principle . . . to ensure the protection of our forces."[32]

The message went on to propose what later became Operation Paul Bunyan—the plan to enter the JSA and cut the tree down. There remained the issue of how much warning to give the North Koreans of the intended action. General Stilwell outlined the alternatives, no notice versus prior notice, and stated the arguments for each view. In a concluding note, he summarized the dilemma of a military leader. "All my military instincts compel me to opt for the first course, but I appreciate that broader considerations may support the second course of action."[33]

The message containing General Stilwell's proposals was quickly received by the JCS, where it was immediately examined and integrated into ISA and JCS recommendations being developed for the second WSAG meeting. As an official noted later, "It was really General Stilwell's proposal that focused attention on going back into the JSA and reaffirming our rights there."

During the evening of August 18, Secretary Kissinger met with the Japanese ambassador to discuss the deployment of U.S. military forces stationed in Japan. He also saw Ambassador Huang Chen, the chief of the People's Republic of China Liaison Mission in Washington. At this meeting, Kissinger reportedly conveyed the outrage of the United States over the killings, and made clear U.S. intentions to redress matters with the North Koreans. He also repeated an earlier American proposal to hold peace talks involving the two Koreas, the P.R.C., and the United States, which would have the objective of seeking a permanent solution to the division of Korea.[34] More importantly, he apparently emerged confident that North Korea could not expect material support from the P.R.C. in this incident.

The JCS were proceeding to carry out the WSAG instructions, and preparations were completed to send orders for the various deployments. The order to put U.N. forces in Korea at a higher level of readiness went out directly to General Stilwell's command. The Pacific Command was instructed to send one F-4 squadron from Kadena Air Base, Okinawa (Japan), to Korea and to prepare the *Midway* to sail. In each of these cases the instructions were given by a general officer on the Joint Staff over secure telephone lines, with written messages used to back up the verbal orders.

Organizationally, the Joint Staff did not undergo any major changes to meet the crisis. The Current Operations Branch in J-3 was already organized to gather information, develop courses of action, and coordinate with other agencies. The other JCS directorates and the military service staffs did, however, send additional personnel to assist J-3, to coordinate Joint Staff recommendations, and to meet round-the-clock manning requirements in accordance with the crisis-action system procedures.

In the State Department, the Korean desk officers and higher officials in the East Asia bureau entered a period of organizational change. After the first WSAG meeting ended at about 5:15, Ralph Scarett, executive director of the bureau, received a telephone call from the assistant secretary instructing him to establish a crisis working group. Scarett notified the Korean desk officers and his administrative staff, and they all began to move their message files and other information sources up to the seventh floor to the State Operations Center. There they established the Korean working group under the direction of Assistant Secretary Hummel, assisted by Deputy Assistant Secretary Oscar V. Armstrong, and William H. Gleysteen of the National Security Council staff.

The Korean working group consisted of a director (Hummel, Armstrong, or Gleysteen, depending on the shift), an executive director (Scarett), the four Korean desk officers, other East Asia personnel, and representatives from the CIA, OSD, JCS, and NSC, for a total of about ten to twelve per shift. The methods of the working group are less formal than those of a task force, but it has the same basic purposes: monitor all crisis-related activities; write and coordinate draft answers to all incoming messages; prepare draft press guidance for the United States and United Nations Command in Korea for clearance by WSAG members; insure consultation with various allied powers; support the department's participation at WSAG meetings with analysis and alternative courses of action; and prepare situation reports twice daily (usually at 6:00 a.m. and 3:00 p.m.) for State Department principals and the White House. The JCS representatives were two colonels, and their duties were to: assist in getting draft messages cleared by the Joint Staff; provide information on military units and capabilities; and assist in a coordinating capacity.

The Operations Center was charged with supporting the group, but the degree of support was not precisely specified. The working group was given a checklist[35] and a large crisis procedures book and was essentially expected to operate independent of the Operations Center staff, which was to resume—as much as possible—its normal routine. Watch officers offered periodically to assist, but their own duties had also increased in the crisis. The Operations Center officers continued to provide briefings to the principals of the department, as well as to the working group, as new information became available. The working group experienced some minor inconveniences in settling into the operations center during the first hours, but these were largely overcome by increasing the administrative staff. The most severe problem the Korean working group faced was some difficulty in obtaining intelligible, high quality, secure voice circuits between the State Operations Center and U.S. embassies in East Asia. It was the consensus of the working group members that although there was an intensive demand for information, they were not overwhelmed by the volume of communications. Administrative techniques, like establishing an incoming message file, were helpful in meeting internal and external information requirements.

As the working group was moving into the Operations Center, it was also examining the issues presented by the tide of events. General Stilwell's recommendations on Admiral Frudden's remarks and the CINCUNC letter to Kim Il-sung were considered, but it was decided to modify them both. (These and other messages to the U.N. Command were drafted by the State Department and were edited and approved in final form by Secretary Kissinger before they were available for review by other executive departments.) State Department officials were generally favorable to General Stilwell's plan to cut down the tree, but most of them thought the proposed numbers of backup military forces were excessive.

In Korea, the time was late Thursday morning, August 19. General Stilwell met with the South Korean minister of defense, and it was agreed that U.S. forces, UNC forces, and all other R.O.K. units would go to a higher level of readiness. The two officials then proceeded to the presidential Blue House to brief President Park on developments, U.S. actual and planned reinforcements, and the proposed operation to cut down the tree. Subsequent planning was conducted by an integrated R.O.K./ U.S. staff at U.N. Command headquarters.

On the diplomatic front, General Stilwell had called for a 10:00 a.m. meeting of the Military Armistice Commission to protest the killings. The North Koreans rejected this proposal and countered with a proposal for a security officers' meeting (which was the lowest of the three levels of meetings, and would only have involved company-grade officers). The U.N. Command rejected the North Korean counterproposal as unacceptable and suggested a concurrent Military Armistice Commission/Security Commission/security officers' meeting for 1:00 p.m. North Korea accepted, but for 4:00 p.m.[36]

The 379th meeting of the Military Armistice Commission opened at 4:00 p.m. with the U.N. representative, Rear Admiral Frudden, presenting a statement which had been coordinated by the departments of State and Defense, the NSC staff, and General Scowcroft. This statement read, in part:

> This was not the eruption of an unplanned argument. It was the deliberate murder of U.N. Command personnel who, while engaged in routine maintenance functions of a type your personnel often perform, were attacked unmercifully by a numerically superior force, wielding axes and clubs.[37]

Admiral Frudden added that the North Korean attack was an open and flagrant act of belligerency that jeopardized the entire framework of the armistice and violated the neutrality of the Joint Security Area. He punctuated his remarks by displaying fifteen photographs of the incident taken by U.N. guards. He concluded by stating, "The U.N. Command views this brutal and vicious act with gravity and concern and warns that such violent and belligerent acts cannot be tolerated. North Korea must bear full responsibility for all consequences of its brutal actions."[38] He also communicated the U.S. demands for: (1) North Korean acknowledgement of its responsibility for the crime; (2) a promise that the security of U.N. forces in the JSA would not be challenged again; and (3) punishment of the men responsible. Lieutenant Pak Chul was signaled out by name as one of the attackers.

For its part, North Korea denied the charges and accused the United States and South Korean forces of "a premeditated, well-organized provocation." North Korean Major General Han Ju-kyong claimed that "the enemy came out with the aim of committing a provocation from our side," rejected a warning

against trimming the tree, engaged in "hurling invectives and
spitting at the security personnel on our side," and then
"pounced upon" the North Koreans, "injuring them by throw-
ing an axe."[39] The North Korean general then produced an axe,
which he claimed had hit one of five injured North Koreans.
General Han accused the United States of raising tensions in
the area and said war could break out if this continued. He
further warned that if the United States continued similar
provocations in the future, it would be held responsible for all
grave consequences.

During the Military Armistice Commission meeting, the
Pyongyang Domestic Service broadcast a supreme command
order to place all North Korean forces in a "war posture."
This action can be seen, however, as taken in response to the
UNC alert that had gone into effect some hours earlier. The
North Korean alert was apparently slow to be implemented
and was defensively oriented.

Shortly after the North Korean alert was announced, the
first of the U.S. military deployments was completed. Twelve
F-4D Phantom fighters and six F-4C Wild Weasel aircraft from
Okinawa began landing at Kunsan Air Base to reinforce the
Eighth Tactical Fighter Wing about 6:00 p.m. Thursday evening,
August 19.

In the United States, the country's attention was focused
on the Republican National Convention, where President Ford
had formally won the nomination for president at about
1:30 a.m. Washington time. At the same time, the Joint Staff
was busy preparing military contingency plans for possible
further deployments of the F-111 squadron and the *Midway*
task force into Korea and the possible use of these forces in a
retaliatory strike against North Korea.

The Joint Staff and the OSD International Security Affairs
Directorate were preparing recommendations for a WSAG meeting the next morning. These recommendations took into
account General Stilwell's proposed plan and were strongly
influenced by estimates of alternative North Korean responses
and possible escalation.

In the State Department, the Korean working group was
also considering possible U.S. actions along with carrying out

its central responsibilities of monitoring and coordinating the flow of crisis communications. Although the working group had interdepartmental membership, the options it was considering were primarily to become State Department recommendations. The interdepartmental representatives to the State working group were officers below the policy level; they were able to assist and coordinate, but they were not authorized to make policy decisions in the name of their departments. The recognition of this situation was one of the primary reasons for establishing the WSAG—a face-to-face meeting of high level officials, each empowered to speak for his agency in matters of policy, and to order implementation of WSAG decisions.

Throughout the night, Under-Secretary Habib and other high officials had been in and out of the State Operations Center, discussing messages and options with Assistant Secretary Hummel and the other working-group directors. At the same time, congressional notification considerations were being investigated by the legal sections of the State and Defense departments, as they examined the War Powers Resolution and its reporting requirements.

The Second WSAG Meeting, Thursday Morning, August 19

The purposes of the second WSAG meeting, which began in the White House Situation Room at 8:00 a.m. Thursday, August 19, were to consider any changes in the situation since the last meeting, to be briefed on the military deployments, to recommend whether and how to proceed with plans to cut down the tree, to consider other options, and to propose any other necessary action. The meeting began with an intelligence briefing from the CIA. Discussion followed on the available options, including General Stilwell's plan to cut down the tree. The tone of this meeting was more purposeful than at the first WSAG meeting, and the following plans were tentatively agreed upon:

○ validation of the F-4 squadron deployment, and agreement, subject to final approval by President Ford in Kansas City, to deploy an F-111 squadron from Idaho to Korea later in the day o   validation of the increased alert status of U.S. and UNC forces in Korea, especially in light of the North Korean move to a war readiness posture

o   recommendation to move the *Midway* task force from its Japanese port to the straits of Korea

o   continuation of the study of the War Powers Resolution and its applicability to executive actions

o   recommendation to accept General Stilwell's basic concept of operations, to enter the JSA with a show of military force and cut down the tree. Stilwell was also asked to amplify his plan with details and forward it for final approval. The no-notice version was accepted.

o   decision to include a flight of three B-52s from Guam in a show of force over South Korea

Of course, all these WSAG decisions were only tentative and were relayed to President Ford via General Scowcroft for final approval. As the principals went back to their departments from the WSAG meeting, Secretary Kissinger departed for the airport and flew to Kansas City. Arriving around noon, the secretary met with the president and General Scowcroft, discussing the deployments, the options, and possible North Korean reactions.

Secretary Kissinger presented the options to the president and outlined the WSAG-recommended course of action—a show of force—but noted that he recommended more forceful action. His reasoning was that more forceful action was necessary to demonstrate the U.S. will to defend its interests, and he believed strongly that North Korea would not do anything in return. General Scowcroft agreed on the necessity of strong action up to the level of the original act—the death of U.S. soldiers—but stressed the importance of assuring that the means chosen would not result in a North Korean reply in which we would be at a disadvantage. Specifically, he pointed out that the use of U.S. artillery near the zone (one 105mm Howitzer battery) could result in an artillery duel in which the U.S. would be at a serious disadvantage. In sum, some other means such as a tactical aircraft strike might be preferable.

The president discussed the issues with Kissinger and

Scowcroft for forty-five minutes, and then tentatively decided on the tree chopping and show-of-force option. He directed that the recommended deployments be implemented but decided to withhold final approval for the tree cutting until General Stilwell's detailed plan arrived from Korea.[40]

The United States at this point was demanding "explanations and reparations" from North Korea for the "premeditated murder" of the two U.S. officers. In a television interview on August 20, Secretary Kissinger elaborated on the specific issue of the crisis. "We cannot permit the principle to be established that Americans can simply be assaulted with impunity any place that some dictator of some aggressive country decides to score some points." When asked whether Americans should be alarmed about the crisis, he replied, "It depends on what it indicates about North Korean intentions. And it also depends on what, or whether, we get any satisfactory response to our demands for explanations and reparation."[41] Reparations were later defined by the State Department to mean "punishment of the people involved."[42]

In accordance with the WSAG recommendations—since approved by the president—the JCS issued execution orders to the U.S. Readiness Command for the F-111 deployment, to the Pacific Command (PACOM) for the *Midway* task-group movement, and to the Strategic Air Command and CINCPAC for the B-52 training mission over South Korea. Within hours, the F-111 squadron of twenty aircraft was airborne from Mountain Home Air Force Base, Idaho, headed for Taegu Air Base, Korea.

The Joint Staff—particularly the J-3 Directorate—at this point, with all the deployments in motion, began to concentrate on "what if?" considerations. Their job was to study in detail the military moves North Korea might take and to plan for possible U.S. military responses. The United States had to be prepared to handle escalation beyond the cutting of the tree itself. This planning went on throughout the night of August 19, during which time General Stilwell's detailed plan was being completed.

In South Korea, President Park tended to be aggressive in his public statements. He said his country would retaliate immediately if North Korean forces "dare commit an illegal provocation again."[43] Later on Friday, Defense Minister Suh Jyong-chul read a speech from President Park to the graduating officers at a junior military academy near Seoul.

> We need a club to deal with a mad dog. . . . Should they [North Korea] dare commit an illegal provocation again, large or small, an immediate punitive action will be taken and they will have to bear all responsibility for such a development. . . . There is a limit to our patience.[44]

Pyongyang domestic radio, for its part, broadcast a message claiming that Ugandan President Idi Amin was supporting the North Korean actions. The U.S. chargé d'affaires and the director of the R.O.K. Joint Staff were in General Stilwell's office almost constantly during the planning phase. The Ministry of Defense offered all assistance, and the operation was planned as a joint R.O.K./U.S. undertaking.

The plan—named Operation Paul Bunyan—was developed with both tactical and strategic/political objectives. The tactical objectives were to cut down the tree and to remove the two illegal North Korean road barriers in the vicinity of KPA 5 and 6. The strategic/political objective was to demonstrate U.S. and UNC resolve that erosion or denial of legitimate rights in the Joint Security Area and the Demilitarized Zone would not be tolerated. The plan proposed a primary task force to enter the JSA and a secondary task force to provide cover and reinforcement, if necessary, to counter any North Korean actions. The primary task force was to enter the JSA precisely at 7:00 a.m., Saturday, August 21 (6:00 p.m. Friday in Washington), thirty minutes before the North Korean Army normally manned its guard posts. The detailed plan was completed Thursday night and was sent to the JCS. When General Stilwell's detailed plan arrived in Washington, it was discussed, debated, and approved by the JCS, the Defense and State departments, and the National Security Council staff. It was forwarded to Kansas City for final decision.

As the time for implementation approached, the JCS initiated another crisis procedure, the formation of a formal crisis-action team and the activation of special communications nets connecting the National Military Command Center and General Stilwell's headquarters in Korea. This crisis-action team was headed by the chief of the Current Operations Division and was composed mainly of officers in the Operations Directorate, but it included members from the other agencies concerned. The wide band, secure, conference communications nets they were assigned were normally used for a multitude of different purposes, but were now specifically reserved for Korean command and control.

In Kansas City, on Friday morning, General Scowcroft briefed President Ford on General Stilwell's detailed operations plan. A final discussion on the entire Korean situation ensued, which included Secretary Kissinger. Based on the continued indications that the North Korean military alert was defensively oriented and his own preferences of the day before, the president decided not to order any reprisal, but approved General Stilwell's plan and his no-notice recommendation. President Ford directed that the operations be carried out so that there would be no mistaking them by the North Koreans, but that the U.N. Command should not advertise them beforehand. His personal belief was that it was essential to reassert U.S. prerogatives firmly, but without overkill. He later stated that his reasons were related to the character of the adversary in North Korea. "In the case of Korea, to gamble with an overkill might broaden very quickly into a full military conflict, but responding with an appropriate amount of force would be effective in demonstrating U.S. resolve."[45]

The president's decision was reached about 10:15 a.m. (EDT) and was immediately flashed to Washington. The execute order was then relayed from the Joint Chiefs of Staff to General Stilwell by secure telephone at 11:45 p.m. Friday night in Korea (10:45 a.m. Washington time). Operation Paul Bunyan was to begin at 7:00 a.m. the next morning, Korean time.

OPERATIONAL IMPLEMENTATION

The time for development of courses of action and decision making had now passed. The forces had been deployed and were in the process of moving to support Operation Paul Bunyan. About 4:45 p.m. Friday, August 20, the principals began to gather in the Emergency Conference Room of the National Military Command Center in the Pentagon. Present were both deputy secretaries of defense, the director of the Central Intelligence Agency, the under-secretary of state for political affairs, the secretary of the army, the chiefs of each of the services, and the director of DIA. The group had immediate access to secure and regular telephones to Korea, message facilities, and all the contingency plans that had been developed by the Joint Staff.

Within an hour, the B-52s from Guam had arrived over their Korean training area, escorted by USAF Korean-based F-4s and Republic of Korea F-5s. These aircraft were assigned flight paths to make their presence visible, but sufficiently far from the DMZ to remain nonprovocative. The primary task force was commanded by Lieutenant Colonel Vierra, the JSA commander. The units inside the JSA were assigned 110 U.N. Command personnel. Sixteen of these were in a U.S. engineering team, with chain saws and axes, 30 were in a security platoon, armed with side arms and axe handles, and 64 were Republic of Korea Special Forces personnel with *tae-kwon-do* (unarmed combat) expertise. Additionally, one JSA security platoon and an R.O.K. force occupied a position within 300 meters of the tree, and another U.S. force was stationed at UNC 2.

The secondary task force was organized under Major General Morris J. Brady, the commander of the U.S. Second Infantry Division and the joint U.S.-Korean I Corps Group. The task force included a U.S. infantry unit airborne in twenty utility helicopters escorted by seven Cobra attack helicopters. These forces were placed so as to be easily monitored on North Korean radar and were intended as a deterrent, or, if needed, for reinforcing or extracting forces on the scene. In addition, U.S. and R.O.K. artillery support was available, USAF fighters and B-52s operated south of the DMZ. Precisely at 7:00 a.m. the engineers, the JSA security platoon, and the R.O.K. force entered the JSA and headed for the tree. Five minutes later, North Korean officials of the Military Armistice Commission were informed that the U.N. force intended peacefully to complete the work begun on August 18, and that if the work party was not molested, there would be no further action. In addition, the Swiss and Swedish members of the Neutral National Supervisory Commission were notified and asked if they requested evacuation. They decided to remain and moved to the Supervisory Commission building to observe.[46]

As the U.N. force moved by truck to the poplar tree and began to work with chain saws, one of the security force platoons drove by truck to the eastern end of the Bridge of No Return, blocking the roadway. North Korean guards began to gather until about 150 of them could be seen across the bridge. At this point, Lieutenant Colonel Vierra moved a second JSA security platoon to reinforce the platoon defending the bridge approach and brought the U.S. force from UNC 2 closer to the tree itself. Either because of surprise, the fear of escalation, the organization of the U.N. force, or for some other reason, the North Koreans did not challenge the operation. If they had resisted, the crisis would have entered a more complex phase, requiring immediate decisions. As a later JCS description noted, "At the time of the tree cutdown, considerable forces were immediately available to protect those directly involved in the operation. Had the North Koreans attempted to interfere with the cutting operation, the U.S. military could have conducted a range of appropriate responses under the immediate direction of the President and the Secretary of Defense."[47]

The U.S. engineers began to work on the thirty-year-old Normandy poplar exactly on schedule. They cut the tree about nine feet above ground, where the trunk divided into three large limbs. The tree operation had been estimated to take forty minutes; it actually took forty-two.

Concurrently with the cutting of the tree, an engineers' work party moved to the illegal North Korean road barriers—KPA 5 and KPA 6—and removed them. The tree and the barriers were removed by 7:45 a.m.; the debris was collected and the work party left the JSA by 8:26.

Shortly after the tree removal, a Pyongyang radio broadcast charged that the U.N. operation was a "grave provocation" that was designed to trap North Korea into the United Nations Command's "war provocation plot." It charged that the United

Nations force entered the Joint Security Area with 300 U.S.
and South Korean soldiers, cut down the tree, destroyed North
Korean guard posts, and smashed barriers, "creating a terrible
war atmosphere."[48] The broadcast also accused the United
States of violating North Korean airspace along the DMZ.

Within an hour after the unopposed operation, Major
General Han Ju-kyong, the senior North Korean representative
to the armistice commission, requested a private meeting with
Admiral Frudden to convey a message from his supreme commander (Kim Il-sung). This meeting took place in the JSA at
noon the same day. At this meeting the following dialogue took
place:

> *General Han Ju-kyong:* I have been instructed by the Supreme
> Commander of the Korean People's Army to convey his message
> to the Commander-in-Chief of the United Nations Command side.
> "It is a good thing that no big incident occurred at Pan Mun Jom
> for a long period. However, *it is regretful that an incident occurred*
> in the Joint Security Area, Pan Mun Jom this time. An effort
> must be made so that such incidents may not recur in the future.
> For this purpose both sides should make efforts. *We urge your*
> *side to prevent the provocation.* Our side will never provoke first,
> but take self defensive measures only when provocation occurs.
> This is our consistent stand." [Italics added.] I hope that you
> convey this message to your side's commander in chief at the
> quickest possible time.
>
> *Admiral Frudden:* The Supreme Commander Korean People's
> Army message to Commander-in-Chief, United Nations Command
> will be delivered by me to CINCUNC in accordance with your
> desires.
>
> *Gen. Han:* I have one thing to add. This morning your side again
> committed provocation by bringing hundreds of completely
> armed personnel in the JSA without any advance notification.
> Such incidents on your part might cause such [sic] one that
> occurred on the 18th. I strongly demand that your side commit
> no such provocations.
>
> *Adm. Frudden:* May I have a copy of the Supreme Commander's
> message to CINCUNC?

Gen. Han: At present I have no copy. I now await your reply to my last statement.

Adm. Frudden: Today I met with you at your request only to receive your Supreme Commander's message to CINCUNC. I have nothing further to discuss at this time. If you have any other subjects to discuss, we may do so at a further meeting.

Gen. Han: I would like to state once more clearly, that the provocation which you committed this morning is a serious one which might cause a serious consequences [sic]. Therefore, I hope that you seriously consider this and take responsible measures so that such provocations may not recur. I propose to conclude our meeting.

Adm. Frudden: I agree to your proposal to conclude the meeting at this time.[49]

This was the first such use of a personal message from Kim Il-sung to the U.N. commander in the twenty-three-year history of the Korean armistice. The meeting itself had lasted only thirteen minutes!

Kim Il-sung's message was immediately flashed to the waiting officials in the U.N. Command, the U.S. embassy in Seoul, and Washington. It arrived at the State Department less than twenty minutes later, at 11:30 p.m. Friday night, August 20, Washington time.[50]

While Kim Il-sung's message was being examined to determine its political meaning, the incident was the subject of comment by several members of Congress. Senate Republican Leader Hugh Scott (Pennsylvania) supported the actions directed by the president and said the "United States should insist on condemnation of North Korean barbarism through proper diplomatic channels. We should make clear we are prepared to defend ourselves along the border, and make sure the next time it is not Americans who get killed in a border foray." But, he added, "Proper security doesn't require U.S. troops."[51]

Senator Charles Percy (R.-Ill.) noted, "It's up to South Korea which has a massive military force of 600,000 that has been equipped by the United States to provide absolute security for our forces, which are symbolic in nature."[52]

Meanwhile, the U.N. Command had analyzed the message from Kim Il-sung, and General Stilwell's opinion was that the message was totally unacceptable—that Kim was not only *not* accepting responsibility for the incident, he was blaming it on the U.N. Command for having inadequate security arrangements.[53] Kim's statement "We urge your side to prevent the provocation. Our side will never provoke first . . ." seemed to U.N. Command officers to indicate this position.

The State Department working group on Saturday also analyzed Kim's verbal message to General Stilwell, and through him to the United States. Department officials were aware of General Stilwell's opinion, but noted two other aspects of the message:

○ a form of an apology: "It is regretful that an incident occurred."

○ a proposal for the separation of forces in the JSA: "An effort must be made so that such incidents may not recur in the future."

Though the message was authoritatively considered to be somewhat conciliatory, it was also ambiguous when compared with the criteria the State Department had established for a North Korean answer. These criteria were transmitted to North Korea at the August 19 Military Armistice Commission meeting and were expanded in public remarks of State Department officials on August 19 and 20. The criteria communicated at the MAC meeting were basically that North Korea:

○ accept responsibility for the killings
○ provide assurances that such incidents would not happen in the future
○ punish the men responsible

Secretary Kissinger, in his television interview on August 20, added the U.S. demands for explanations and reparations. Officials in the Korean working group were surprised, and commented that they were "amazed at the message," that it represented "uncharacteristic behavior of North Korea." One official noted privately that the message was "not exactly what the State Department had requested," but it was "more than we had expected."

The members of the Korean working group considered Kim's statement to partially meet U.S. demands, but not wholly. They also knew that Kissinger wanted to be tough in this crisis. Further, there was genuine concern that if the message were to be officially accepted outright as complete reparation for the two murders, an opportunity for enhancing long-term stability in the JSA would be lost. Specifically, such a move would transfer the initiative in the situation to the media—much of which was perceived as being overly sensitive to escalatory implications of using force and insufficiently sensitive to the security benefits of additional North Korean concessions. The working group believed that accepting the note would allow the press to write off the crisis and undermine the momentum and leverage the United States had created. This concern was voiced by one official who later said, "None of us wanted to have the media call off the crisis and have the U.S. lose the initiative with North Korea." The termination of the crisis, it was felt, would prevent the United States from insisting that North Korea follow through on the second part of Kim's message—the separation of forces to prevent future incidents. (This separation of forces was considered especially important because the intermingling of forces in the JSA had been the cause of thousands of low-level but tense incidents over the years.) There was some concern that the United States not be seen to be gloating over the message as a victory. The group also knew that Secretary Kissinger wanted to keep open the option of reprisal against North Korea.

The Korean working group, operating on Kissinger's previous generalized instructions, decided on Saturday, August 21, to release a statement that would acknowledge the North Korean message but would preserve the initiative for the United States and the United Nations in Military Armistice Commission negotiations. The release did not have specific clearance from Secretary Kissinger. The next morning, Sunday, August 22, at 6:00 a.m., the Korean working group was terminated. Later that day, the State Department press office, in response to numerous media inquiries, held a short news briefing.

The following verbal statement was made by Press Officer John Ordway:

> The United States does not find acceptable a North Korean statement indirectly expressing regret for the killing of two American officers in the Demilitarized Zone between North and South Korea. We consider this a back-handed acknowledgement that the North Koreans were wrong in the brutal act that they committed during a tree-trimming incident in the DMZ. . . .
>
> We do not find this message to be acceptable since it does not acknowledge responsibility for the deliberate and premeditated murders of the two U.N. Command officers. We're very skeptical about this message. We do not intend to lower our guard any, nor fall for any propaganda ploys.[54]

Murrey Marder, of the *Washington Post*, reported the State Department release in a Monday morning headline, "U.S. Says Message Fails to Admit Guilt in 'Brutal Murders.' " The story gave the reasons for the technical rejection of the note, but went on to report that Mr. Ordway had expressed the belief that tensions on the DMZ were expected to subside, "with the dispute now expected to shift to diplomatic channels."[55] The military forces in Korea were reported to remain on alert status, however.

The story commented that the North Koreans had signaled their intention to halt the military escalation by their response on Saturday, but "North Korea avoided anything that could be termed an apology for the killings by North Korean forces, and continued to charge the United States with initiating a 'provocation.' "[56]

When Secretary Kissinger read the negative interpretations in the Monday morning press accounts, he decided that the department should put out a more balanced interpretation of the North Korean message. He so instructed the press office, and later that day Mr. Robert L. Funseth appeared at a news conference to make three points on Korea:

> First: we recognize that the North Korean statement expresses regret over the incident, and we consider this a positive step.

> Second: nevertheless this does not change the tragic fact that two American officers were brutally beaten to death without provocation.
>
> Third and final point: therefore, we are calling for a meeting of the Military Armistice Commission tomorrow to insist upon North Korean assurances respecting the safety of our personnel in the Demilitarized Zone.[57]

The president, on the other hand, emphasized the indirect, strategic signals the U.S. actions conveyed to North Korea, the People's Republic of China, and the Soviet Union. Press Secretary Nessen held a press briefing on the same day as the State Department release, in which he said, "The United States is anxious to cooperate in the relaxation of tension, but we want to make sure there is no miscalculation concerning our firmness in that area."[58]

Meanwhile, most South Korean officials were greatly satisfied with the apparent outcome of the crisis, but some were privately urging military retaliation. An Information Ministry official who asked not to be identified, said, "The North Koreans must reply immediately with some sign of regret or condolence. If they don't reply after one or two weeks, your strategists must take military measures, a surgical strike."[59]

Despite Mr. Funseth's characterization, the next morning's *Washington Post* headline read, "State Department Reverses Stand on N. Korea's Regrets." The article, by Murrey Marder, reported that the department sought to reduce tension in Korea by retroactively accepting North Korea's message as "a positive step." The article then reiterated the Sunday press statement and the wording of Funseth's statement on Monday. Marder noted that the reason given for the apparent reversal was "a more considered reaction." The article went on to report a Funseth comment about obtaining North Korean assurances of safety for U.S. personnel, but this important statement of objectives was overshadowed by the more prominent headline.

With the circulation of the news that the State Department had accepted Kim Il-sung's message as a "positive step," and the publication of editorials drawing lessons from the incident, the Korean tree crisis can be said to have ended. Both the perceived threat and the felt need for further response had diminished, at least in the mind of the public, despite the fact that the negotiations over the separation of forces in the JSA had not yet begun.

AFTERMATH AND OUTCOMES

The aftermath of the crisis, following the removal of the tree and Kim Il-sung's conciliatory statement, can be summarized under four headings: Joint Security Area changes; U.S. public reaction; congressional hearings; and international political results.

Joint Security Area Changes

The objective military results of the U.S. action were reflected in the changes in Joint Security Area operating procedures. Although there were certainly individuals who thought the United States should have taken even stronger action, the position of the military in Korea, as expressed by General Stilwell, was that the tree and barrier removal had been a complete success—achieving their objective without incident. It should be noted as well that General Stilwell's perception of U.S. action in relation to the challenge conforms to standards of customary international law; that is, that an injured nation is justified in taking reprisal action in a degree equivalent to, but not exceeding, the level of the injury. Although, technically, the U.S. would have been justified in inflicting a physical quid pro quo—killing two Koreans—it was the considered view of policy officials that felling the tree coupled with a demonstration of force majeure would effectively reestablish U.S. prerogatives in the zone and cause the North Koreans to back down. The operation was seen in Korea and the United States as a clear signal to North and South Korea, as well as to other adversaries and allies, that the United States took seriously and was prepared to defend its authority under the terms of the armistice to operate freely and without interference in the JSA and that it also took its commitment to South Korea seriously.[60]

As precautionary measures, the *Midway* task force and the

air force fighter squadrons were retained in the Korean area, and the B-52s continued their flights daily.[61] These moves were considered essential by a number of NSC and ISA officers to give depth and credibility to the show of force. The B-52s continued their training flights over South Korea into the month of September, and the F-4 and F-111 squadrons were redeployed to Okinawa and Idaho respectively in mid-September.

The negotiations to conclude the crisis were initiated at a Military Armistice Commission meeting on August 25 and concluded on September 6. In these sessions the North Koreans proposed that security personnel be restricted to their respective sides of the JSA.[62] The innovation in this proposal was that the military demarcation line within the JSA was to be observed as the line to physically separate the military personnel of the two sides. This proposal, in effect, meant that there was no longer a Joint Security Area, that North Korea would lose its primary access road into the JSA across the Bridge of No Return, and would also abandon four guard posts which were south of the new line. (The U.N. Command had no guard posts or any other facilities north of the demarcation line.)

The new Joint Security Area agreement became a supplement to the "Agreement on Military Armistice Commission Headquarters Area, Its Security and Its Construction." It was signed on September 6 and became effective on September 16. The principal features of this new agreement were:

○ joint establishment and marking of the military demarcation line (MDL) through the JSA

○ restriction of military personnel from crossing over to the opposing side

○ removal of all guard posts presently constructed and manned from the opposing side's area

○ restriction of military personnel from crossing the MDL at the MAC conference site area and moving freely in the area of the other side

○ allowing of vehicles to cross the MDL only with approval of the opposing side

○ requirement that each side insure the safety of the personnel of the opposing side who legally cross the MDL o   prohibition on construction of barriers that obstruct observation of the opposing side

Two important footnotes to this agreement are of special interest. One is that this joint survey of the JSA to mark the exact military demarcation line was the first such joint venture since 1953. The second point is that the agreement was the first substantive change in the JSA procedures since 1958.

In the period September 6–15, a joint observer team surveyed the demarcation line and supervised its actual marking by the construction of concrete posts spaced ten meters apart. In addition, a North Korean Army work crew dismantled the four guard posts—KPA 5, 6, 7, and 8—which were now on the United Nations side of the line.

It was never learned for certain whether any of the North Korean soldiers involved in the incident were ever punished. Lieutenant Pak Chul disappeared immediately after the fight, came back about a week later, left the area, and did not return until late September, when he was seen briefly. He left again and has not been seen by U.N. Command personnel since.

In reviewing the military activities during the crisis, there was widespread agreement that the forces were deployed with speed, efficiency, and effectiveness. The other deployments, the military planning, and the cooperation between the JCS and the U.N. Command and between UNC and the R.O.K. military were similarly lauded.[63] The primary objectives of the military forces—to assert the U.N. Command's right of self-defense and freedom of movement in the JSA and to show the capability of U.S. forces to mount a coordinated operation with the Republic of Korea, without resorting to excessive force or triggering an escalation—had been fully demonstrated.

U.S. Public Reaction

The media in the United States are both reporters and shapers of public opinion. Media reaction can be sampled by examining several press editorials which commented on the results of the U.S. action. In most of these editorials, the issue was cast in a broad context, that of the role and utility of U.S.

forces in Korea, not in the more narrow context of U.S. management of the specific crisis.

The *Washington Post* published an editorial on the "Korean Incident" on August 24, the morning after Secretary of State Kissinger had accepted the North Korean statement as "a positive step." The *Post* editorial did not comment directly on the advisability of the U.S. government actions, but it noted that the North Koreans were evidently impressed enough by the U.S. show of force to take efforts to reduce the level of tension. It went on to state, "It is American steadfastness that keeps the peace, such as it is, in Korea."[64]

The *New York Times'* treatment focused on the U.S. military actions in the crisis and stated that the deployment of air and naval units into the area was a "necessary precaution." The deployments and the show of force were effective, it argued, in convincing North Korea of the firm commitment of the United States to deter any aggressive actions.[65] The *Times* also linked the tree incident with the larger Korean question in an editorial the previous day, stating that North Korea's display of aggression underscored the "continuing need for a strong and patient United States presence."[66]

Newspaper editorials from the Midwest and West Coast tended to express one of three general positions with regard to the U.S. response—disappointment that it had not been stronger; concern that it had been excessive; and, in larger numbers of editorials, support. Thus, the *Chicago Defender* called the U.S. actions a "namby-pamby approach to a serious incident,"[67] while the *Chicago Sun Times* accused the United States of "irrationality" in the deployment of two fighter squadrons and B-52s in a situation that "does not merit such excessive response."[68] The *San Diego Union* was more circumspect in its belief that the North Koreans were not at all intimidated by the show of force and might, in fact, welcome it to propagandize to the world that the United States was about to start a war.[69]

The majority of American newspaper editors agreed with government decisions and action. The *Milwaukee Journal* called them "a proper course," making a symbolic but "important point";[70] the *Pittsburgh Press* argued that the reaction was "wholly defensible" and commended candidate Carter for not making it a partisan political issue.[71] The *Chicago Tribune* applauded the initial rejection of the Kim Il-sung "apology" and noted that U.S. behavior had been "responsible" in devising "a nearly perfect symbolic response."[72] The *Cleveland Plain Dealer* argued that the continued defense of South Korea was essential and that the U.S. show of force "was both prudent and necessary."[73]

Many columnists also supported the government's actions. Joseph C. Harsch, writing in the *Christian Science Monitor*, called the deployments and the tree cutting both "necessary and desirable." He called the North Koreans "probably the most primitive, bigoted, irrational, and fanatic" of all the Communist powers.[74] Further, he saw in the North Korean murders a deliberate test of United States readiness to use force and to act promptly.

Joseph Kraft's column stressed the connection of the tree incident with overall relations between North and South Korea, with the North seeing an opportunity to influence the Colombo conference as well as the U.N. resolution on Korea coming up in September. He stated that the strong United States reaction made sense, but he went on to argue for an overall review of U.S. policy in Northeast Asia.[75]

Precise data on U.S. public opinion during or after a crisis are always very difficult to obtain; this crisis followed the rule. No known opinion surveys specifically asked U.S. citizens how they felt about their government's action. What is available, and in one sense more important, is data on the issue of how the crisis affected public opinion on the president's performance, which was itself an issue in the presidential campaign. Even this issue is difficult to separate from the other issues that were affecting presidential popularity during the same period. There are public opinion polls on the popularity of both presidential candidates before and after the Korean tree incident. One such poll produced the responses recorded in Table 2.

The Gallup opinion data in Table 2 indicate that President Ford's popularity increased from 32 percent before the crisis to 36 percent after it. Having said this, it must be immediately noted that Ford's nomination coincided with the crisis and that Carter increased his own popularity by 2 percent from June to

Table 2. Candidate Popularity: Pre- and Post-Crisis*

Time Period of Poll	*Ford*	*Carter*	*Other*	*Undecided*
June 11–14: Before either convention; before crisis	37%	55%	3%	5%
August 6–9: After Democratic convention; before Republican; before crisis	32%	57%	3%	8%
August 27–30: After both conventions and crisis	36%	54%	10%	10%

* Question: "Suppose the presidential election were being held today, if President Gerald Ford were the Republican candidate and Jimmy Carter were the Democratic candidate, which would you like to see win?"

Source: *Gallup Opinion Index—Political, Social and Economic Trends,* Report no. 131, June 1976; no. 133, August 1976; no. 134, September 1976 (Princeton, N.J.: American Institute of Public Opinion, 1976).

July, after nomination by the Democratic National Convention. Thus, one could argue that just being nominated would account for an increase in popularity among the voters. At the same time, there were numerous economic, social, and other political factors which a broad-gauged survey like the Gallup poll cannot isolate. The only scientifically valid conclusion that can be drawn from the data is that President Ford's popularity did not decrease over the period he made decisions to act in Korea.

Congressional Reaction

In the Congress, the Korean tree incident became intertwined with two other areas of interest—human rights and the War Powers Resolution. A third issue—the role of U.S. troops in Korea—was tangentially affected by the tree incident, but few congressmen claimed it was a strong factor in arguments either to withdraw or to retain those forces.

Broadly stated, the human rights issue concerned how U.S. policies should be designed so as to induce countries in which civil liberties were restricted to lessen repression. The human rights issue had been before the Ninety-fourth Congress in the form of House Resolution 506, which expressed regret over the South Korean government arrest and sentencing of eighteen distinguished citizens for their part in a March 1 declaration requesting the rescinding of the Presidential Emergency Decree. On August 31, this resolution was amended to indicate the "sense of the House of Representatives" that it "deplores the killing on August 18, 1976," and "conveys sympathy to the families," and called on the North Korean government to desist from actions which raise tensions on the DMZ.[76] The amendment and the resolution passed the House by a unanimous voice vote, without objection.

Two weeks after the deaths in Korea, the General Accounting Office (GAO) published a report entitled *Executive-Legislative Communications and the Role of the Congress During International Crises.*[77] This report was the result of a survey taken by the GAO between February and May 1976 at the request of Congressman Dante B. Fascell (D.-Fla.), chairman of the Subcommittee on International Political and Military Affairs of the House Committee on International Relations. The report is significant because it was a part of the aftermath of the *Mayaguez* crisis and is an indicator of congressional opinion during the Korean tree hearings. Based on responses from only 44 percent of the 537 legislators, and despite other limitations in the data,[78] the GAO proposed several conclusions, three of which are most relevant for our study: (1) of those congressmen who had received information from the executive branch during the *Mayaguez* crisis, 59 percent said that they had been "informed" rather than "consulted"; (2) 55 percent of those responding indicated that they expected the future role of Congress in crises to be "significantly more active," and 29 percent thought it would be "slightly more active"; and (3) 68 percent said they would support a system, such as a Congressional Operations Center, whereby information would automatically flow to the Congress during a crisis.

The desire of the Congress to have a larger role in government policy making during international crises was documented not only in the GAO report but in the Korean crisis hearings held on September 1, 1976. On that day, Representative Fascell, chairman of the Subcommittees on International Political and Military Affairs and International Organizations, called for combined hearings on the incident.[79] Executive-branch witnesses included Assistant Secretary Arthur Hummel and Korean Country Director Edward Hurwitz from the State Department, Deputy Assistant Secretary of Defense (East Asia and Pacific Affairs) Morton Abramowitz, and Brigadier General Anderson Atkinson, assistant deputy director for operations, JCS.

Congressman Fascell began by indicating the committees' desire to know how the crisis and past incidents related to overall U.S. security interests in the western Pacific. Secretary Hummel testified first, relating U.S. security interests to information on the North Korean August 5 speech, the Nonaligned Nations Conference, the pending U.N. debate, and the JSA events immediately prior to the incident. Secretary Abramowitz then testified on the military aspects of the crisis itself and the long history of incidents on the DMZ. General Atkinson offered to show the committee the photographs of the incident. Until then the entire hearing had been devoted to the crisis and to U.S. policy in the area.

At this point, Congressman Fascell invited Representative Elizabeth Holtzman (D.-N.Y.) to the witness table to make a statement. She stated that her intention was to raise the War Powers issue and the question of whether the president had complied with the resolution's provisions. She drew the committees' attention to Section 4 of the War Powers Resolution which

> requires the President of the United States, in the absence of a declaration of war, to report to the Congress within 48 hours when ". . . U.S. Armed Forces are introduced . . . into the territory, airspace or waters of foreign nations while equipped for combat except for deployments which relate solely to supply, replacement, repair or training of such forces," or when U.S. Armed Forces ". . . are introduced in numbers which substantially enlarge U.S. Armed Forces equipped for combat already located in a foreign nation." The President is required in these circumstances to set forth "(A) the circumstances necessitating the introduction of U.S. Armed Forces; (B) the constitutional and

legislative authority under which such introduction took place, and the estimated scope and duration of the hostilities or involvement."

I am advised that no report was filed by the President under the War Powers Resolution. Although the handling of this incident may have been appropriate in every sense, still in all it seems to me that the intent of the War Powers Resolution should have been followed and obeyed. It is an important piece of legislation which requires that the Congress of the United States is to be consulted about the use of American forces abroad when this might lead to hostilities and when there is an additional enlargement of present forces abroad. It requires the President to consult closely with the Congress in these respects.[80]

Mr. Hummel then submitted a copy of the legal memorandum from the acting legal advisor of the State Department entitled "War Powers and Korean Deployments," dated August 27. In this memorandum the Department of State set out its reasoning in concluding that the War Powers Resolution did not apply. The legal advisor argued that Section 4(a)(1) of the resolution was not applicable since hostilities were not present and involvement in pending hostilities was not "clearly" imminent. Subsection 2 of the resolution was deemed not applicable because the United States only reinforced—did not introduce—U.S. military forces in Korea. The third and final subsection was ruled as not binding because,

I believe it would be an undesirable precedent to construe the Resolution as requiring a report in a situation where a relative handful of people have been added to an existing force of some 41,000 men. Although in terms of tactical aircraft the increment is significant, I believe we should interpret 4(a)(3) as concerned primarily, if not entirely, with numbers of military personnel, rather than with items of equipment.[81]

The wording of the Department of State justification was discussed for some minutes, but little agreement was reached. Several of the congressmen were distressed that the executive branch could unilaterally decide not to report under the resolution, and several others disagreed with the justification given.

At one point, Congressman Fascell argued directly with the logic of the contention that aircraft and naval deployments were not required to be reported, and he accused Mr. Abramowitz of a "semantic, circuitous evasion" on this point.[82] Representative Donald M. Fraser (D.-Minn.) entered the discussion and called the memorandum "ridiculous," saying the State Department would either have to get some new lawyers or the law would have to be changed to more clearly express the intent of the Congress.

The hearing then turned back to discussions of the incident, the JSA procedures, North Korean intentions, and a very general exchange on the WSAG meetings. Congressman Fascell adjourned the subcommittee meeting at 4:30 p.m., after two hours and twenty minutes.

International Political Results

The international results of the crisis fall into three main categories: opinions expressed by uninvolved nations; official press statements from Communist states indirectly involved; and postcrisis political actions of North Korea. The international media followed the Korean developments quite closely both in the press and on television.

European editorial opinions were generally quite supportive of the U.S. actions, and many linked the response to the larger issue of troop deployment and status. The independent Viennese newspaper *Die Presse* remarked, "The 42,000 American troops . . . are fulfilling . . . both a military and political role in the Far East which even a most highly armed South Korea could never fulfill alone." The U.S. troop presence was, *Die Presse* noted, "a precondition for the state of non-war."[83] Along the same lines, the Swedish moderate newspaper *Svenska Dagbladet,* remarked:

> If the most recent crisis, which now fortunately appears to be winding down, has shown anything it is that the U.S. presence is still indispensable as a guarantee against an armed North Korean attack against the border to the South.[84]

In Paris, *Le Monde* emphasized the domestic aspects and attempted to explain U.S. actions as being due in large measure

to the election campaign.[85] Similarly, the Washington correspondent for the West German *Koelner Stadt-Anzeiger* was of
the opinion that the incident would probably not have serious
international political or military consequences.[86]

In the Far East, Japan's independent moderate newspaper
Yomiuri ran a correspondent's opinion that Kim's message was
a "diplomatic defeat for North Korea." It said, "The biggest
miscalculation of the Pyongyang side was the unexpectedly
strong reaction from the Ford administration, which has adopted
a policy of unchanging support for South Korea."[87]

In Singapore, an editorial in *The Nation* said that Kim's

> expression of regret over the weekend—his first to the United
> States on any matter—was a surprise. So was yesterday's U.S.
> State Department description of the gesture as a "positive step"
> after unnamed American officials had said that the U.S. rejected
> the non-apology. Ironically, the American response last week
> might has [sic] secretly gladdened hearts in Peking, as it amounted
> to a reaffirmation of the U.S. military commitment in Asia after
> Communist victories in Indochina, the U.S. military pullout from
> Thailand and the forthcoming fade-out from the Philippines.[88]

In a strategic-bargaining sense, the Communist nations,
principally the Soviet Union and the P.R.C., were the indirect
targets of U.S. actions in Korea. They were the recipients of
implicit bargaining signals, and in the case of China, received
direct diplomatic communication from Secretary of State
Kissinger. The degree of their prior knowledge and consent had
been a vital issue in the 1950 North Korean invasion across the
thirty-eighth parallel, and these countries were clearly the
pivotal geopolitical factor in considering any regional conflict
involving North Korea.

The Soviet Union was very restrained in its reaction, and it
maintained a relative silence for several days after the killings.
The first significant mention of the incident did not appear
until late on August 20, two days after the original event. This
broadcast cited "news agency reports" of "heightened tensions"
and "provocative actions" by the U.S. forces in Korea. A
Pravda article written in Pyongyang cited the South Korean
news agency as reporting the increased U.N. alert and blamed

it on a "psychosis in South Korea" provided by an incident in the JSA in which "people were killed."

A statement in this dispatch indicates the Soviet restraint. "The Korean Central News Agency notes that the clash was provoked by the American–South Korean side. A KCNA statement issued today . . . declares this a premeditated criminal action."[89] *Pravda*'s New York correspondent filed a dispatch on Saturday, August 21, but it too was a mildly worded description. Neither of these two *Pravda* reports were distributed by Tass, the Soviet news agency. Finally, on August 29, an *Izvestiya* editorial lightly chastised the United States for using "threats and sabre-rattling" methods which were inconsistent with détente.[90]

Peking was even more restrained in its public communications. We noted earlier that the P.R.C. did not respond publicly to North Korea's harsh August 5 denunciations of the United States until August 15 and then only reprinted—with amplification—its ally's charges. Similarly, after the incident, the P.R.C. waited two days before distributing verbatim selected North Korean News Agency dispatches, mostly from the *Nodong Sinmun* of Pyongyang. On August 23, the New China News Agency (NCNA) reported a Peking news conference of the North Korean ambassador where he strongly denounced U.S. imperialism for its recent grave provocations against North Korea. The restrained nature of the Chinese reporting seemed apparent.

North Korean attitudes were expressed in published Communist party statements and actions by third countries at the United Nations. Just as U.N. representatives at the Military Armistice Commission had been impressed with the reduction in hostility from their North Korean counterparts, so were observers startled to note a change in tone of the official North Korean press in the weeks following the crisis. The anti-American invective which had characterized North Korean press statements over the past year subsided somewhat after the 380th meeting of the Military Armistice Commission on August 25. Neither North Korean press nor radio carried any account of Kim Il-sung's message expressing "regret."

The reader will recall that allies of North Korea had, in mid-

August, presented at the U.N. a resolution denouncing the U.S. role in South Korea. On September 20, less than a month after the successful U.S. operation to cut down the tree, these same allies withdrew their resolution.[91]

In summary, the Korean tree crisis—like so many other modern military confrontations—had a diverse and debatable set of outcomes. Its several results could not be called conclusive because the conflict of values between North Korea on the one side and South Korea and the United States on the other was not resolved. Yet, there was at least a temporary discontinuance of hostile acts in the JSA and along the DMZ generally. Although the long-term political differences between the two Koreas were not resolved, the political influence of North Korea has receded in the region, with the nonaligned nations, and in the United Nations. On this basis, it is possible to characterize the political outcome as at least semiconclusive.

The outcomes can be divided into two parts. The first aspect of conflict resolution was compellence—the forcing of North Korea to call the incident "regretful" and the associated demonstration of U.S. resolve. This compellence was achieved by the use of military force and was generally reinforced by U.S. domestic opinion, by world public opinion, and by official opinion in the People's Republic of China and the Soviet Union. The withdrawal of the North Korean resolution at the United Nations can very likely be attributed to this factor.

The second part of the conflict resolution can be described as diplomatic ratification—the agreement and implementation of new procedures in the Joint Security Area. This agreement was achieved through diplomatic negotiations, but it extended from the compellence component; traditional diplomacy alone could not have achieved a new agreement.

The new JSA procedures improved the physical security of U.S. forces, and thus represented an advancement of U.S. military interests. At the same time, there was little doubt that the operation—in demonstrating U.S. will, resolve, and capability—served a long-term foreign policy interest. Both military and foreign policy benefits might be transitory outcomes of the incident, but crisis resolution does not necessarily imply permanent solutions. There may be no permanent solutions in the relations among nations. But if short-range solutions do not detract from long-range interests, they may be the best terms possible.

Analysis and Conclusions

The rigorous standard by which we judge ourselves is what makes us different from the totalitarian regimes of the Left and Right.

—Henry Kissinger

This study of crisis behavior and crisis management has had several purposes up to this point: to review the major approaches of other analysts; to outline a conceptual framework; to discuss the U.S. organizational processes in handling crises; to inventory the U.S. command and control communications available to decision makers; and to develop two case studies. The purpose of this chapter is to apply the conceptual framework to the analysis of the two cases and within the limitations of our data to draw what conclusions seem appropriate. The conclusions fall into three categories: those primarily having to do with crisis research (Conclusions 1 and 2); those focused on the crisis decision-making process (Conclusions 3 through 12); and those in the section at the end, which attempt to evaluate the overall decision-making process and the two crisis decisions. Some of the conclusions became quickly apparent during the research and will appear obvious to the reader; others were not at all obvious and were only reached after much discussion and analysis.

CRISIS VERSUS ROUTINE POLICY MAKING

Conclusion 1. Crisis policy making is significantly different from routine. It can be differentiated from the routine policy process by its speed and rapid elevation to the highest levels of government and by the activation of task force–type organizations. However, international crises occur with sufficient frequency that they should not be treated as abnormal *situations. Crisis management procedures should be developed as an adjunct to the regular policy process.*

Specifically, crisis policy planning appears to differ from routine in that a crisis involves:

- ○ a heightened consciousness of threat and risk among the media and the public; a relative increase in attention given to the process and substance of presidential decisions; and increased expectations of presidential decisiveness and action
- ○ relatively greater opportunity for *presidential* determination of a national policy priority
- ○ the focused attention of many high-level officials for an unusual length of time
- ○ the tendency (due to time constraints) for high-level involvement in normally low-level functions
- ○ unusually high uncertainty about the details of the situation, the crisis event, the intentions of the adversary, and the potentials for success of the alternatives (due to the lack of appropriate information, often stemming from surprise)
- ○ increased difficulty in the evaluation of options, of interdepartmental and intergovernmental coordination and consultation
- ○ a higher probability of miscalculation due to the limited information available and reduced time for analysis and evaluation

This is not to say that the opportunity for the president to vary from past policies is unlimited, or that he has comprehensive control of the vast governmental apparatus. Allison, in particular, stresses in his study of the Cuban missile crisis that organizational processes and individual initiative played a large role in the U.S. response to the Soviet move.[1] The results of our research do indicate that, on balance, the president and his advisors have *relatively* more opportunity for decision independent of bureaucratic constraints during a crisis than they do in routine policy making. In summary, crisis decision making tends to be accompanied by centralization, elevation, optimization, and lack of information.

CRISIS TYPES AND CHARACTERISTICS

Conclusion 2. The crisis definition developed in Chapter 2 appears to be a useful one, but it could be refined, as follows: "An international political/military crisis situation is characterized by: a change in the international or domestic environment, which may be abrupt or gradual, but which generates a threat to important national goals or objectives as defined by individuals or policy-making groups experiencing the crisis, with significantly increased probability of military action and/or war, and the perception of a short time for response." However, for a governmental crisis to begin, the critical factor is the authoritative decision by a responsible official that the international situation constitutes a crisis.

Both case studies seem to justify the validity of the four elements in our basic definition. The seizure of the *Mayaguez* and the murder of the two U.S. officers both represented "a change in the international environment," and both changes came as a surprise to U.S. policy makers. Changes in the domestic environment were not addressed in our two cases, but we believe the concept of internal change is valuable and should be retained for future studies.

There was a clear "threat to important national goals or objectives as defined by the group experiencing the crisis." In the case of the *Mayaguez,* the principle of freedom of the seas—vital to the national existence of an essentially maritime nation—had been challenged. In addition, the standing of the United States as a great power—particularly in the wake of the recent defeat in Vietnam—had been called into question. The murder of two officers who were part of the U.S. forces that constituted the visible element of our security commitment to Korea was a flagrant challenge to U.S. resolve and good faith toward its commitments.

In both cases the "probability of military hostilities . . . was significantly increased." In the case of the *Mayaguez,* the isolated nature of the incident on the high seas, the absence of any U.S. diplomatic relations with the Cambodian authorities, and the enormous imbalance of force between the two countries virtually assured that the United States would exercise its advantage in this area. With respect to the Korean incident, the provocation was itself military. While the larger challenge was to the ability of the United States to exercise and defend prerogatives within the JSA, the reassertion of that capability could only have been military. It is doubtful whether a solely diplomatic U.S. response would have commanded the attention of Kim Il-sung and his North Korean advisors.

Finally, both case studies considered here involved "short time for response." In the case of the *Mayaguez*, the time constraints were imposed by the nature of the crisis event—the seizure of a ship—and the (correct) belief that the objectives of the United States (the release of the ship and its crew) would be incomparably more difficult if ship and crew were moved to the Cambodian mainland. In the case of the DMZ murders, the clearly premeditated nature of the act made it apparent that this was not an isolated accident, but a direct challenge to the United States. Here there was no deadline forced on the United States by the crisis event or a North Korean ultimatum. The deadline was self-imposed, as a result of the dynamics of the crisis situation. Each day after the murders represented a diminution of apparent U.S. concern over the crisis event. Although the U.S. ability to react within a three-day time period was not challenged, this period could not have been stretched indefinitely. Crisis events do have the effect of heightening the political awareness of citizens, but the attention thus generated does not last forever. Retaliation conducted six months later certainly would not have been perceived as responsive to the importance of the challenge. Internationally, the absence of a timely quid pro quo would have been perceived as representing a setback to U.S. international prestige and political interests. The result was a high degree of perceived urgency in resolving the crisis.

However, this sense of urgency depends on the crisis. Differences in the situation (e.g., the degree to which "important national goals or objectives" are threatened), may make a substantial difference in the conduct of crisis management. Where a crisis contains substantial risk of escalation to nuclear war, the performance of actors and the decision unit may be substantially different from their performance in lower-order crises.

KEY POLICY MAKERS

Conclusion 3. An international crisis affords a U.S. president relatively more opportunity to make decisions and control implementation than routine policy making.

Conclusion 4. During periods of routine policy making, key policy makers tend to develop their objectives based on their individual and organizational backgrounds; but during an international crisis, these policy makers tend to agree quickly on U.S. national objectives and are less influenced by their bureaucratic position than during normal periods of noncrisis.

A crisis situation presents the president with an unusual opportunity to lead the policy process; he can define the crisis, initiate organizational and interdepartmental procedures for crisis management, set deadlines, and generally guide the process of decision making. He can have great influence on the process of implementation through the elaborate network of command and control communications which are available to him on a daily basis but which are not used until needed. The media, the Congress, interest groups, and the public have relatively less effect on the crisis decision-making process because of their lack of information and the pace of events.

Based on the data in the *Mayaguez* case, there is little doubt that the president played a central role in the decision to use military forces to obtain the release of the crew and ship. President Ford sensed the importance of assuring allies and adversaries of his ability to act to protect U.S. interests and commitments. Throughout his twenty-six years in the Congress, he had been a vigorous proponent of American strength and leadership and felt very strongly the vital importance of the United States continuing to lead the free world in its containment of communism.

At home, Ford faced the parallel task of restoring the confidence of the American people in the presidency. He considered it his personal responsibility to fulfill the expectations of U.S. citizens for presidential leadership and vigorous action. This was balanced by his long experience in the House of Representatives, which convinced him of the value and indeed the necessity of consultation with advisors and of basing executive decisions on a broad collegial base. This combination of characteristics led President Ford to take a personal leadership role in the *Mayaguez* decision and to follow its implementation closely. Nothing exemplified this position so much as the newspaper photo of the president in formal attire, having just come from a state dinner, checking on the progress of the *Mayaguez* relief force.

In response to the will of Congress as expressed in the War Powers Resolution, the president personally instructed John Marsh to initiate and follow through on reporting crisis developments. The intention of his instructions was to comply with the *intent* of the War Powers Resolution, without prejudice to an ultimate challenge to the *constitutionality* of the resolution itself. President Ford's position, since elaborated in an address at the University of Kentucky,[2] represents an important contribution to the judicial history of the resolution in view of his unique experience as both legislator and president since its enactment.

The role of the president in the Korean DMZ crisis was much less visible, although equally commanding. His decision not to return to Washington indicated that he did not consider the level of threat to U.S. goals and objectives to be high and that he apparently wished to avoid any hint of politicization of the event. He also knew that, as directed, Dr. Kissinger would activate the WSAG in his absence, and that he would be kept fully informed by General Scowcroft of its recommendations. Thus, by President Ford's decision, the initiative for preliminary assessment and development of options was delegated from the NSC to the WSAG. That this process of delegating was allowed was a firm indication of President Ford's faith in the NSC system, of which the WSAG was a functioning part.

When Dr. Kissinger flew to Kansas City after the second WSAG meeting on the DMZ crisis, the president, General Scowcroft, and he discussed the alternatives and recommendations.

Dr. Kissinger presented the range of options, summarized the collective views of the WSAG members, and gave his own preference. General Scowcroft presented his views as well, with particular emphasis on the comparative efficacy of alternative military measures in achieving U.S. objectives and controlling events. The president personally decided to authorize the tree chopping and show of force.

In sum, our conclusion is that President Ford entered both crises with a clear sense of needing an outcome which demonstrated U.S. strength, resolve, and ability to act to defend its interest, but to do so in such a deliberative fashion as to assure consistency with American values and thereby command broad-based American support.

The secretary of state's role was also prominent in both crises. While this could be said of his entire role in the field of foreign policy since 1969, his roles in these two crises were different. He was certainly more dominant in the Korean episode than in the *Mayaguez,* and this difference was due largely to the president and General Scowcroft being away from Washington during the Korean crisis. In the case of the *Mayaguez,* the president decided that *he* was going to be the principal crisis manager; in the Korean DMZ crisis he retained control over decisions but delegated management aspects to the NSC subgroup. Although this observation may not surprise laymen and students of American government, it is clearly contrary to the routine predictions of some bureaucratic-politics analysts, who tend to predict that the initiative in role selection can be manipulated by lower-level officials.

In the *Mayaguez* crisis, there is every indication that the final selection of options was fully in consonance with Secretary Kissinger's desires. The strong military reaction against Cambodia would appear to be consistent with the secretary's belief system summarized in Chapter 3 (to advocate executive authority, firmness, deterrent and symbolic effects, and sufficient force).

On the other hand, the U.S. response to the DMZ crisis was more restrained and did not appear to be consistent with the secretary's belief system. Dr. Kissinger remained convinced that the United States should have retaliated against North

Korea to deter its leaders from future provocations.

Further analysis of the case data indicates that the organizational representatives at both the NSC and the WSAG were quick to agree on the nature of the U.S. interests that were threatened by the two incidents. In this collective activity, it appears that the dominant influence on their attitudes and behavior was not their institutional representation, but the objective situation. Thus, their organizational positions did not influence their perception as much as on routine issues.

CONTEXT—THE STRUCTURE OF THE SITUATION

Conclusion 5. The context of a crisis structures the situation in such a way as to set limits on the character and method of responses. The characteristics of the adversary's provocation establish salients which—though not impenetrable—are important thresholds tending to limit responses.

The context of a crisis includes the impact of recent history and the onrush of other issues that collectively establish the relationship of the United States with allies and adversaries. Context reflects the strength of our political leadership at home and abroad and thus bears on crisis decision making. Context, then, makes every crisis unique, because it is the product of a distinctive network of relationships, trends, issues, and events. It is important to distinguish these contextual factors from the objective characteristics insofar as possible, because contextual factors are nonscientific (in the sense that they are not reproducible) and tend to retard rather than enhance the development of theory.

The *Mayaguez* crisis was strongly affected by at least three international and three domestic situational factors. The international environment included: the precipitous withdrawal by evacuation under fire of U.S. personnel from Indochina in April 1975; the depressed and declining state of the international economy as a result of the Arab oil embargo and associated price rises of 1973; and the shock to international confidence caused by the first resignation of a U.S. president in the nation's 200-year history. In the background as an environmental—

but not a decisive—factor lay the balance and relationship of the superpowers. Militarily, the strategic nuclear situation could still be characterized as bipolar and one of approximate parity, although many officials in the administration were warning of the strength and momentum of the Soviet build-up. Diplomatically, the U.S.-Soviet relationship was relatively cordial, based at least on mutual respect if not trust.

Domestically, the *Mayaguez* incident occurred at a time of economic recession. The resignation of President Nixon, the recent withdrawal from Southeast Asia, and the setback in the Middle East peace talks combined to make the American people seriously question the abilities of their political leadership. In the public opinion polls, only 39 percent of the respondents approved of the way President Ford was doing his job (see Table 1).

Thus, the context of the recent past structured the decision-making climate and reduced the viability of several possible options. First, the internal domestic turmoil caused by the Vietnam War made unlikely any proposal for the use of U.S. ground forces on the mainland of Cambodia. Second, given the personalities and their role perceptions described in the previous conclusion, the possibility that the United States would take no action to release the crew and the ship was made extremely remote. Third, the recognition by President Ford of the *Pueblo* analogy tended to increase the time pressure and to further weaken the position of any who would have argued against strong action. Fourth, the possibility that a diplomatic initiative would be successful was rendered very unlikely because of the lack of formal channels and direct communications with the new Cambodian government. Fifth, the likelihood that a show of force would have the desired effect on the Cambodians was extremely low. The context of the failure in Vietnam and the precedent of the *Pueblo* show of force strengthened the arguments of many Orientals that the United States was just a "paper tiger." It would have been exceedingly difficult for a U.S. policy maker to argue that a show of force would be effective in Cambodia, where a ruthless regime, already known to be slaughtering thousands, was now in power. The *Mayaguez* actions, then, became a part of the context of the Korean DMZ crisis a year later.

By August 1976, the position of the United States in the eyes of its allies was greatly improved. Under U.S. leadership the International Energy Agency had been organized and was well on its way toward establishment of a firm basis for assuring confidence among the industrialized democracies in their ability to deal with future energy embargoes.

At the time of the Korean crisis, the economy was on the rise in most industrialized states. Although there had been a change in the political leadership of almost every Western country in the preceding twelve months, there was a general consensus that the means of restoring economic strength were at hand. Under U.S. leadership, two summit conferences (Rambouillet in November 1975 and Puerto Rico in June 1976) had produced renewed confidence in our ability collectively to cope with threats to the international economy and, for the first time, to coordinate with our allies in the development of domestic economic policies.

As a result of the Sinai II Agreement (September 1975), respect for the creative diplomacy and leadership of the United States was renewed, as evidenced by statements of political leaders throughout the world. The U.S. initiative toward creating an environment conducive to a peaceful settlement of the Rhodesian problem enhanced the United States as a moral force for peace in the world. In short, as a result of the series of actions noted above, and the increase in real investment in U.S. defense resources for the first time in more than eight years, the respect for the United States as a leader by both allies and adversaries was at a post-Watergate high.

At home, the United States was in the middle of an election year, with Jimmy Carter having been nominated as the Democratic candidate and the Republican Convention to select a nominee in progress. The campaign had been dominated in the international context by a challenge to the morality of U.S. foreign policy and concern for human rights. Candidate Carter expressed the view that the United States could make a substantial reduction in its defense expenditures and should place less emphasis on the use of force in the world. In the Republican party, President Ford was being challenged severely by Ronald

Reagan for weakness in dealing with the Soviet Union and for inattention to human rights. At the convention, President Ford had won a challenge in the Rules Committee on a procedural vote, which implied enough votes to gain the nomination. In this situation, the timing of the crisis even by a few days might have substantially changed the picture. As it was, the DMZ incident did not become an issue at the national convention.

How, then, did the context affect the Korean crisis? First, the confluence of factors leading up to the Nonaligned Conference in Sri Lanka most likely influenced North Korea to stage the incident. When the conference representatives failed to support North Korea's actions in the crisis, the North Koreans lost any incentive to prolong or amplify the crisis. Second, the increased international prestige of the United States would have strengthened our ability to use major force, although the same rise in prestige might also have tended to lessen the need for any overly strong U.S. military response. Third, the overwhelming military retaliation during the *Mayaguez* incident probably reduced the perceived necessity to use violent force in Korea. Although we cannot know what influenced Kim Il-sung's apologetic response, it is very likely that the object lesson of *Mayaguez* was not lost on him. Fourth, the nearly complete lack of support by the P.R.C. and the Soviet Union meant Kim Il-sung would not use the incident to play one of his allies against the other. Thus, incentives to escalate the crisis were lessened, if not removed. The context of the *Mayaguez* crisis constituted a comparatively severe challenge to the U.S. ability to control events. In the Korean case, this challenge was not present.

Both crises were strongly affected by their contexts. There was a high degree of agreement on the background factors, the selection of historical analogies, the realm of political feasibility, and the perceived need for action. Contextual factors supported and channeled the key policy makers' basic dispositions.

SURPRISE

Conclusion 6. Crises continue to surprise policy makers and military forces. Despite the world's most sophisticated intelli-

gence network, U.S. intelligence gathering and analysis are not sufficient to predict specific international crises before they occur. Although there were several political indicators that a crisis might occur off the shores of Cambodia in May 1975 and on the Korean DMZ in August 1976, the indicators were both ambiguous and hidden amid a background of other, less significant intelligence "noise."

A major function of intelligence systems is to prevent the political leadership from being surprised by events which may constitute a threat to its interests—a crisis. Analyses of why crises occur, particularly in states having sophisticated intelligence systems, usually focus upon bureaucratic impediments or inadequate analysis. For example, in the United States, there is less doubt about our ability to collect information than there is about our ability to analyze that information correctly, and to get it to policy-level officials. This presumption as to the adequacy of our ability to collect information is subject to one qualification, however; it concerns the implications of resource allocation for implicitly setting priorities among potential threats and attributing relative importance to given areas. Specifically, the intelligence community devotes the bulk of its collection resources to indicators of the greatest threat— strategic nuclear war. Fewer resources are devoted to collection of information on indicators of lower-order attack. Finally, the fewest resources are devoted to collecting information in areas considered of marginal threat or political interest.

We do not question that even at the lowest level of threat, U.S. investments in intelligence gathering provide a base line sufficient to collect enough information to forecast potential crises. We note, however, that this information, once obtained, must be analyzed and weighed within the intelligence community by persons who, by their low standing, in terms of resources, may be hesitant to report information to decision makers.[3] This is not to say that a hypothetical desk officer who constitutes the total U.S. investment in collecting information on Nepal would hesitate to report information that he clearly believed signaled a crisis. It does imply, however, that his low standing may induce a certain reticence which biases downward the probability that indicators of crisis in perceived low-threat environments will be reported.

The more important problems which result in officials being caught by surprise are bureaucratic impediments and inadequate analysis. Bureaucratic impediments concern the problem of information flow to policy-level officials. That is, if it is accepted that the amount of time cabinet officers devote to intelligence is limited to fifteen minutes, there is pressure to assure that only the most vital information is included in that time. The compilation of morning intelligence briefings is normally the responsibility of generalists in the operation centers. They are faced with a problem of setting priorities among perhaps seventy-five pages of reports from throughout the world with little more to guide them than the degree of pressure they may expect from several assistant secretaries. This completely procedural issue may determine what goes in and what stays out. This situation is particularly relevant to the opportunities which existed for warning officials before the Korean DMZ crisis. Potential indicators included the Mao/Hua letters and previous incursions in August as well as the expectation that some event could take place in conjunction with North Korean initiatives at the Colombo conference. These are the very kinds of long term indicators which in and of themselves on a given day would not have competed successfully with other information for the attention of higher-level authorities.

The filtering system does not relieve the desk officer from the responsibility to collect indicators regularly and to insert at appropriate moments assessments that clearly imply the potential for crisis in a given area. Such an aggregated set of indicators of hostile intentions can be visualized as an "intentions staircase," as we have done in Figures 9 and 10.[4] Some of the problems in constructing such staircases include the designation of appropriate categories and potential crises, the assessing of relationships among the indicators, and the establishment of subjective probabilities. Even with their limitations, the concept of incremental intentions and the graphing of crisis indicators seem to have merit as analytical tools.

It is entirely appropriate to consider whether Southeast and Northeast Asian desk officers, DOD action officers, and

FIGURE 9

A STAIRWAY OF INCREMENTAL INTENTIONS: MAYAGUEZ CRISIS—APRIL-MAY 1975

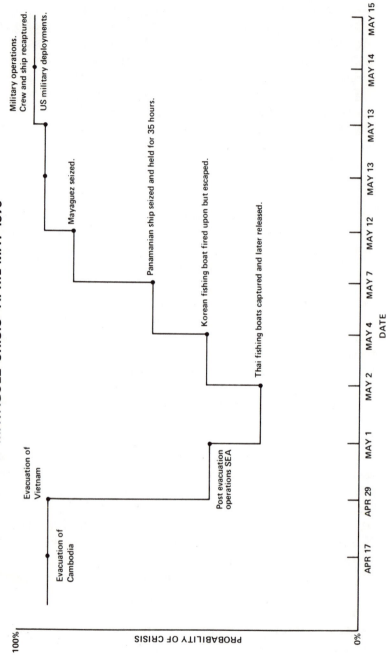

FIGURE 10

A STAIRWAY OF INCREMENTAL INTENTIONS:
KOREAN TREE CRISIS

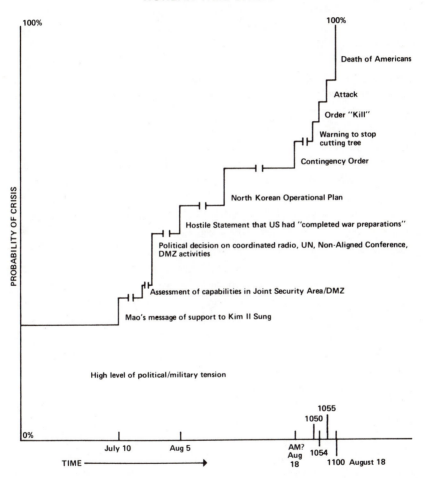

analysts had the resources and data from which to deduce a high probability of crisis sometime after May 7, 1975, in Cambodia, and August 5, 1976, in Korea. If so, such a general warning might have gotten into the key policy makers' intelligence briefings. After interviewing officials at various levels of the government, the authors tend to believe that such a demand is expecting too much from governmental organizations. First, it fails to consider the total volume of intelligence indicators, most of which never produce any significant event—the background noise. Second, it tends to overvalue in retrospect those indicators which were linked to the crisis event, and to undervalue the others. Third, it neglects the fact, in the Korean case, that some precautions had already been taken as a matter of course—that this particular tree trimming was not a purely routine affair. It is impossible to say in retrospect what would have happened if the UNC had been warned specifically. Fourth, if general warnings were encouraged, they could create a "wolf-crying" syndrome; reports of potential crises could become so common as to vitiate their credibility. Still, although it may be too much to *demand* strategic warnings from analysts, the *desirability* of such warnings cannot be denigrated. The goal of intelligence analysts must still be to design tactical indicators that can be used to produce strategic warnings with high confidence. These analysts, operations personnel, and policy makers need to be particularly sensitive to the integration of political and technical indicators. The fact that no known analysis connected the Mao/Hua letter, North Korea's warnings on August 5, the Nonaligned Conference, and the situation in the JSA, can be understood, but cannot be a proud achievement of the intelligence community.

The authors' view is that there was little possibility of strategic warning in the case of the *Mayaguez* incident. To the extent that earlier seizures were known and were reported, one may say that strategic warning did in fact exist. The seizure of the Panamanian vessel was reported to the White House Situation Room and to the president. It may be reasonably asked, however, whether knowledge of the seizure *and release* of a third-country vessel ought to have been recognized as a signal of the possible seizure by Cambodia of a vessel of the United

States or any other great power, in view of the chaos in Phnom Penh and clear asymmetry of force vis-à-vis the United States. It would have been difficult to judge that such seizure served the political or any other interests of Cambodia.

It is on this point of the subjective aspects of warning indicators that many intelligence failures have hung and controversies have raged. The linkage of indicators with assumptions of national purpose and rational intentions through an analytical framework is fraught with difficulty. Thus, the Israeli intelligence service in October 1973 tended to ignore the many tactical indicators of Egyptian attack because they did not agree with strategic assumptions.[5]

It may be useful to comment on the value of strategic warning, if it can be obtained. That is to say, had the United States recognized in advance the crisis potential of the *Mayaguez* seizure or of the events preceding the murders in the JSA, what could we have done? The scale of possible actions could range from a simple diplomatic warning to a major show of force. Even the lowest level of action on this spectrum, however, holds implications of risk. Such a warning to Cambodian authorities might conceivably have had some effect, but that is doubtful.

In the case of the Korean incident, if U.S. authorities had issued a diplomatic warning, it might have been used by the North Koreans for propaganda purposes to document the warmongering charges they were making in Colombo. This is not to imply that we believe that strategic warning serves no purpose—certainly it does. Strategic warning could have served the very useful purpose of triggering contingency planning within the bureaucracy in Washington so as to be better prepared once the crisis event took place. Ideally, strategic warning may prevent the crisis event; at a minimum, it performs another valuable function—the reduction of surprise.

In both crises, it must be acknowledged that strategic warning did exist. On the larger question—what was done—it must be said that no actions were taken, either offensive or defensive, vis-à-vis the offending parties. As a preventive measure in the *Mayaguez* case, the Hydrographic Office of the Defense Mapping Agency could have issued a warning to commercial carriers about the possibility of seizure off Cambodia. Ultimately, such a warning was issued, but not until well into the crisis. However, it is doubtful whether such a warning would have stopped vessels from traveling in those waters, nor is it likely that such a warning would have been seen by the Cambodian authorities as a demonstration of U.S. firmness or resolve.

With respect to the failure to issue strategic warnings and its effect on subsequent high-level efforts to resolve the *Mayaguez* crisis, there is the possibility that this failure may have created underlying doubts as to the competence of the intelligence community. However, during the NSC/WSAG meetings there was no evidence of unwillingness to accept intelligence community judgments. As the crisis evolved, additional resources were concentrated on the crisis areas.

In summary, crises present nearly insurmountable obstacles for intelligence analysts in attempting to reduce the element of surprise. These obstacles consist of a lack of appropriate information; professional differences among the intelligence, policy-making, and operational communities; and organizational hierarchies which transmit information imperfectly. The result is that we can reduce—but cannot eliminate—surprise as an element in crises.

CRISIS EVENT RECOGNITION

Conclusion 7. Indicators of crisis for use by watch officers and policy-making officials need to be refined, and procedures on notification of top officials should be reexamined. For example, the death of two U.S. officers after a physical assault by North Korean soldiers contained many of the classic characteristics of an international crisis; yet the notification of the president and top U.S. officials was delayed because policy makers did not recognize the seriousness of the situation.

The crisis event, or trigger mechanism, as it is often called, is the specific international or domestic action that precipitates the development of crisis conditions for a government. The ability to recognize this event, and more importantly, to recognize the general characteristics of situations that have the potential to create crises is a desirable quality in watch officers, administrative officials, and policy makers. With this in mind, Charles Hermann and Robert Mason have attempted to define the properties of crisis-precipitating events in the hopes that such definition will expand our knowledge of this variable and provide some assistance to government officials.[6]

Hermann and Mason list eight properties of crisis events and hypothesize that the more of these eight properties an event has, the more likely it is to precipitate a crisis. We will describe these properties and then apply them to the *Mayaguez* and Korean cases to see if they are helpful in discerning a crisis. With slight modifications they propose the following list:

Anticipated undesirability to recipient. This property emphasizes the displeasure of high officials, the creation of a threat to important values or goals.

Physical assault. This dimension concerns the use of force and the degree to which seizure or other physical actions were practiced.

Military instrumentality. In conjunction with the last property, this one labels the person or organizational group responsible for the action. A physical assault is likely to create the conditions for a crisis, especially if it is conducted by military forces.

Effect. The effect of an event is the degree of perceived hostility that accompanies the action itself. That is, to what extent did the creator of the event transmit feelings of hostility or premeditation to the recipient?

External consequentiality. What potential effect will this event have on nations other than the direct recipient? To what degree will it affect or change that nation's relations with other states?

Specificity. This property attempts to measure whether the initiator is specific with regard to: the issue; the recipient; resources; or the time frame. To what degree does this event portend a clear threat in the future from the nation in question?

Commitment. Commitment involves the decision by an adversary to dedicate assets and resources to the fulfillment of a policy. Expressions of hostility in official statements are often hollow rhetoric, but if they are followed by the commitment of resources, the potential for a crisis is heightened.

Implementation time. This relates to our definition of crisis. If a crisis must be characterized by a shortness of time for response, then the degree to which an international or domestic event creates a deadline is an important factor.

Applying these criteria to the *Mayaguez* crisis event—the seizure of the ship—one can see their utility. Of the eight properties, the most prominent appears to be "physical assault," followed by "military instrumentality." The only property that does not seem to be present in any degree is "specificity," in that the Cambodian government and the soldiers who seized the ship remained silent about their objectives, the demands on the United States, and the dimensions of the problem their action was intended to resolve. However, the majority of the criteria were met, and one would expect—if these criteria had been used—that they would have led to an unambiguous identification of the crisis situation which would have been transmitted swiftly to Washington and then to the highest levels of government.

The first requirement—the recognition of an important and potentially dangerous situation—was accomplished by the agencies in the field. Both Mr. Neal of Delta Exploration Company and the Department of State officials in the Jakarta embassy recognized the importance of the seizure and transmitted the information to Washington. The second requirement—the notification of high-level officials—took somewhat longer to accomplish. In this respect, the major agencies involved did not vary much in the time they took to notify their highest officials. The initial message was received at the NMCC, the State Department, and the White House at 5:12 a.m. The acting chairman of the Joint Chiefs of Staff was notified at 6:45, the president at 7:30, and the secretary of state at 8:00.

In the Korean case, the initial message left the U.N. Command between 10:00 and 11:00 p.m. Washington time. Notification actions were initiated in the NMCC, White House, and State Department between 11:00 and 12:00 the same night, but none of the senior officials were informed of the incident until the following morning.

The death of two U.S. officers in the Joint Security Area

appears to contain all of the crisis properties except commitment of large numbers of resources and perhaps short implementation time. Yet the physical assault by military forces and the resultant deaths indicated a high degree of hostility and anticipated undesirability.

In both cases there were a large number of crisis properties present in the precipitating event, and the events were promptly relayed from field units to Washington. In the nation's capital the notification problem became an organizational problem—one of passing information upward through successive layers of hierarchy. Here the crisis-precipitating qualities of the events apparently did not seem unique or precise enough to warrant the extra effort and responsibility that notification would entail. In the final analysis, there was an underestimation of that most critical quality—anticipated undesirability—as it would be defined by the highest policy officials.

This analysis produces the conclusion that either the crisis properties are not sufficiently precise and extensive to be used as indicators, or that alerting procedures should be changed. While one can propose that organizations direct their operations centers to bypass intervening levels and to target critical information to the highest level immediately, this is a judgment that each organization must make.

If the crisis properties are not precise enough, then there is value in proposing additional properties that would make the crisis more unambiguous. The *Mayaguez* crisis suggests the concept of a "target," for example a U.S. ship or aircraft (commercial or military), as a potential crisis indicator. The Korean incident suggests that events which produce a U.S. death are unusual in themselves, and when combined with other less specific properties can be used to predict a crisis.

The two crises investigated in this study do not offer a valid opportunity for judging the final value of the list of eight properties. However, the cases tend to reaffirm the utility of a crisis properties list, and to suggest that such a list should be distributed not only to watch officers and operations centers, but to administrative and middle-level policy makers as well. Of course, the situational context of the event will strongly influence its undesirability, but having even subjective criteria for crisis recognition and warning is of great value.

ORGANIZATIONAL AND INTERDEPARTMENTAL PROCEDURES

Conclusion 8. Organizational procedures were effective in searching for information, developing courses of action, and especially in deploying aircraft and ships to the regions of crisis. The interdepartmental procedures in the Korean crisis tended to be used by the Department of State to retain departmental options and influence while restricting somewhat the influence of other organizations.

Organizational procedures impose constraints on individual behavior and can aid or hinder crisis performance. People do best in crises what they have been doing or practicing in normal situations. Thus, a warning notice to mariners—a unique requirement—was not transmitted until some nineteen hours after the *Mayaguez* had been captured, due to the failure to delegate specific responsibility and develop internal guidelines on the subject. Similarly, the procedures of the Pacific Command did not assure distribution to subordinate units of all critical intelligence material, with the result that the estimates of enemy strength which had been developed by DIA and the Pacific Command intelligence staff never did reach the marine ground assault commander, and PACOM did not know this.

Another shortcoming of organizational procedure involved the ad hoc integration of units for the assault on Koh Tang. Island assault is one of the most difficult military maneuvers. It requires an extremely well trained air-ground team like the Marine Corps to make it successful. The assault force for Koh Tang was hurriedly assembled from among many, diverse military services and units, flown to the region, and employed in a very short time frame. The units had had no opportunity to work together; their command and control relationships and communications networks were unorthodox and made combat support and monitorability very cumbersome and difficult.

By contrast, the procedures for operating U.N. forces in Korea had been well established, modified as conditions changed, and practiced by both air and ground elements of the U.N. Command. The deployment of two squadrons of high performance jet fighters over long distances without incident in such a short time period was also a credit to the organizational procedures that made these feats possible. When combined for the operational implementation of the crisis plan, the established and practiced procedures undoubtedly enhanced the likelihood of a smooth, successful mission.

Organizational procedures also helped to shape and structure the search for information and development of a course of action in both cases. Organizational specialization was apparent among the lower departmental levels in these two decision processes. The intelligence community developed a threat estimate and an analysis of the adversary's intentions. The JCS Operations Directorate (J-3) led in the development of military options and target planning, while JCS Plans and Policy (J-5) and International Security Affairs worked on the political-military aspects of the options. The Department of State concentrated on specific guidance for commanders and ambassadors and diplomatic contacts with allies and the U.N.

Well established NSC procedures were the foundation of interdepartmental leadership in both crises. The procedures included interdepartmental coordination on messages relating to instructions, directions, negotiating positions, and press releases. Secretary Kissinger tended to approve State task force proposed drafts of these messages, which then became final versions—contingent upon approval by JCS and OSD. For messages dealing with diplomacy or the political dimension of the problem, this is as it should be. In matters of military concern—deploying forces—the Pentagon took the lead. Due to the dynamics of the situation and the perceived necessity to conduct a great number of consultations and actions, the intergovernmental deadlines tended to be very short.

THE DECISIONAL UNIT

Conclusion 9. The decisional unit in a crisis tends to be a small, high-level group of policy makers. This group tends to have twelve to fifteen members, but will vary according to presiden-

tial style and the level of response proposed. The size of the unit tends to increase with an increase in perceived threat and with an increase in the level of response.

The *Mayaguez* and Korean DMZ crises were resolved by decisional units that had many similarities to those used to decide previous U.S. crises. In 1950, President Truman's decision group for crises varied from five to fifteen members, with twelve to fourteen being average;[7] in 1962, the Cuban missile crisis was decided by a group averaging fourteen to fifteen. The NSC meetings on the *Mayaguez* varied from twelve to sixteen; the WSAG meetings on the DMZ incident averaged twelve. This size may have been arbitrary in previous crises (e.g., in the 1950 Korean War decision it may have been determined by the ability of the Blair House dining room to seat only fourteen), but by 1969 it was a matter of presidential decision. Both Presidents Nixon and Ford dictated an NSC attendance rule of "principals plus deputy for State and Defense; principals only for other agencies." Despite this rule, members (except for Kissinger) usually sought to bring additional aides. It would appear from this data that presidents tacitly or overtly agree that the size of twelve to fifteen is considered optimum for managing an international political/military crisis. That size is small enough to promote candor in discussion, and reduce (but not eliminate) the possibility of premature public disclosure of U.S. actions, and large enough to insure participation of the major foreign affairs agencies as well as representatives of other sectors (e.g., congressional liaison and legal counsels). (The problem of size contributes to executive reluctance to include congressional members in the basic decision-making process. But, in truth, this structural factor is undoubtedly overshadowed by more fundamental misgivings about the potential erosion of the separation of powers.)

In contrast to the 1950 and 1962 crises, the *Mayaguez* and DMZ decisional units were formal, structured committees of the NSC system supported by highly structured professional staffs. They were not composed of ad hoc groupings dominated by a White House majority. In fact, it was one of the goals of

President Nixon and Henry Kissinger in 1969 to formalize, regularize, and rationalize the decision-making system.

A second part of our proposition is that the decisional unit will vary according to the choice of the president. Thus, in the 1950 Korean case, President Truman selected the men who would attend; in 1962 President Kennedy did the same. In the *Mayaguez* crisis, it was President Ford's personal decision to exercise control of the decisional unit and of the subsequent military operation. His reasons for injecting himself directly into the decision-making process, as opposed to leaving it to the WSAG, were several: (1) the perceived necessity for urgent action due to the possibility of early movement of the vessel and crew to a safe haven on the Cambodian mainland (such as happened when the *Pueblo* was seized); (2) the timing of the crisis, so soon after the fall of Cambodia and Vietnam to Communist forces; and (3) the fact that this was President Ford's first major international crisis after assuming office and his perception that the United States needed to rebuild both at home and abroad some of the self-confidence and prestige which had been lost in Southeast Asia.

During the DMZ crisis, President Ford was attending the Republican National Convention in Kansas City, along with several of his cabinet members, General Scowcroft, and one other statutory NSC member, the vice-president. His secretary of state, Henry Kissinger, was in Washington and, as chairman of the WSAG, called it into session as the crisis-management body responsible within the NSC system. President Ford had immense faith in the NSC system and his staff's ability to manage the situation in Washington, and saw no need to preempt the process. The president may also have been motivated by a desire to keep the crisis free of domestic political overtones. Once it was clear to him that the country was not threatened, he saw no need for great involvement. His stand during the crisis—whether hard or soft—was not expected to be of great importance to the American public unless distorted or challenged, which can happen during political campaigns. If he had assembled the NSC in Kansas City or returned to Washington with General Scowcroft and Vice President Rockefeller, it would have indicated a grave concern for the situation which he did not feel and saw no reason to imply.

The third part of our proposition argues that the decision-making group tends to expand as the anticipated level of response increases. The evidence for this is less clear. In 1950, President Truman authorized two groups of five and six members respectively to recommend a relatively uncontroversial action—to alert the United Nations—and, when time was a severe constraint, to give General MacArthur permission to use one regimental combat team on the Korean mainland. (In this second case, General MacArthur had stated the urgent need for U.S. forces to bolster the confused South Korean Army and to defend the Han River line.) General MacArthur's request for a two-division force was denied, however, until President Truman had time to discuss it with his advisors.

In the *Mayaguez* and Korean DMZ crises, the NSC and WSAG appear to have been conducted in an open and frank manner, like the NSC Executive Committee of the Cuban missile crisis and the ad hoc decision-making group associated with the Korean War decision. The president did not enter the NSC with a specific, preconceived proposal of his own, but solicited information, discussion, and advice on international and domestic aspects of the situation. Similarly, although the secretary of state let it be known that he was in favor of a retaliatory military action against North Korea, he did not curtail or limit the discussion in the WSAG.

A final point needs to be made about the decisional unit. With an organizational policy of keeping the decisional unit small, there is an added danger of insulating the group—usually composed of high-level generalists—from the very specialists in the executive branch and elsewehre who may have specific knowledge of the cultural and political factors operative on the scene. A concerted attempt needs to be made to seek this information from area specialists and others and to assure that it is injected into the decision-making process. How this is done is an important consideration, but it is less important in the long run than the strong desire to seek this information. In the *Mayaguez* and Korean decision processes, area specialists and desk officers were afforded virtually unimpeded access to high officials.

DECISIONS

Conclusion 10. Crisis decisions tend to be the product of the key policy makers' belief systems and the unique situational context. The primary role of the domestic environment is to express public values which establish the limits of acceptable actions during the crisis. The decisions thus chosen tend to be novel responses to the international environment and rational adaptations to the specifics of the situation. They are only secondarily influenced by internal organizational procedures, congressional attitudes, and the decisional unit.

This section will be limited to a discussion of the substantive decisions on the two crisis cases. It will review the objectives and perceived alternatives and will attempt to render conclusions on the reasons for U.S. actions. An evaluation of the decisions and the decision-making process will be included at the end of this chapter.

In the *Mayaguez* case, two primary objectives were articulated and developed at the first NSC meeting: to get the ship and crew back safely, and to do it in a way that demonstrated U.S. resolve without being excessive. The possible measures available to accomplish these objectives were never really stated together in any rank order in the White House, but rather were discussed variously at one or another NSC meeting.

These NSC discussions demonstrated two of the major frustrations of the key policy makers—the limited utility of the political use of military force, and the difficulty of fulfilling the two (occasionally contradictory) objectives. (For example, the bombing of the mainland with B-52s would demonstrate U.S. resolve, but might not compel the Cambodians to release the crew.)

The alternatives, the objectives, and the situational context described earlier interacted to determine the limits of the key policy makers' debate and decisions. Thus, the perceived precipitous decline in U.S. prestige after the fall of Saigon and Phnom Penh provided incentives for a strong military reaction to the *Mayaguez* seizure. This was reinforced by President Ford's personal interpretation that the American people expected any U.S. response to: (1) be successful; and (2) reflect firmness without being excessive. Further, President Ford and Secretary Kissinger shared a belief that small incremental applications of military force had proven to be ineffective in the Vietnam context, and that show-of-force demonstrations and diplomacy had been ineffective in the *Pueblo* crisis.

When the diplomatic efforts to reach the Cambodian government proved ineffective, President Ford decided on military measures which were consistent with his belief that the amount of force should: (1) be sufficient and applied efficiently; but (2) not involve "overkill" of the targets. The decisions to direct a seaborne boarding party to recover the *Mayaguez,* assault Koh Tang with marines to recover the crew, and attack the facilities at Kom Pong Som were deemed sufficient to accomplish the U.S. objectives; the alternative of using B-52s was rejected as representing overkill; and the option of seizing a Cambodian island was discarded as probably ineffectual.

Thus, the options were selected more because of the beliefs of the key policy makers, the nature of the seizure, the lack of precise information on the crew's location, and the context than because of the element of surprise, organizational factors, or the specifics of the NSC decision-making unit. The record reflects that congressional considerations were not a decisive factor in the decision-making process. Attention to Congress was more to legitimize the action than to seek information. This may have been a reflection of the enormous frustration within the executive branch over congressional forays into foreign policy during the period 1973–76 where, in each case, Congress had represented the special interest of a minority. In no case was there evidence of an ability to achieve a *national* perspective. This is not to say that congressional sentiment was not considered. The views of specific members and the overall issue of congressional tolerance were often raised in the meetings and always conditioned the thinking of the principal decision makers. Nevertheless, the Congress was looked upon by the White House as a ponderous and essentially negative influence capable of hindering, but unlikely to be constructive, in the crisis process.

In the Korean case, the three final options included a show of force, attacks on selected DMZ targets, or retaliation deeper into North Korea. Again, the core beliefs of President Ford led him to accept the WSAG recommendation and select the show-of-force option. He rejected the two reprisal options as not being consistent with U.S. objectives and, *in the context of the North Korean adversary,* as being needlessly risky. In strategic bargaining terms, the U.S. response did not have to compel North Korea to undo anything it had done (as was the case with the Cambodians), but only to restrain it from doing anything worse and to extract a statement of apology and/or a promise not to repeat such attacks. These objectives, one could argue, were easier to accomplish and, thus, did not require as much compellence as did the Cambodian action.

The primary concern of the WSAG officials and the president was focused on achieving the international objectives, and although they were well aware of the domestic political situation, their actions were not primarily directed toward the domestic audience. In fact, President Ford consciously rejected the opportunity to exploit the crisis for partisan political purposes and downplayed the domestic publicity of the entire affair. Here again, congressional attitudes were not prominent. In fact, the president's congressional staff was receiving its first briefing on the crisis while decisions were being made by the president in a separate room in Kansas City.

The unique ingredient in the Korean decision was the role of the field commander—traditionally only a peripheral actor in crisis decisions. General Stilwell's suggestion that the tree cutting was necessary to insure respect for the basic U.S. prerogative in the zone was uncommon in recent years in that: (1) it came from a military field commander; (2) it had an impact on the final crisis decision; (3) it proposed action that was consistent with standards of international law; and (4) it was effective. It was a quid pro quo that did not escalate the situation and at the same time prevented escalation by the adversary. Moreover, it reflected not only an understanding of military capabilities and limitations, but also an appreciation of international political, legal, and moral standards and domestic political values.

The discussion above leads us to conclude that U.S. crisis decisions tend to be the product of the key policy makers' belief systems and the unique situational context. The role of partisan political factors appears to be overdrawn in the literature. The role of the domestic environment appears to be to impart general criteria to decision makers.

OPERATIONAL IMPLEMENTATION

Conclusion 11. The political success of crisis actions requires that the president not only make the final decisions, but monitor operational implementation to control the use of force. The tactical success of operational implementation is extraordinarily dependent upon intelligence information, communications, organizational procedures, and the presence of an operational military command with combined arms resources.

The first factor—presidential control of the use of force—has been a perennial issue in American civil-military relations. It was highlighted by the Truman-MacArthur controversy and more recently by the conduct of the Vietnam War. Apart from these instances, it is an open question as to what—in the normal course of events—constitutes an appropriate limit to presidential management of tactical military operations. In general, professional military officers believe that their competence in the execution of tactical military operations is superior to that of civilians, untrained and untested in these matters. That seems a reasonable assumption so long as the operation is clearly and exclusively military. What is often neglected, however, is the continuing need to focus on the use of force as an instrument in achieving a basically political objective. Subsequent events—political, diplomatic, or other—may alter the situation and make it desirable either to end or alter operations. These new factors are normally not available at the tactical level, and indeed may only be known by the president. Such would have been the case, for example, during *Mayaguez*, if an ambassador had brought to the president a diplomatic response from the Cambodian authorities during the course of the operation indicating willingness to release the crew and the ship. There can often be sources of information even within the military that are unavailable at the tactical level because of compartmentalization, but that can often influence the president toward a different course of action. These introductions of new information can, and indeed should, result in the president directing new courses of military action. At the tactical level, these may be seen as apparently unnecessary intrusions. They are, however, justified by information as it is interpreted by the National Command Authority.

A final point should be made concerning the role of the president in managing military operations. It concerns the constitutional mandate provided the commander in chief. By designating the president as commander in chief of the armed forces, we believe that the intent of the framers of the Constitution went beyond formalizing the concept of civilian control. That is, it was not merely their intention to prevent military coups by uniformed officers, but rather to assure that, even during the normal course of events in war or peace, the president of the United States serve as the commanding officer as surely as a general, a lieutenant colonel, or a captain would in commanding a unit. The president bears ultimate responsibility and has the superior informational resources and thus is most able to exercise competent command.

Those opposing this view point to the assumed lack of experience in military tactics of most "civilian" presidents. The authors submit that this assumption is invalid. No president—particularly during the nuclear era—can assume his responsibilities without extremely detailed briefings on the capabilities and limitations of strategic and general-purpose forces. In addition, every president without exception in the postwar period has served in the military and has had close personal acquaintance with the general capabilities of tactical as well as of strategic units. Most important, the president has at hand competent military advisors—the Joint Chiefs of Staff—who are able to answer questions on tactics, capabilities, limitations, and so forth, which are beyond the president's competence. Ultimate command must rest with the president, for seldom is any operation purely military.

When asked to analyze the issue of presidential control of the use of force, President Ford reaffirmed the traditional American prescription that civilian leaders should be the final decision makers in matters of crisis management. He then expanded his view to include two other points.

> The president should not dictate every detail, but he should be given options as we were in these two cases. He ought to be able to see the total picture of the B-52 bombing (for instance) and the types of weapons proposed for use. But he should not get involved in the numbers of bombs on each aircraft and the numbers of flights, etc. Second, the president should retain final control and the right to change orders as the operation is being implemented because Washington has access to information that is not necessarily available to field forces.[8]

Thus, the first wave of navy aircraft was instructed to hold its bombs when the Cambodian message arrived with a proposal to release the *Mayaguez,* but was allowed to proceed when it was confirmed that the crew was not mentioned.

We submit that the proper role of the president in crisis management must of necessity extend to managing even the tactics of an operation so as to bring to bear the full range of informational resources available within the U.S. government and to assure the integration of diplomatic, political, and economic resources—none of which can be successfully integrated below the level of the commander in chief.

The second factor in the success of operational implementation is the quality of intelligence information. That the tactical success of a military operation is dependent upon intelligence estimates of enemy intentions and defenses can hardly be doubted. A major reason for the large marine and air force casualties in the assault on Koh Tang was the presence of an enemy force much larger than had been predicted by the initial intelligence estimate. A second—and more accurate—intelligence report was sent to the on-scene forces, but was never received due to a communications breakdown.

The size of the defending forces and the fact that their presence was unknown to local staff and to the assaulting troops highlight a crucial point. Military operations (especially amphibious assaults) have traditionally been planned without knowing precise enemy strength. Military planners have learned through experience that certain tactics can reduce—but not eliminate—the consequences of being wrong, and these tactics have become the basis for operational procedures. Two of the classic tactics to minimize surprise on an assault landing are pre-strike reconnaissance and preassault bombardment.

During *Mayaguez,* prestrike reconnaissance could have identified the size of the defending force, and had photographs been requested of the small boats crossing to the mainland, the location of the entire crew would have been known. Preassault bombardment would have been inappropriate in this case, because of fear of hitting the *Mayaguez* crew. Had it been known that the entire crew had been moved to the mainland, the assault would have been unnecessary.

The point to be made is this: operational military procedures have evolved over time to meet many contingencies. Continual review of standard procedures is necessary before planning an operation to reaffirm their applicability in the special circumstances of a crisis. Organizational changes may be necessary, but deviations from accepted doctrine must be fully justified, or else the strengths of proven techniques may be lost.

There were many complications in the *Mayaguez* operation: the remote area of the target; the distance from friendly forces; and the dispersed nature of the operating units. U.S. forces were converging on the scene from Okinawa, the Philippines, and Thailand, and the *Coral Sea* task force was en route to Australia when it turned around. These dispersed units were temporarily assigned to an ad hoc organization which required unorthodox interservice arrangements. Thus, the marines were transported to the beach by air force helicopters, supported by air force tactical aircraft, while the navy—the traditional supporting arm of the Marine Corps—was used to strike interdiction targets on the mainland. Although the political assumptions which prompted this unusual assignment of forces can be appreciated, in retrospect they seem less persuasive. Further, it seems likely that if the NSC members had known of the other military options at hand, their decision would have been different. The lessons of these two crises clearly indicate the value of fighting with units that have a common bond of equipment, training, and employment doctrine.

One of the difficult decisions in the *Mayaguez* case was to balance the diplomatic consequences of employing the Thailand-based military units against the military risks of not using them. Although no prescription is possible for all cases, the important considerations in this case were the degree of uncertainty in the intelligence estimates, the presence or absence of complete tactical communications, the use of proven operational procedures, and the existence of combined arms capabilities under an established military command. When these conditions are maximized, an operation can be conducted under a minimum of military risk. A failure of any of these conditions jeopardizes not only the military tactical success of the operation, but the political success as well. (The validity of this conclusion was proven in the wake of the *Mayaguez* crisis, when the president was lauded for his resolute action and the success of having the crew returned, but criticized for the number of casualties.)

Although the primary task of the Korean operation was much easier, the implementation of Operation Paul Bunyan stands as a clear contrast to the *Mayaguez*. Intelligence on the North Korean forces near the Joint Security Area was accurate and complete; predictions about their probable intentions in not interfering with the tree cutting were correct. Tactical communications between General Stilwell and his operational forces were complete, and strategic communications to the National Military Command Center and on to the president were easily arranged and soon available. Proven operational procedures were used, and the operations plan was written by an established military command organization with combined arms forces assigned. As further insurance of success, the bulk of the operational air and ground forces had an extensive history of interservice and international coordination and cooperation in combined exercises with both U.S. and R.O.K. forces. The U.S. Eighth Army had been in Korea for over twenty-five years, and its staff had an intimate knowledge of the area of operations, the capability of U.N. forces, and the adversary. The ad hoc organizational arrangement of putting the I Corps commander in charge of the back-up task force was the only deviation from the normal chain of command, and it was an appropriate adaptation to the unique circumstances of the situation. Thus, the Korean crisis implementation was successful and demonstrated once again that tactical success is a precondition for political success. Perceptions may vary over the skill and values of the decision makers, but it the operation is a tactical success, the political outcomes of the crisis are much more likely to be favorable.

OUTCOMES

Conclusion 12. International political military crises can be analyzed by their outcomes in three interrelated areas—tactical, domestic, and international. Tactical accomplishment of military objectives appears to be a necessary condition for the achievement of international political conclusiveness. Domestic outcomes tend to be independent of precise tactical results in that most crisis decisions generate popular support for the president.

The two crises studied in this volume were unusual in that their outcomes were achieved by military means. Both were relatively conclusive in a tactical and an international sense. The outcome of the *Mayaguez* crisis concluded in the termination of the hostile Cambodian action and the resolution of the threat to U.S. interests. The Korean crisis outcome was at least semiconclusive in that there was a temporary discontinuance of hostile acts and a clear decline in North Korean political influence.

The commitment of military forces appears to enhance the probability of a conclusive outcome, although it undoubtedly increases the risk of escalation. The risk of escalation, on the other hand, can be minimized by the careful selection of proper objectives in the decision-making process, the use of sufficient military forces, provisions for extensive communications, and presidential control. Escalation was never really a concern in the *Mayaguez* case, since the incident was remote from other Communist powers, and Cambodia had a very limited military capability. Escalation was a possibility in the Korean case, but it was reduced to some degree by the political distance of North Korea from the P.R.C. and the Soviet Union and the application of a decisively higher threat of force.

The relationship between domestic popularity and decisive

presidential action in a crisis is not nearly as clear as many policy makers seem to think. This relationship is illustrated by the story of President Theodore Roosevelt and the North African rebel Raisuli. The story has recently been retold in the Hollywood movie *The Wind and the Lion,* in which Raisuli captures and rides into the desert with a beautiful American socialite, and Teddy Roosevelt negotiates her release. In reality, the victim was not an American beauty but a Greek-American businessman named Perdicaris. President Roosevelt did, however, order a cable sent to the U.S. consul general in Tangier with the instructions, "Perdicaris alive or Raisuli dead!" Perdicaris was returned in due time, but the immediate effect of the note was domestic. It was read at the 1904 Republican National Convention then meeting in Chicago, to the reportedly delirious applause of the assembled delegates.

The Roosevelt-Raisuli episode suggests that the U.S. president will be supported by increased popularity if he acts successfully in a crisis, *but* that he will suffer an immediate loss of popularity if he does not act or if he acts unsuccessfully. A part of this suggestion has been confirmed by experience; the president who acts successfully is invariably rewarded with an increase in his popularity rating as measured by opinion polls. In the *Mayaguez* and Korean cases, President Ford's popularity increased by 12 percent and 4 percent respectively, although it is difficult to determine precisely the degree to which the crisis affected each rise.

The other half of the suggestion—the loss of popularity with a lack of action—is not well substantiated. Although the data is not conclusive, the president's performance in a crisis does not seem to be directly reflected in opinion polls. What seems to happen is that crises divert citizens' attention away from their more mundane daily pursuits and cause them to perceive an external threat to the nation. For the most part, citizens neglect the objective outcomes and respond to the crisis by giving support to the president.[9]

Despite these general tendencies for crisis to be beneficial, certain crises clearly produce more positive results than others. Of the two crisis studies, *Mayaguez* was more important than the Korean incident with regard to far-reaching political consequences. *Mayaguez* came in a more critical context, when there were genuine doubts—both internationally and domestically—about the ability of the United States to control events. More importantly, President Ford thought the crisis had a significant bearing on the international influence of the United States, on his presidency, and on the confidence of the country.

> Although we were successful in the evacuation of Phnom Penh and Saigon, it was sort of a subdued feeling that we had accomplished something in those two instances, but to have an affirmative action go right, gave me a great sense of confidence. It did not only ignite confidence in the White House, among the people here, it had an electrifying reaction as far as the American people were concerned. It was a spark that set off a whole new sense of confidence for them too. We had all gone through a very, very difficult eight months. This sort of turned the corner and changed the course.[10]

President Ford was correct in his assessment that his management of the *Mayaguez* crisis was greeted with remarkable public acclaim, but this support was challenged by many members of Congress. Congressional concerns were voiced over the unusually strong military response, over the "disproportionately high" casualty figures, and over the alleged lack of meaningful congressional consultation required by the War Powers Resolution. The criticisms were centered in hearings before the House Subcommittee on International Political and Military Affairs of the Committee on International Relations, chaired by Congressman Dante Fascell, the same subcommittee which held hearings on the Korean DMZ incident. Although the *Mayaguez* hearings and the subsequent General Accounting Office report requested by Congressman Fascell challenged several aspects of the operation, the basic theme in both sets of hearings was executive compliance with the consultation requirements of the War Powers Resolution.

The reader may recall that President Ford opposed the War Powers Resolution when he was the House Republican leader, and it was passed only over President Nixon's veto. The resolution was passed in a period when the United States was still at war in Southeast Asia, shortly after the Watergate break-in, when there was widespread opposition to the growth of executive power and special concern with an executive decision-making process that was perceived as closed and secretive.

President Ford provided the Congress with information as required by the War Powers Resolution during six international crises (including *Mayaguez*), while reserving for a calmer environment the question of whether the resolution was constitutional. He specifically did not report the Korean incident under the War Powers format, and the Department of State provided Congress with a justification of that position (see Appendix D). Thus, the primary *domestic political* outcomes of both crises were discussions and arguments over the issue of executive compliance with the War Powers Resolution.

The question remains whether the War Powers Resolution is an effective and appropriate mechanism to aid in U.S. crisis decision making and management. President Ford, in an April 12, 1977, speech before the University of Kentucky, attempted to open national debate on the issue in an era removed from emotionalism in the wake of Vietnam and Watergate. He raised broad objections to the resolution, noting that "the inherent weakness from a practical standpoint was conclusively demonstrated" by his experiences in six crises.

"When a crisis breaks, it is impossible to draw the Congress into the decision-making process in an effective way," Ford said, citing the following reasons:

○   Many key legislators were not in Washington during his six crises, and communication with them was difficult, slow, and in some cases impossible.

○   Congressmen have too many other concerns to keep up with foreign policy developments.

○   Crisis situations demand timely decision making which is inconsistent with the time required to develop a congressional consensus among scattered and perhaps disagreeing congressional leaders.

○   Sensitive information about military operations needs to be protected, rather than distributed widely to congressional leaders.

○   Consultations with congressional leaders would not

insure support by other legislators, particularly independent younger members.

In conclusion, President Ford said, "There is absolutely no way American foreign policy can be conducted or military operations commanded by 535 members of Congress on Capitol Hill, even if they all happen to be on Capitol Hill when they are needed."[11]

The War Powers issue highlights two fundamental aspects of the U.S. governmental system: the expectation that action will proceed from a broad consensual base; and the maintenance of separation of powers. Thus, it is the responsibility of the president to not only comply with the law, but to develop a consensus sufficiently broad to support his decisions. Congressional leaders can play a very important role in this consensus—when they are invited to by the executive. Forcible—even if legal—involvement of large numbers of legislators could not only jeopardize the security and speed of the decision-making process, it could fundamentally compromise the constitutional separation of powers between the executive and legislative branches.

Further objections to the War Powers Resolution can be based on historical and foreign policy consideration.[12] Historically, precedent supports broader presidential authority, as argued in the Federalist Papers (nos. 38 and 74). Only five of the several hundred foreign hostilities involving U.S. forces have resulted from congressional declarations of war. In the rest, the president was required to make a crisis decision in the national interest.

In a crisis situation, the very existence of the War Powers Resolution suggests unreliability in U.S. behavior. The resolution tends to require broadening the base of decision making and may engender public debate in a period when quiet diplomacy is needed to avoid conflict. With respect to adversaries, it reduces the deterrent effect of any probable U.S. response.

The international outcomes of the two incidents in this study are among the most favorable crisis resolutions in recent years. The U.S. actions on *Mayaguez* had the twin objectives of getting the crew back and doing so in a manner that demonstrated

U.S. resolve. These goals were not changed during the crisis, and both were conclusively achieved. The techniques of attaining the release of the crew are not altogether clear, because the men were set free before the main military effort. Diplomatic efforts could have had some effect on the Cambodian decision to release the crew, but the weight of the evidence indicates the more likely cause was the application of U.S. military power both to interdict the area between the island and the mainland and to seize Koh Tang. Thus, the decisive technique was the application of military force, and the substantive international outcome was the forced submission—or compellence—of the Cambodians to release the crew.

The second international objective—the demonstration of U.S. resolve and ability to act decisively—was primarily achieved by the size and character of the U.S. military reaction. These characteristics were most conclusively demonstrated by the marine landings and by naval air attacks on Cambodian mainland targets.

The magnitude and destructiveness of these attacks have been criticized by some as being out of proportion to the objective of recovering the crew. These arguments have tended to underestimate the difficulty of getting U.S. citizens returned after capture by foreign governments. They ignore the sordid history of the *Pueblo* crew and the extreme difficulty in negotiating the release of U.S. prisoners of war from the Viet Cong and the North Vietnamese. These arguments also tend to deny either the existence or the validity of the U.S. objective of demonstrating resolve to international allies and adversaries. While the question of economy of effort must be considered, to deny a state the legal and moral right to such action is to deny an important aspect of sovereignty and international security enforcement. Critics tend to overemphasize the rights of the aggressor and to undervalue the rights of the victim. The United States did not militarily seize a Cambodian ship and forcibly detain a Cambodian crew. The United States was the aggrieved party and used what forces were available for the safe release of the *Mayaguez* crew.

In conclusion, the U.S. actions in the *Mayaguez* crisis produced the release of the crew through compellence, the demonstration of decision making and popular resolve through the use of force, and the enhancement of U.S. credibility in the minds of adversaries. Although deterrence in the commonly used sense can be said to have failed because the Cambodian attack was not prevented, the swift use of force in the *Mayaguez* crisis most probably had some deterrent effect on the North Koreans, inhibiting, if not the initial attack, at least any attempts at escalation.

The outcomes of the Korean crisis included widespread allied and nonaligned international support for the U.S. actions, the relative absence of criticism (implying tacit support) from Communist nations, and a sudden decline in the international prestige and influence of North Korea. The crisis actions were at least semiconclusive, in that they produced a temporary discontinuance of hostilities on the Korean peninsula, but did not resolve the underlying value conflicts of the two political systems there. The outcomes were produced by the military application of force to produce the North Korean apology, and diplomatic negotiation to ratify the new arrangements in the Joint Security Area.

As a final note, the two crises can be compared not only with each other but with U.S. actions in other crises. Two such comparisons will briefly be made. In January 1968, after the capture of the U.S.S. *Pueblo* by the North Koreans, the U.S. actions consisted primarily of sending Task Force Seventy-seven with five aircraft carriers into the Straits of Korea in a show of force. After the EC-121 was shot down by North Korea on April 15, 1969, the U.S. again mounted only a show of force, this time ordering Task Force Seventy-one and its four carriers to Korea. The outcomes of these crises included an unabated conflict—the continuance of hostilities and an unresolved value threat. These outcomes were of no discernible benefit to the United States and tended to further weaken an uneven U.S. political influence.

The *Mayaguez* and Korean crises tended, on the other hand, to have results that were both positive and conclusive. Both internationally and domestically, the crises produced outcomes that were favorable to the U.S. government. The international and domestic outcomes were dependent upon the tactical results, and in each case the primary objectives of the decision makers were achieved. In *Mayaguez,* the key factor was the return of the crew. In the Korean case, the success was due in large part to the crisis innovation—a unique enhancement of the basic show of force technique by the addition of a specific military objective which was both appropriate to the situation and symbolic for the defense of U.S. forces. This innovation—the decision to cut down an ordinary, but tactically significant and strategically symbolic, poplar tree—appears in retrospect to have been the key determinant of the U.S. success. It was a necessary signal to insure the more basic right of a military commander to provide for the self-defense of his troops. As such, it provided a valuable intermediate point between bluffing with a show of force and the initiation of military hostilities with the actual use of force. Such policy innovations are a valuable addition to the U.S. techniques of crisis decision making and management.

EVALUATION

One of the objectives of this study was to determine how best to organize to cope with international crises. This objective implies a qualitative evaluation which in turn presumes normative criteria against which alternative organizational approaches may be judged. In the course of our study, involving numerous interviews and the review of the considerable literature on the subject, we have encountered many opinions on criteria against which both the system and substance of the decision-making process may be evaluated. These criteria emerge from the individual and collective expressions of praise, criticism, and recommendations for change made by participants in and academic observers of crisis resolution. Each comment reflects a judgment of good or bad performance based upon implied standards of behavior. In each case the comment is of course conditioned by the individual's perspective—military, congressional, executive, or popular as reported through the media. In the aggregate, however, these viewpoints represent a social mosaic, a statement of values, limits, and expectations which the leadership of the United States seeks to reflect in its deliberations. In this section we will attempt a statement of these criteria and then use them as a basis for evaluating both the process and substance of decision making during the two crises being considered.

The Decision-making Process

What requirements must be fulfilled in shaping a crisis decision-making group? What must it be able to do? Are there limits within which it must operate? The following criteria address these questions and provide ways of evaluating the crisis decision-making process.

Knowledge. The participants in the decision-making group must possess or be able to get information quickly; they must have not only objective data but also resources—both military and diplomatic—available in working to resolve the crisis. The group members must be knowledgeable concerning the capabilities and limitations of these resources and must be able to contribute *timely recommendations* for their employment. The group members must also be knowledgeable concerning the *international and domestic context* in which decisions will be made and carried out. They must be able to assess the degree of support from allies and the probable reactions of adversaries. They must have a grasp of congressional and public sentiment so as to be able to reach decisions in keeping with American priorities and values and thus commanding the respect of the American people.

Simplicity. The decision-making unit should not be complex in its structure and procedures. It must be able to pull together facts, formulate options, evaluate risks, and make decisions with clarity and balance, but without bureaucratic layering or technical preoccupation.

Speed. Related to simplicity is the need for promptness. While not all crises are equally time-sensitive, the effectiveness of decisions once taken is conditional upon implementation before conditions change. In addition, governments experiencing crisis are ipso facto embroiled in the unknown, the unique, and the nonroutine; accordingly, great benefit can accrue to the player who maintains *the initiative.* Each side can simplify its problem by requiring the adversary to react rather than being reactive itself. Further, although Americans expect their government to be deliberate and thoughtful out of concern for the potentially catastrophic effect of military escalation, there is normally an important element of expectation both at home and abroad. Delay is often viewed as indecisiveness and ineffectuality. There will always be uncertainty; however, a key to effective decision making lies in being able to define and accept uncertainties, to recognize that waiting will not change them, and to move with resolve and flexibility.

Manageable size. Again, related to the foregoing qualities of simplicity and speed is the value of avoiding unmanageable size. As mentioned above, the decision-making group must include competent representation from the political (State Department), military (Defense Department/JCS), and intelligence (CIA) elements of the national security community as well as others competent to articulate congressional, legal, and public considerations and to be responsible for management of the process (NSC). Beyond this number—perhaps as many as twelve—additional voices normally become redundant impediments to action. Even this number goes beyond the limit normally considered optimal in business management practice.

Once the decision-making unit is formed, it must also have a structured sense of mission and methodology. It must be able to define the problem, establish criteria for approaching its resolution (e.g., promptness and economy of force), and proceed with the collection of information and formulation of options. Once decisions are made, the group must be able to communicate them promptly to appropriate subordinates for execution and be able to monitor implementation so as to be able to evaluate responses and adapt to new circumstances as the crisis evolves.

It is a major conclusion of the authors that the NSC (during *Mayaguez*) and the WSAG (during Korean DMZ) met the above criteria. In general, the methodology developed and pursued in managing crises during the Nixon and Ford administrations was rational and consistent. The approach of considering at each meeting the same standard topics—the facts (presented by the director of the Central Intelligence Agency); the motives and objectives of the adversary; U.S. interests and objectives;

the interests and objectives of the third parties, to include great powers; and alternative means of pursuing U.S. interests and objectives (diplomatic as well as military)—was lucid and inductively sound.

The efficacy with which this system operated, however, was more often conditioned by the adequacy of available information or the functioning of the implementative system below the decision-making unit than by the decision makers themselves. More specifically, seldom, if ever, have these authors observed a failure to have occurred because of: the lack of capability of actors to cope with the issue due to stress or inability to understand facts and make rational decisions; failure of the decision-making unit to generate options and consensus on them; or stress leading to a breakdown in the functioning of the decision-making unit. The last point deserves particular comment. In both the *Mayaguez* the Korean tree incidents, which took place during approximately seventy-two hours of around-the-clock meetings or analysis, at no time did the authors learn of abnormal stress, irrational behavior, or other-than-normal thought processes by any of the principal contributors to the decision-making unit.

A further comment is perhaps in order with respect to the level of the decision-making unit. In the case of the *Mayaguez,* the unit was the NSC; it was the Washington Special Actions Group in the Korean case. Where time permits, advantages accrue from convening the crisis unit first at a lower level. These advantages include allowing the president's advisors to collect all available information and to evaluate it before confronting the president with potentially contradictory and often erroneous data. As one of the NSC members commented later to the authors, "We were reluctant to offer options based on that soft information because by past crises we knew how much initial information tended to be incorrect."

It is true that when the president presides over the decision-making unit he inevitably dominates the scene, if not the discussion. Further, increased pressure is placed on the unit when information-gathering and decision-making steps are compressed into one meeting. The authors did not find this to be a dysfunctional element in the handling of the *Mayaguez* recovery, however.

Convening a crisis management group at a lower level offers opportunities for diplomatic initiatives without involving the president, preserving that option for escalatory purposes should the need arise, and offering the possibility for resolution of the crisis at the lowest possible level. Such resolution promotes, but cannot guarantee, action based on agreement and consensus (conflict invariably escalates decisions), a tendency toward less use of force (higher degrees of violence tend to be more politically controversial and thus invite presidential decision), and bureaucratic economy of effort.

On balance, it is the authors' view that the cases studied reflect relatively close adherence of the decision-making unit to the above-stated criteria and requirements. In both cases, the unit was convened quickly. It contained knowledgeable representation of each element of the national security community with expertise to contribute, but no more than that. It brought to the surface all available knowledge which bore on the problem in the *Mayaguez* crisis. In the Korean case, first reports of the incident did not include important historical/ contextual considerations. Specifically, principals in Washington were not informed of the August 6 incident, nor of the warning which had been issued immediately prior to the attack. Had they been aware of these considerations, it is conceivable that the additional facts might have had an impact upon the tone of the first WSAG meeting and the initial official public statements.

In the two crises considered, the decision-making units exhibited the principle of simplicity. One knowledgeable person represented each major bureaucratic entity. Each representative had excellent control over and communications with his resources. In both cases the unit operated expeditiously to develop facts, options, and recommendations. Once decisions were taken, there was prompt, effective implementation and continuous monitoring at the highest level.

Evaluating the Decisions

In the course of this study, three criteria have emerged that appear useful in evaluating the quality of crisis decisions per se as distinct from the process through which they were reached.

All governments are accountable in varying degrees for their performance. In the United States, this accountability is through several channels, but the ultimate judge is the electorate, the American people. From opinions expressed in interviews and media reports, the following seem to comprise an American standard against which the performance of the U.S. political leadership is measured during crises.

Thoughtfulness. For many years the American people were content to leave the management of international crises to the political and military leadership with little insistence upon participation. This remains essentially true today. However, the advent of nuclear weapons and the ultimate calamity always possible through escalation, the perceived blurring of the events and decisions which led to our involvement in Vietnam, the presence of divided partisan control over the executive and legislative branches during the Nixon/Ford years have raised citizen interest in establishing a higher standard of quasi-public deliberation during decision making which may involve major international entanglements. This is not to say that Americans expect a national referendum on each small decision. Rather, they seek to assure that decision makers are aware that it is not acceptable to make decisions peremptorily, without careful reflection which takes into account basic values. In sum, the decisions must be made thoughtfully and after due deliberation and regard for American standards of fairness, respect for others, and avoidance where possible of violence and long-term military engagement.

Firmness. Americans do not support vacillation. They expect their leaders to lead, to be clear, forthright, and firm. Particularly when Americans lives or property have been lost, the American impulse is toward firmness. It must not be reflexive— a knee jerk—but rather thought out and appropriate in strength to the task.

Success. Whether as an outgrowth of our competitive economic system or a simple expression of national pride, Americans like to win.

We believe that the decisions taken during the *Mayaguez* and Korean incidents met these standards rather well. In each case, the meetings of the NSC and WSAG resulted in a consensus of the political leadership which was stated publicly. The American people were given time to comment and the public attitude toward alternative courses of action was discussed in subsequent meetings. The decisions taken reflected firmness, but not overkill. They reflected sensitivity to the escalatory risk. They reflected efforts to use peaceful means and to apply force only after deliberation. Once the decision to use force was taken, however, it was applied decisively, not in small increments—this attribute perhaps reflecting a lesson learned from Vietnam. Finally, the decisions were vindicated by success.

The United States paid a high price to recover the *Mayaguez* and her crew, but the military actions achieved results, demonstrated firmness, and restored confidence in the ability of the United States to act and protect its interests. On the Korean DMZ, the response achieved the immediate results of obtaining a North Korean apology and enhanced long-term American security interests. Thus, the importance of successful crisis management stems not simply from the immediate crisis situation, but from the significance of international crises as tests of stability, national character, will, and resolve.

Appendix A:
Chronology of the *Mayaguez* Crisis

Time/Date			Action
Washington	Cambodia		
	April 17		Phnom Penh falls.
	April 25		A Cambodian "Special National Congress" confirms Sihanouk as chief of state of the new government of Cambodia.
	April 29		Saigon falls and last U.S. personnel are evacuated from Indochina.
	May 2		A group of Thai fishing boats is seized and later released by Cambodian authorities.
	May 4		Korean ship is fired upon by Cambodian patrol boat, but escapes.
	May 6		Seven South Vietnamese vessels are seized by Cambodia.
	May 7		Panamanian ship is seized and released about 35 hours later by Cambodian authorities.
3:10 to 3:18 a.m.	May 12 Monday	2:10 to 2:18 p.m.	S.S. *Mayaguez* is boarded by Cambodian personnel about 6–7 miles from Cambodian island of Poulo, which lies about 60 miles south/ southwest of Cambodian mainland.

Time/Date		
Washington	*Cambodia*	*Action*
3:18 a.m. May 12 Monday	2:18 p.m.	Mr. John Neal of Delta Exploration Company in Jakarta, Indonesia, receives a mayday call from the *Mayaguez*: "Have been fired upon and boarded by Cambodian armed forces at 9°48′ N/102°53′ E. Ship is being towed to unknown Cambodian port."
4:00 to 5:00 a.m. May 12 Monday	3:00 to 4:00 p.m.	Mr. Neal loses communication with the *Mayaguez*, gives up trying to reach the ship, and informs the U.S. embassy in Jakarta.
4:45 a.m. May 12 Monday	3:45 p.m.	U.S. Defense Attaché Office, Singapore, repeats that local shipping agency had relayed mayday: "Being boarded by Cambodian army and commandeered at position 9°48′N/ 102°23′E." Vessel identifies itself as an American flag ship.
4:54 to 6:55 a.m. May 12 Monday	3:54 to 5:55 p.m.	U.S. embassy in Jakarta sends Washington a series of unclassified messages informing them of the incident. Embassy indicates that vessel was under own power slowly following one gunboat to Kompong Som; no casualties.
5:12 a.m. May 12 Monday	4:12 p.m.	National Military Command Center at the Pentagon and other addressees receive notification of the incident from U.S. embassy, Jakarta. The message is received by the State Department's intelligence watch, but is not passed to State's Operations Center.
5:30 a.m. May 12 Monday	4:30 p.m.	General Scowcroft calls President Ford and informs him that a merchant ship has been seized.
5:55 a.m. May 12 Monday	4:55 p.m.	*Mayaguez* anchors near Poulo Wai, close to the point of seizure.

Time/Date		
Washington		*Cambodia*	*Action*

Washington		Cambodia	Action
6:20 a.m.	May 12 Monday	5:20 p.m.	NMCC officials discuss possible aircraft reconnaissance with Pacific Command (CINCPAC).
7:30 a.m.	May 12 Monday	6:30 p.m.	JCS orders CINCPAC to launch reconnaissance aircraft to find ship.
7:40 a.m.	May 12 Monday	6:40 p.m.	During his regular morning intelligence briefing, the president is further briefed on the *Mayaguez* seizure.
8:00 a.m.	May 12 Monday	7:00 p.m.	Secretary of state is informed of the seizure at his morning briefing.
9:30 a.m.	May 12 Monday	8:30 p.m.	Secretary of state discusses seizure with the president; NSC meeting called for noon.
9:37 a.m.	May 12 Monday	8:37 p.m.	CINCPACFLT, Hawaii, directs nearest surface ships to proceed to area at best speed to provide assistance.
9:57 a.m.	May 12 Monday	8:57 p.m.	P-3 aircraft is launched from Thailand to locate *Mayaguez.*
10:05 a.m.	May 12 Monday	9:05 p.m.	P-3 aircraft from Cubi Point, Philippines, en route to scene.
10:19 a.m.	May 12 Monday	9:19 p.m.	Destroyer, U.S.S. *Holt,* and a supply ship, U.S.S. *Vega,* leave Philippines for seizure area.
12:05 p.m.	May 12 Monday	11:05 p.m.	First meeting of National Security Council.
May 12 Monday 1:50 p.m.		May 13 Tuesday 12:50 a.m.	White House announces seizure of ship. President calls it an "act of piracy," demands immediate release of ship, and states that failure to do so will have the most serious consequences.
May 12 Monday 2:12 p.m.		May 13 Tuesday 1:12 a.m.	Aircraft carrier, U.S.S. *Coral Sea,* and escorts are directed to proceed to vicinity of Kompong Som. An

	Time/Date	
Washington	*Cambodia*	*Action*

		amphibious ready group is directed to prepare to proceed to seizure area.
May 12 Monday 4:30 p.m.	May 13 Tuesday 3:30 a.m.	A representative of the People's Republic of China is summoned to the office of the deputy secretary of state and given a message for the Cambodian authorities, demanding the release of the ship. The P.R.C. representative refuses to accept the message.
May 12 Monday 6:00 p.m.	May 13 Tuesday 5:00 a.m.	Voice of America broadcast to Cambodia carries news story of *Mayaguez* incident. (News reporting continues periodically over Voice of America throughout crisis.)
May 12 Monday 6:24 p.m.	May 13 Tuesday 5:24 a.m.	Second destroyer, U.S.S. *Wilson,* underway toward seizure area from South China Sea, 1200 miles away.
May 12 Monday 9:16 p.m.	May 13 Tuesday 8:16 a.m.	P-3 aircraft reports: (1) positive visual identification of *Mayaguez,* anchored off Poulo Wai; (2) one minor hit on low identification pass; and (3) two gunboats in vicinity.
May 12 Monday 9:43 p.m.	May 13 Tuesday 8:43 a.m.	*Mayaguez* departs Poulo Wai, heads for Kompong Som.
May 12 Monday 9:44 p.m.	May 13 Tuesday 8:44 a.m.	Marine amphibious ready group is ordered to prepare for movement.
12:10 a.m. May 13 Tuesday	11:10 a.m.	A representative of the U.S. Liaison Office in Peking delivers a message to the Cambodian embassy there protesting the ship's seizure and demanding its release. A message is also delivered to the Foreign Ministry of the People's Republic of China.
12:30 a.m. May 13 Tuesday	11:30 a.m.	The first mariners' warning to avoid the area is disseminated through the Defense Mapping Agency Hydrographic Center.

Time/Date			
Washington		*Cambodia*	*Action*
2:18 a.m.	May 13 Tuesday	1:18 p.m.	*Mayaguez* stops and anchors 1 mile north of Koh Tang.
4:00 a.m.	May 13 Tuesday	3:00 p.m.	Thai premier informs United States that Thailand will not permit use of its bases for U.S. action or retaliation against Cambodia. U.S. chargé d'affaires promises that the United States will inform the Thai government before undertaking any action involving Thai-based planes.
4:45 a.m.	May 13 Tuesday	3:45 p.m.	A-7 aircraft place ordnance in the water in vicinity of *Mayaguez* as a warning not to get underway.
5:40 to 6:00 a.m. approx.	May 13 Tuesday	4:40 to 5:00 p.m. approx.	*Mayaguez* captain and crew are moved by two small boats to a location about 75 yards off the beach at Koh Tang.
6:17 a.m.	May 13 Tuesday	5:17 p.m.	JCS orders CINCPAC to maintain surveillance of *Mayaguez* and prevent its movement into a Cambodian mainland port.
6:33 a.m.	May 13 Tuesday	5:33 p.m.	Pilot reports that personnel are disembarking on Koh Tang and that ground fire has been received during low reconnaissance passes.
7:15 a.m. approx.	May 13 Tuesday	6:15 p.m. approx.	Aircraft report that small boats are off-loading personnel onto Koh Tang and that personnel have been moved toward interior of island.
7:35 a.m.	May 13 Tuesday	6:35 p.m.	Aircraft pilots observe crew on island but cannot ascertain numbers.
9:41 a.m.	May 13 Tuesday	8:41 p.m.	JCS authorized CINCPAC to use riot control agents and/or gunfire to disable the ship without risking sinking it.
—	May 13 Tuesday	—	*Mayaguez* crew spends night aboard fishing vessel anchored just off Koh Tang.

Time/Date		
Washington	*Cambodia*	*Action*
10:30 a.m. May 13 Tuesday	9:30 p.m.	President convenes second NSC meeting.
12:00 noon May 13 Tuesday	11:00 p.m.	JCS directs that Koh Tang be isolated by fire to prevent movement of all boats.
12:10 p.m. May 13 Tuesday	11:10 p.m.	JCS directs that 125 USAF security police be transferred from Nakhon Phanom to Utapao, and a marine battalion at Okinawa be placed in readiness for air movement to Utapao.
May 13 Tuesday 3:12 p.m.	May 14 Wednesday 2:12 a.m.	Marine battalion is directed to move from Okinawa to Utapao by airlift.
May 13 Tuesday 5:50 to 11:00 p.m.	May 14 Wednesday 4:50 to 10:00 a.m.	White House contacts 10 House and 11 Senate members regarding the military measures directed by the president to prevent movement of the *Mayaguez* and its crew to the mainland, and to prevent any Cambodian reinforcement.
May 13 Tuesday 6:30 p.m.	May 14 Wednesday 5:30 a.m.	Helicopter crashes, killing 18, during deployment of air force security police from Nakhon Phanom to Utapao.
		Unconfirmed field report indicates a 30-foot craft with approximately 40 people aboard departed Koh Tang. (Post-crisis information confirmed this was the *Mayaguez* crew.)
May 13 Tuesday 7:04 p.m.	May 14 Wednesday 6:04 a.m.	Three patrol boats attempting to move from Koh Tang are turned back by warning fire from USAF aircraft.
May 13 Tuesday 7:10 p.m.	May 14 Wednesday 6:10 a.m.	JCS orders U.S.S. *Hancock* with amphibious ready group/marine assault unit to sail from Philippines to Koh Tang area as soon as possible.

Time/Date		
Washington	*Cambodia*	*Action*

May 13 Tuesday 8:12 p.m.		May 14 Wednesday 7:12 a.m.	President orders Cambodian patrol boats attempting to leave Koh Tang to be sunk.
May 13 Tuesday 8:20 p.m.		May 14 Wednesday 7:20 a.m.	A Cambodian patrol boat is sunk after attempts to divert it from going to the mainland are unsuccessful.
May 13 Tuesday 8:45 to 11:15 p.m.		May 14 Wednesday 7:45 to 10:15 a.m.	Vessel spotted headed for Kompong Som with possible Caucasians huddled in bow. Attempts to stop it by firing across its bow and dropping riot control agents are unsuccessful.
May 13 Tuesday 10:40 p.m.		May 14 Wednesday 9:40 a.m.	President convenes third meeting of the National Security Council.
12:00 p.m. to 2:00 a.m.	May 14 Wednesday	11:00 a.m. to 1:00 p.m.	Unknown to Washington, the small boat with *Mayaguez* crew anchors for a short time about 1½ miles out of Kompong Som harbor, then departs for Koh Rong Som Lem, where crew is taken ashore.
12:29 a.m.	May 14 Wednesday	11:29 a.m.	U.S. aircraft continue to attack and sink patrol boats trying to leave island.
12:48 a.m.	May 14 Wednesday	11:48 a.m.	Acting chairman, JCS, briefs CINCPAC and major subordinate commanders on the 10:40 p.m. Tuesday NSC meeting and provides planning guidance for military operations to recover the ship and crew.
5:00 a.m.	May 14 Wednesday	4:00 p.m.	Thai prime minister protests the landing of marines at Utapao despite Thailand's request that its facilities not be involved in U.S. action to recover the *Mayaguez.*
7:15 a.m.	May 14 Wednesday	6:15 p.m.	U.S. Liaison Office reports that Chinese Foreign Ministry returned the message for the Cambodian

	Time/Date		
Washington		*Cambodia*	*Action*

		authorities, who would not accept it.
8:00 a.m. approx.	May 14 Wednesday 7:00 p.m. approx.	Unknown to Washington, *Mayaguez* captain is informed that he and selected crew members will be released if they return to the *Mayaguez* and request that U.S. aircraft be withdrawn from Cambodian airspace.
11:15 a.m. to 12:00 noon	May 14 Wednesday 10:15 to 11:00 p.m.	White House staff notifies 11 House and 11 Senate leaders by telephone that three Cambodian patrol craft have been sunk and four others immobilized in an effort to prevent removal of the *Mayaguez* crew to the mainland.
morning	May 14 Wednesday afternoon	Senate Foreign Relations Committee unanimously adopts a resolution supporting the president.
May 14 Wednesday between 1:00 and 2:00 p.m.	May 14–15 Wed.-Thur. between 12:00 p.m. and 1:00 a.m.	U.S. Ambassador Scali delivers a letter to U.N. Secretary General Waldheim requesting his assistance in securing release of the *Mayaguez* and its crew.
May 14 Wednesday 3:00 to 5:00 p.m.	May 15 Thursday 2:00 to 4:00 a.m.	State and Defense officials brief members of House International Relations Committee, Senate Foreign Relations Committee, and House Armed Services Committee.
May 14 Wednesday 3:15 p.m.	May 15 Thursday 2:15 a.m.	Destroyer U.S.S. *Wilson* estimates arrival off Koh Tang in about 5 hours.
May 14 Wednesday 3:52 p.m.	May 15 Thursday 2:52 a.m.	President Ford convenes fourth meeting of National Security Council.
May 14 Wednesday 4:45 to 5:10 p.m.	May 15 Thursday 3:45 to 4:10 a.m.	President issues orders to execute military plan to recover *Mayaguez* and crew.

	Time/Date	
Washington	*Cambodia*	*Action*

Washington	Cambodia	Action
May 14 Wednesday 4:52 to 5:20 p.m.	May 15 Thursday 3:52 to 4:20 a.m.	JCS issues verbal orders to CINCPAC to seize and secure *Mayaguez*, conduct a marine helicopter assault on Koh Tang, and destroy all Cambodian craft that intervene in operation. CINCPAC is also ordered to conduct strikes from the U.S.S. *Coral Sea* against targets in Kompong Som complex, with first time on target to be 8:45 p.m. to coincide with estimated capture of *Mayaguez*.
May 14 Wednesday 4:58 p.m.	May 15 Thursday 3:58 a.m.	Arrival of U.S.S. *Coral Sea* (already within range for launching aircraft) estimated at 12:15 a.m., or a little over 7 hours later.
May 14 Wednesday 5:15 p.m.	May 15 Thursday 4:15 a.m.	First troop-carrying helicopter departs Utapao. Tactical aircraft launch to provide continuous coverage for the operation, and an airborne command post assumes on-scene control.
May 14 Wednesday 5:45 p.m.	May 15 Thursday 4:45 a.m.	U.S.S. *Holt* is in position to receive helicopters with marine boarding team.
May 14 Wednesday 5:55 p.m.	May 15 Thursday 4:55 a.m.	B-52 aircraft in Guam are placed on 1-hour alert.
May 14 Wednesday 6:40 p.m.	May 15 Thursday 5:40 a.m.	President Ford and other National Security Council members brief 17 congressional leaders on military plans.
May 14 Wednesday 7:00 p.m.	May 15 Thursday 6:00 a.m.	U.N. issues a statement that the secretary general has communicated with Cambodians in an attempt to solve the problem of the U.S. merchant vessel by peaceful means.
May 14 Wednesday 7:00 to 7:22 p.m.	May 15 Thursday 6:00 to 6:22 a.m.	Three helicopters carrying security forces arrive at U.S.S. *Holt*.

Time/Date	
Washington	*Cambodia*	*Action*
evening of May 14 Wednesday	morning of May 15 Thursday	State Department advises various embassies in Washington that the United States is taking military action to secure the release of the ship and its crew.
May 14 Wednesday 7:07 to 7:26 p.m.	May 15 Thursday 6:07 to 6:26 a.m.	Phnom Penh domestic radio broadcasts a 19-minute message by Cambodian government, stating it is prepared to release the *Mayaguez*. No mention is made of crew. Broadcast is monitored by U.S. Foreign Broadcast Information Service and relayed to Washington. Secretary Kissinger receives summary at 8:15 and informs president at 8:29. The president directs that a public statement be issued promptly calling for release of the crew and offering to cease military operations upon receipt of Cambodian promise to release crew.
May 14 Wednesday 7:09 to 8:15 p.m.	May 15 Thursday 6:09 to 7:15 a.m.	Eight helicopters carrying about 175 marines begin to arrive Koh Tang. Groundfire causes heavy losses. 131 marines are landed.
May 14 Wednesday 7:20 to 8:00 p.m. approx.	May 15 Thursday 6:20 to 7:00 a.m. approx.	Unknown to Washington, Cambodian authorities on Koh Rong Som Lem release *Mayaguez* crew and several fishermen on a Thai fishing boat.
May 14 Wednesday 8:05 p.m.	May 15 Thursday 7:05 a.m.	First aircraft for mainland strikes are launched from U.S.S. *Coral Sea*.
May 14 Wednesday 8:10 p.m.	May 15 Thursday 7:10 a.m.	Destroyer U.S.S. *Wilson* arrives on scene.
May 14 Wednesday 8:25 to 9:22 p.m.	May 15 Thursday 7:25 to 8:22 a.m.	U.S.S. *Holt* pulls alongside *Mayaguez* and places security force on board. No personnel are found. *Mayaguez* is declared secure.

Time/Date		Action
Washington	*Cambodia*	*Action*
May 14 Wednesday 8:45 to 12:00 p.m. approx.	May 15 Thursday 7:45 to 11:00 a.m. approx.	During this period, air strikes are carried on against Cambodian mainland.
May 14 Wednesday 9:15 p.m.	May 15 Thursday 8:15 a.m.	White House announces that it has sent an urgent message to Cambodian authorities demanding release of the crew and offering to promptly cease military operations.
May 14 Wednesday 9:24 p.m.	May 15 Thursday 8:24 a.m.	State Department instructs Ambassador Scali to deliver letter to president of U.N. Security Council stating that the United States had taken certain measures to achieve the release of the *Mayaguez*.
May 14 Wednesday 10:35 p.m.	May 15 Thursday 9:35 a.m.	P-3 aircraft, investigating small craft proceeding toward Koh Tang, notes 30 Caucasians aboard vessel waving white flags.
May 14 Wednesday 10:49 to 11:00 a.m.	May 15 Thursday 9:49 to 10:00 a.m.	U.S.S. *Wilson* intercepts boat carrying *Mayaguez* crew. Captain reports that all of his crew and five Thais are on board. Meanwhile marine landing party on Koh Tang continues to receive heavy fire. President directs that supporting fire be continued while arrangements are made to withdraw from Koh Tang.
12:27 a.m.	May 15 Thursday 11:27 a.m.	White House announces recovery of the *Mayaguez* and its crew.
12:55 a.m.	May 15 Thursday 11:55 a.m.	JCS orders cessation of all offensive operations and withdrawal of all forces from operational area as soon as possible, consistent with safety and self-defense.
1:05 a.m.	May 15 Thursday 12:05 p.m.	Captain and crew board *Mayaguez* which is under tow by U.S.S. *Holt*.

	Time/Date		
Washington		*Cambodia*	*Action*
1:30 a.m. approx.	May 15 Thursday	12:30 p.m. approx.	A second wave of about 100 marines in 3 helicopters successfully lands on Koh Tang to assist in covering withdrawal.
2:00 to 2:30 a.m.	May 15 Thursday	1:00 to 1:30 p.m.	President Ford's report of U.S. actions is delivered to Senate and House leadership.
3:34 a.m.	May 15 Thursday	2:34 p.m.	Initial efforts to withdraw forces from the island begin.
4:45 a.m.	May 15 Thursday	3:45 p.m.	Thai premier presents memorandum to U.S. chargé d'affaires in Thailand protesting the sending of marines to Thailand for U.S. military actions against Cambodia.
7:15 to 9:15 a.m.	May 15 Thursday	6:15 to 8:15 p.m.	Marine personnel are extracted from Koh Tang by helicopters and landed on U.S.S. *Coral Sea.*
10:09 a.m.	May 15 Thursday	9:09 p.m.	U.S. embassy in Thailand reports view that if U.S. Marines are withdrawn speedily, U.S.-Thai relations will be improved.
12:44 p.m.	May 15 Thursday	11:44 p.m.	Department of State instructs all diplomatic posts to inform local officials at the highest level of specific circumstances surrounding *Mayaguez* incident.

Appendix B:
Chronology of the
Korean DMZ Crisis

Washington	Time/Date Korea	Action
	July 10	Mao Tse-tung sends personal message to Kim Il-sung on 15th anniversary of People's Republic of China (P.R.C.)/North Korea pact.
	July 28	The Korean People's Army (KPA) is informed through the joint duty officer that not more than 150 United Nations Command (UNC) personnel will be in the Joint Security Area (JSA) from August 1 to August 31 for the purpose of construction, beautifying the area, and routine maintenance.
	July 29	UNC informs KPA that up to 50 additional personnel will take part in JSA maintenance during August.
	August 2	UNC survey team visits tree in JSA.
	August 5	North Korea issues strongly worded formal statement that United States/R.O.K. has finished war preparations.
	August 6	South Korean maintenance personnel examine the tree which obstructs view near UNC Guard Post 3. KPA guards tell them to leave the tree alone.

Time/Date		
Washington	*Korea*	*Action*
August 17 Tuesday 10:06 p.m.	August 18 Wednesday 11:06 a.m.	At approximately 10:30 a.m. a UNC work crew accompanied by a seven-man security detail and three UNC officers enter the JSA and begin to prune the tree. At about 11:06 a.m., the North Koreans attack, killing two U.S. officers.
August 17 Tuesday 10:15 p.m. approx.	August 18 Wednesday 11:15 a.m. approx.	UNC message notifies United States authorities of the incident.
August 17 Tuesday 11:15 p.m.	August 18 Wednesday 12:15 p.m.	Department of State Korean desk officer receives call from U.S. embassy in Seoul on killings.
10:00 a.m.	Aug. 18 Wednesday 11:00 p.m.	President Ford briefed on Korean situation by Lt. Gen. Scowcroft.
August 18 Wednesday 3:30 p.m.	August 19 Thursday 4:30 a.m.	WSAG meets, recommends options: move F-4s from Japan to Korea; increase defense posture in the R.O.K.; alert the *Midway* task group; and alert the USAF on a possible F-111 deployment.
August 18 Wednesday 4:35 p.m.	August 19 Thursday 5:35 a.m.	CINCUNC forwards proposed operations concept.
August 18 Wednesday evening	August 19 Thursday morning	Secretary Kissinger discusses WSAG recommendations with President Ford by telephone.
August 18 Wednesday 5:30 p.m.	August 19 Thursday 6:30 a.m.	Korean working group forms in State Department.
August 18 Wednesday evening	August 19 Thursday morning	Kissinger meets with P.R.C. ambassador and consults with Japanese officials.
August 18 Wednesday 10:00 p.m.	August 19 Thursday 11:00 a.m.	R.O.K./U.S. forces in Korea ordered to an increased level of readiness.

Time/Date		
Washington	*Korea*	*Action*

August 18 Wednesday 10:18 p.m.	August 19 Thursday 11:18 a.m.	JCS orders CINCPAC to deploy one F-4 tactical fighter squadron from Kadena air base, Okinawa, Japan, to South Korea.
		Midway is put on alert to sail for Korea strait.
		Strategic Air Command is ordered to prepare to fly B-52 training missions from Guam to Korea.
August 18 Wednesday 10:00 p.m.	August 19 Thursday 11:00 a.m.	UNC cancels 379th meeting of Military Armistice Commission (MAC) when North Koreans fail to appear.
August 18 Wednesday 12:00 a.m.	August 19 Thursday 1:00 p.m.	North Korea agrees to a MAC meeting at 4:00 p.m. in response to a UNC request.
1:30 a.m.	Aug. 19 Thursday 2:30 p.m.	Republican Convention in Kansas City nominates President Ford.
3:00 a.m.	Aug. 19 Thursday 4:00 p.m.	379th MAC meeting begins. North Koreans accuse United States of provoking the incident and claim that some of their men have been injured.
		U.S. United Nations representative reads letter to supreme commander, KPA, stating that UNC views this brutal and unprovoked assault with gravity and concern; warns the North Koreans that such violent and belligerent actions cannot be tolerated; and warns that North Korea must bear full responsibility for all the consequences of its brutal actions.
4:23 a.m.	Aug. 19 Thursday 5:23 p.m.	Pyongyang Domestic Service broadcasts a supreme command order placing all North Korean forces in a "war posture."

Time/Date			
Washington		*Korea*	*Action*
			State Department directs U.S. representative to the U.N. to transmit UNC special report on the incident to the U.N. Security Council with a request that it be circulated as a U.N. document.
8:00 a.m.	Aug. 19 Thursday	9:00 p.m.	WSAG meets, chaired by Kissinger; recommends F-111 deployment, Stilwell's plan, and B-52 flights.
10:30 a.m.	Aug. 19 Thursday	11:30 p.m.	Kissinger flies to Kansas City after WSAG to meet President Ford and Lt. Gen. Scowcroft.
11:00 a.m.	Aug. 19 Thursday	12:00 p.m.	Moscow Radio broadcasts commentary calling for withdrawal of U.S. troops and arms from South Korea.
August 19 Thursday 11:00 a.m.		August 20 Friday 12:00 a.m.	Pyongyang Domestic Service reports that UNC was warned at August 19 meeting that if it continued "similar provocations in the future, it will be held responsible for all grave consequences."
August 19 Thursday evening		August 20 Friday morning	Nonaligned conference passes resolution condemning U.S. action.
			JCS issues order to CINCPAC and CINCSAC for B-52s from Anderson AFB, Guam, for training mission over South Korea.
7:00 a.m.	Aug. 20 Friday	8:00 p.m.	JCS activates crisis-action team and special communications nets.
10:15 a.m.	Aug. 20 Friday	11:15 p.m.	President approves General Stilwell's plan to cut down the tree and conduct show of force.
August 20 Friday 4:45 p.m.		August 21 Saturday 5:45 a.m.	Principals meet in NMCC to monitor operation.

Time/Date		
Washington	*Korea*	*Action*
August 20 Friday 6:00 p.m.	August 21 Saturday 7:00 a.m.	UNC personnel enter the JSA to cut down the tree and remove two illegal North Korean road barriers.
August 20 Friday 6:15 p.m.	August 21 Saturday 7:15 a.m.	UNC representative in JSA informs North Korean representative that UNC work party has entered JSA to peacefully complete the work commenced on August 18.
August 20 Friday 6:45 p.m.	August 21 Saturday 7:45 a.m.	Work party completes tree cutting.
August 20 Friday 7:26 p.m.	August 21 Saturday 8:26 a.m.	Work party and security platoon depart the JSA without incident.
August 20 Friday 11:00 p.m.	August 21 Saturday 12:00 noon	A private meeting of MAC senior members is held at the request of the North Koreans. North Korean representative delivers a message to the UNC commander from the KPA supreme commander, which terms the August 18 incident "regrettable."
August 20 Friday evening	August 21 Saturday morning	Pyongyang Domestic Service charges that the UNC tree-felling operation was a "grave provocation" designed to trap North Korea into the UNC's "war provocation plot."
	Aug. 22 Sunday	State Department representative announces U.S. does "not find the message acceptable because there is no acknowledgement of responsibility."
	Aug. 23 Monday	State Department accepts North Korean message.
3:00 a.m.	Aug. 25 Wednesday 4:00 p.m.	At the 380th MAC meeting, the UNC representative calls the North

Time/Date		
Washington	*Korea*	*Action*
		Korean statement of August 21 a "positive step." The North Koreans call for a joint effort to prevent similar incidents in the future and propose that security personnel be restricted to their respective sides of the JSA.
	September 6 Monday	MAC representatives sign a revised JSA agreement.
	September 7 Tuesday	U.N. forces reduce readiness posture JCS directs redeployment of forces.
	September 16 Thursday	Division of JSA into north and south portions is completed.

Appendix C:
The War Powers Resolution

Resolved by the Senate and House of Representatives of the United States of America in Congress assembled,

Short Title

Section 1. This joint resolution may be cited as the "War Powers Resolution".

Purpose and Policy

Section 2. (a) It is the purpose of this joint resolution to fulfill the intent of the framers of the Constitution of the United States and insure that the collective judgment of both the Congress and the President will apply to the introduction of United States Armed Forces into hostilities, or into situations where imminent involvement in hostilities is clearly indicated by the circumstances, and to the continued use of such forces in hostilities or in such situations.

(b) Under article I, section 8, of the Constitution, it is specifically provided that the Congress shall have the power to make all laws necessary and proper for carrying into execution, not only its own powers but also all other powers vested by the Constitution in the Government of the United States, or in any department or officer thereof.

(c) The constitutional powers of the President as Commander-in-Chief to introduce United States Armed Forces into hostilities, or into situations where imminent involvement in hostilities is clearly indicated by the circumstances, are exercised only pursuant to (1) a declaration of war, (2) specific statutory authorization, or (3) a national emergency created by attack upon the United States, its territories or possessions, or its armed forces.

Consultation

Section 3. The President in every possible instance shall consult with Congress before introducing United States Armed Forces into hostilities or into situations where imminent involvement in hostilities is clearly indicated by the circumstances, and after every such introduction shall consult regularly with the Congress until United States Armed Forces are no longer engaged in hostilities or have been removed from such situations.

Reporting

Section 4. (a) In the absence of a declaration of war, in any case in which United States Armed Forces are introduced—

(1) into hostilities or into situations where imminent involvement in hostilities is clearly indicated by the circumstances;

(2) into the territory, airspace or waters of a foreign nation, while equipped for combat, except for deployments which relate solely to supply, replacement, repair, or training of such forces; or

(3) in numbers which substantially enlarge United States Armed Forces equipped for combat already located in a foreign nation; the President shall submit within 48 hours to the Speaker of the House of Representatives and to the President pro tempore of the Senate a report, in writing, setting forth—

(A) the circumstances necessitating the introduction of United States Armed Forces;

(B) the constitutional and legislative authority under which such introduction took place; and

(C) the estimated scope and duration of the hostilities or involvement.

(b) The President shall provide such other information as the Congress may request in the fulfillment of its constitutional responsibilities with respect to committing the Nation to war and to the use of United States Armed Forces abroad.

(c) Whenever United States Armed Forces are introduced into hostilities or into any situation described in subsection (a) of this section, the President shall, so long as such armed forces continue to be engaged in such hostilities or situation, report to the Congress periodically on the status of such hostilities or situation as well as on the scope and duration of such hostilities or situation, but in no event shall he report to the Congress less often than once every six months.

Congressional Action

Section 5. (a) Each report submitted pursuant to section 4(a)(1) shall be transmitted to the Speaker of the House of Representatives and to the President pro tempore of the Senate on the same calendar day. Each report so transmitted shall be referred to the Committee on Foreign Affairs of the House of Representatives and to the Committee on Foreign Relations of the Senate for appropriate action. If, when the report is transmitted, the Congress has adjourned sine die or has adjourned for any period in excess of three calendar days, the Speaker of the House of Representatives and the President pro tempore of the Senate, if they deem it advisable (or if petitioned by at least 30 percent of the membership of their respective Houses) shall jointly request the President to convene Congress in order that it may consider the report and take appropriate action pursuant to this section.

(b) Within sixty calendar days after a report is submitted or is required to be submitted pursuant to section 4(a)(1), whichever is earlier, the President shall terminate any use of United States Armed Forces with respect to which such report was submitted (or required to be submitted), unless the Congress (1) has declared war or has enacted a specific authorization for such use of United States Armed Forces, (2) has extended by law such sixty-day period, or (3) is physically unable to meet as a result of an armed attack upon the United States. Such sixty-day period shall be extended for not more than an additional thirty days if the President determines and certifies to the Congress in writing that unavoidable military necessity respecting the safety of United States Armed Forces requires the continued use of such armed forces in the course of bringing about a prompt removal of such forces.

(c) Notwithstanding subsection (b), at any time that United

States Armed Forces are engaged in hostilities outside the territory of the United States, its possessions and territories without a declaration of war or specific statutory authorization, such forces shall be removed by the President if the Congress so directs by concurrent resolution.

Congressional Priority Procedures for Joint Resolution or Bill

Section 6. (a) Any joint resolution or bill introduced pursuant to section 5(b) at least thirty calendar days before the expiration of the sixty-day period specified in such section shall be referred to the Committee on Foreign Affairs of the House of Representatives or the Committee on Foreign Relations of the Senate, as the case may be, and such committee shall report one such joint resolution or bill, together with its recommendations, not later than twenty-four calendar days before the expiration of the sixty-day period specified in such section, unless such House shall otherwise determine by the yeas and nays.

(b) Any joint resolution or bill so reported shall become the pending business of the House in question (in the case of the Senate the time for debate shall be equally divided between the proponents and the opponents), and shall be voted on within three calendar days thereafter, unless such House shall otherwise determine by yeas and nays.

(c) Such a joint resolution or bill passed by one House shall be referred to the committee of the other House named in subsection (a) and shall be reported out not later than fourteen calendar days before the expiration of the sixty-day period specified in section 5(b). The joint resolution or bill so reported shall become the pending business of the House in question and shall be voted on within three calendar days after it has been reported, unless such House shall otherwise determine by yeas and nays.

(d) In the case of any disagreement between the two Houses of Congress with respect to a joint resolution or bill passed by both Houses, conferees shall be promptly appointed and the committee of conference shall make and file a report with respect to such resolution or bill not later than four calendar days before the expiration of the sixty-day period specified in section 5(b). In the event the conferees are unable to agree within 48 hours, they shall report back to their respective Houses in disagreement. Notwithstanding any rule in either House concerning the printing of conference reports in the Record or concerning any delay in the consideration of such reports, such report shall be acted on by both Houses not later than the expiration of such sixty-day period.

Congressional Priority Procedures for Concurrent Resolution

Section 7. (a) Any concurrent resolution introduced pursuant to section 5(c) shall be referred to the Committee on Foreign Affairs of the House of Representatives or the Committee on Foreign Relations of the Senate, as the case may be, and one such concurrent resolution shall be reported out by such committee together with its recommendations within fifteen calendar days, unless such House shall otherwise determine by the yeas and nays.

(b) Any concurrent resolution so reported shall become the pending business of the House in question (in the case of the Senate the time for debate shall be equally divided between the proponents and the opponents) and shall be voted on within three calendar days thereafter, unless such House shall otherwise determine by yeas and nays.

(c) Such a concurrent resolution passed by one House shall be referred to the committee of the other House named in subsection (a) and shall be reported out by such committee together with its recommendations within fifteen calendar days and shall thereupon become the pending business of such House and shall be voted upon within three calendar days, unless such House shall otherwise determine by yeas and nays.

(d) In the case of any disagreement between the two Houses of Congress with respect to a concurrent resolution passed by both Houses, conferees shall be promptly appointed and the committee of conference shall make and file a report with respect to such concurrent resolution within six calendar days after the legislation is referred to the committee of conference. Notwithstanding any rule in either House concerning the printing of conference reports in the Record or concerning any delay in the consideration of such reports, such report shall be acted on by both Houses not later than six calendar days after the conference report is filed. In the event the conferees are unable to agree within 48 hours, they shall report back to their respective Houses in disagreement.

Interpretation of Joint Resolution

Section 8. (a) Authority to introduce United States Armed Forces into hostilities or into situations wherein involvement in hostilities is clearly indicated by the circumstances shall not be inferred—

(1) from any provision of law (whether or not in effect before the date of the enactment of this joint resolution), including any provision contained in any appropriation Act, unless such provision specifically authorizes the introduction of United States Armed Forces into hostilities or into such situations and states that it is intended to constitute specific statutory authorization within the meaning of this joint resolution; or

(2) from any treaty heretofore or hereafter ratified unless such treaty is implemented by legislation specifically authorizing the introduction of United States Armed Forces into hostilities or into such situations and stating that it is intended to constitute specific statutory authorization within the meaning of this joint resolution.

(b) Nothing in this joint resolution shall be construed to require any further specific statutory authorization to permit members of United States Armed Forces to participate jointly with members of the armed forces of one or more foreign countries in the headquarters operations of high-level military commands which were established prior to the date of enactment of this joint resolution and pursuant to the United Nations Charter or any treaty ratified by the United States prior to such date.

(c) For purposes of this joint resolution, the term "introduction of United States Armed Forces" includes the assignment of members of such armed forces to command, coordinate, participate in the movement of, or accompany the regular or irregular military forces of any foreign country or government when such military forces are engaged, or there exists an imminent threat such forces will become engaged, in hostilities.

(d) Nothing in this joint resolution—

(1) is intended to alter the constitutional authority of the Congress or of the President, or the provisions of existing treaties; or

(2) shall be construed as granting any authority to the President with respect to the introduction of United States Armed Forces into hostilities or into situations wherein involvement in hostilities is clearly indicated by the circumstances which authority he would not have had in the absence of this joint resolution.

Separability Clause

Section 9. If any provision of this joint resolution or the application thereof to any person or circumstance is held invalid, the remainder of the joint resolution and the application of such provision to any other person or circumstance shall not be affected thereby.

Effective Date

Section 10. This joint resolution shall take effect on the date of its enactment.

CARL ALBERT
Speaker of the House of Representatives

JAMES O. EASTLAND
President of the Senate pro tempore

IN THE HOUSE OF REPRESENTATIVES, U.S.,

November 7, 1973.

The House of Representatives having proceeded to reconsider the resolution (H. J. Res. 542) entitled "Joint resolution concerning the war powers of Congress and the President", returned by the President of the United States with his objections, to the House of Representatives, in which it originated, it was

Resolved, That the said resolution pass, two-thirds of the

House of Representatives agreeing to pass the same.

Attest:

W. PAT JENNINGS
Clerk

I certify that this Joint Resolution originated in the House of Representatives.

W. PAT JENNINGS
Clerk

IN THE SENATE OF THE UNITED STATES

November 7, 1973.

The Senate having proceeded to reconsider the joint resolution (H. J. Res. 542) entitled "Joint resolution concerning the war powers of Congress and the President", returned by the President of the United States with his objections to the House of Representatives, in which it originated, it was

Resolved, That the said joint resolution pass, two-thirds of the Senators present having voted in the affirmative.

Attest:

FRANCIS R. VALEO
Secretary

Appendix D:
Department of State
Memorandum on the Applicability
of the War Powers Resolution to the
Korean DMZ Crisis

August 21, 1976

Subject: *War Powers and Korean Deployments* *

The War Powers Resolution requires that "the President in every possible instance shall consult with Congress before introducing United States Armed Forces into hostilities or into situations where imminent involvement in hostilities is clearly indicated by the circumstances . . ." Given what I know of the situation in Korea, I would not interpret this requirement as applicable to the strengthening of our armed forces there, even when accompanied by a heightened alert status. More difficult is the question whether the sending of reinforced patrols into the DMZ would qualify, but, so long as they are engaging merely in acts which we are entitled to take under the Armistice Agreement and which we have consistently taken, then I do not think the prospect of increased North Korean aggressiveness triggers the consultation requirement. In any event, consultation is only required where "possible;" and, to the extent that it is possible, it is clearly desirable in any case.

The Resolution requires reporting within 48 hours in three

---

*Note: The following are the relevant, substantive portions of a memorandum sent to the secretary by the acting legal adviser on August 21, 1976, explaining why it was not recommended that the secretary propose to the president a War Powers Report in connection with events in Korea and the augmentation of United States armed forces there.

circumstances. The possibly relevant one with respect to the presently planned deployment is Sec. 4(a)(3)—"numbers which substantially enlarge United States Armed Forces equipped for combat already located in a foreign nation." Whether the proposed additions are substantial enlargements depends upon an analysis of what is already there and what is being added.

I believe it would be an undesirable precedent to construe the Resolution as requiring a report in a situation where a relative handful of people have been added to an existing force of some 41,000 men. Although in terms of tactical aircraft the increment is significant, I believe we should interpret 4(a)(3) as concerned primarily, if not entirely, with numbers of military personnel, rather than with items of equipment. Certainly the text speaks of "numbers," and the examples given in the legislative debates referred only to numbers of personnel. I am satisfied that this interpretation is reasonable and fully defensible and that a contrary interpretation would create a precedent that would haunt us in many future cases.

George H. Aldrich
Acting Legal Advisor

Notes

CHAPTER 1

1. Hearings before the Preparedness Investigating Subcommittee of the Senate Committee on Armed Services, 89th Cong., 2d sess., Aug. 25, 1966, as quoted in Charles F. Hermann, ed., *International Crises* (New York: Free Press, 1972), p. 3.

2. Barry M. Blechman and Stephen Kaplan, *The Use of the Armed Forces as a Political Instrument* (Washington, D.C.: Brookings Institution, 1976).

3. Unfortunately, there have been very few studies of crisis from the perspective of comparative politics, resulting in an ethnocentric bias in most U.S. academic efforts. One recent and notable attempt to correct this deficiency and link crisis research with the larger field of comparative politics is Davis B. Bobrow et al., "Understanding How Others Treat Crises," *International Studies Quarterly* 21 (March 1977): 199-221. In this article, Bobrow and his colleagues at the University of Maryland contrast Western and Chinese views on crisis and recommend a multi-method research strategy to analyze national decision-making systems with restricted information access, as with the P.R.C. and the Soviet Union.

4. Jan F. Triska and David D. Finley, *Soviet Foreign Policy* (New York: Macmillan, 1968), p. 317.

5. Kenneth E. Boulding, *Conflict and Defense* (New York: Harper & Row, 1963), p. 250.

6. Oran R. Young, *The Intermediaries: Third Parties in International Crises* (Princeton: Princeton University Press, 1967), p. 10.

7. James A. Robinson, "Crisis: An Appraisal of Concepts and Theories," in Hermann, *International Crises*, p. 23.

8. Hermann, *International Crises*, p. 13. See also Charles F. Hermann, *Crises in Foreign Policy: A Simulation Analysis* (Indianapolis: Bobbs-Merrill, 1969), p. 29.

9. Margaret G. and Charles F. Hermann, "Maintaining the Quality of Decision Making in Foreign Policy Crises: A Proposal," in *U.S. Commission on the Organization of the Government for the Conduct of Foreign Policy, Report* 2 (June 1975): 125.

10. Michael Brecher, "Toward a Theory of International Crisis Behavior," *International Studies Quarterly* 21 (March 1977): 43.

11. The difficulty with diversity in definitional phases of study is the near impossibility of data comparison and evaluation across cases. Thus, the Brookings and Brecher studies cited above do not use the same criteria and both are different from a CACI Corporation inventory of crises cited in Leo Hazlewood, John J. Hayes, and James R. Brownell, Jr., "Planning for Problems in Crisis Management," *International Studies Quarterly* 21 (March 1977): 75-106. These studies, respectively, list 215, 450, and 290 crisis cases, although their criteria and time periods are different.

12. The classic explanation of the approaches and their differing requirements is found in J. David Singer, "The Level-of-Analysis Problem," in *The International System,* Klaus Knorr and Sidney Verba, eds., (Princeton: Princeton University Press, 1961), pp. 77-92. For another summary of scholarly approaches to the study of crisis, see Raymond Tanter, "Crisis Management: A Critical Review of Academic Literature," *Jerusalem Journal of International Relations* 1 (Fall 1975): 71-97. Tanter's review is especially good on the concepts of rationality, decision theory, and stress.

13. Representatives of the simulation efforts are: Hermann, *Crises in Foreign Policy;* Ithiel de Sola Pool and Allen Kessler, "The Kaiser, the Tsar, and the Computer: Information Processing in a Crisis," *American Behavioral Scientist* 9 May 1965 pp. 31-38; and Ole R. Holsti, Richard A. Brody, and Robert C. North, "Measuring Effect and Action in International Reaction Models: Empirical Materials from the 1962 Cuban Crisis," *Journal of Peace Research* 1 (1964): 170-189.

14. The method and philosophy of the rational/analytic framework have been the subjects of countless articles and books. The summary here is developed from the presentation by John D. Steinbruner, *The Cybernetic Theory of Decision* (Princeton: Princeton University Press, 1974), Chapter 2, "The Analytic Paradigm."

15. For an extensive review and criticism of the rational/analytic approach to the field of international politics, see Graham T. Allison, *Essence of Decision* (Boston: Little, Brown & Co., 1971), Chapter 1.

16. Glenn H. Snyder, *Deterrence and Defense* (Princeton: Princeton University Press, 1961), p. 12.

17. Ibid.

18. Hermann, *International Crises,* p. 296ff.

19. Thomas C. Schelling, *The Strategy of Conflict* (Cambridge, Mass.: Harvard University Press, 1960).

20. Oran R. Young, *The Intermediaries*, and *The Use of Force: Bargaining During International Crises* (Princeton: Princeton University Press, 1968). Another excellent work on strategic negotiations is Glenn H. Snyder, "Crisis Bargaining," in Hermann, *International Crisis*, pp. 217-258.

21. Albert and Roberta Wohlstetter, *Controlling the Risks in Cuba*, Adelphi Papers, no. 17 (London: Institute for Strategic Studies, 1965).

22. Roberta Wohlstetter, *Cuba and Pearl Harbor: Hindsight and Foresight* (Santa Monica, Cal.: Rand Corporation, 1965) and *Pearl Harbor: Warning and Decision* (Palo Alto, Cal.: Stanford University Press, 1962).

23. Triska and Finley, *Soviet Foreign Policy*, p. 347.

24. Hannes Adomeit, *Soviet Risk-Taking and Crisis Behavior: From Confrontation to Coexistence?* Adelphi Papers, no. 101 (London: Institute for Strategic Studies, 1973), p. 34.

25. Robert Jervis, *The Logic of Images in International Relations* (Princeton: Princeton University Press, 1970).

26. Richard C. Snyder, H. W. Bruck, and Burton Sapin, *Foreign Policy Decision-Making: An Approach to the Study of International Politics* (New York: Free Press, 1962).

27. Richard G. Head, "Introduction to Defense Policymaking," in *American Defense Policy*, R. G. Head and Ervin J. Rokke, eds., 3d ed. (Baltimore: Johns Hopkins University Press, 1973), p. 266.

28. Glenn D. Paige, *The Korean Decision* (New York: Free Press, 1968), pp. 276-278.

29. Snyder, Bruck, and Sapin, *Foreign Policy Decision-Making*, p. 65.

30. James E. Dougherty and Robert L. Pfaltzgraff, Jr., *Contending Theories of International Relations* (New York: Lippincott, 1971), p. 331.

31. The four best explanations of the problems associated with the assumption of rationality are Steinbruner, *Cybernetic Theory of Decision;* Sidney Verba, "Assumptions of Rationality and Non-Rationality in Models of the International System," in *International Politics and Foreign Policy*, ed. James N. Rosenau (New York: Free Press, 1969), pp. 217-231; Allison, *Essence of Decision;* and Charles E. Lindblom, "The Science of 'Muddling Through,'" *Public Administration Review* 29 (Spring 1959): 79-88.

32. Dougherty and Pfaltzgraff, *Contending Theories*, p. 317.

33. This approach was strongly argued by Woodrow Wilson in *Political Science Quarterly*, June 1887, pp. 197-222.

34. The critiques of the policy-administration dichotomy, as it came to be called, are numerous, starting with Herbert A. Simon, *Administrative Behavior*, (New York: Free Press, 1947). In the field of policy analysis the major works have been Warner R. Schilling, Paul Y. Hammond, and

Glenn H. Snyder, *Strategy, Politics and Defense Budgets* (New York: Columbia University Press, 1962); Richard E. Neustadt, *Presidential Power* (New York: New American Library, 1964); and Roger Hilsman, *To Move A Nation* (New York: Doubleday, 1967).

35. Graham T. Allison, "Conceptual Models and the Cuban Missile Crisis," *American Political Science Review,* September 1969, pp. 689-718.

36. Morton H. Halperin, "Why Bureaucrats Play Games," *Foreign Policy,* Spring 1971, pp. 70-90. Allison and Halperin collaborated in what is perhaps the best explanation and most useful article for participants in the policy process, "Bureaucratic Politics: A Paradigm and Some Policy Implications," *World Politics* 24 (Spring 1972), Supplement 40-79. For the most comprehensive treatment of the subject, see Morton H. Halperin, *Bureaucratic Politics and Foreign Policy* (Washington, D.C.: Brookings Institution, 1974). The classic in using the bureaucratic perspective to look at both sides in two case studies is Richard E. Neustadt, *Alliance Politics* (New York: Columbia University Press, 1970). See also, I. M. Destler, *Presidents, Bureaucrats, and Foreign Policy* (Princeton: Princeton University Press, 1972).

37. One of the important contributions of bureaucratic politics is the formal statement of what most bureaucrats have known informally for a long time—that many so-called "decisions" are not strategic choices at all, but merely political problems to be manipulated as the situation warrants. Thus, in his excellent summary of "types of outcome," Ted Warner specifies seven categories of bureaucratic decision: (1) decisive political choice; (2) compromised policy; (3) logrolling; (4) lowest common denominator; (5) contradictory policy; (6) paper policy; and (7) no policy at all. To this list we can add (8) unstable policy; and (9) slow policy. See Edward L. Warner, "Bureaucratic Politics: A Thematic Outline," in Richard G. Head, *Study Guide to American Defense Policy,* 3d ed. (Baltimore: Johns Hopkins University Press, 1973), p. 95.

38. Allison, "Conceptual Models," p. 706ff.

39. Ole R. Holsti, "The Belief System and National Images," *Journal of Conflict Resolution* 6 (1962): 244-252. Holsti's investigation into cognitive theory and its application to politics was only one of many efforts by political scientists and psychologists. For a relatively complete listing of cognitive research efforts, see the bibliography in Robert Axelrod, *Structure of Decision: The Cognitive Maps of Political Elites* (Princeton: Princeton University Press, 1976).

40. Joseph de Rivera, *The Psychological Dimension of Foreign Policy* (Columbus, Ohio: Charles E. Merrill, 1968).

41. Ibid., pp. 432-433.

42. Henry A. Kissinger, *American Foreign Policy* (New York: W. W. Norton, 1969), p. 22.

43. Tanter, "Crisis Management," p. 81.

44. Charles F. Hermann and Linda P. Brady, "Alternative Models of International Crisis Behavior," in Hermann, *International Crises*, pp. 283-284. The Hermann/Brady definition was strongly influenced by Margaret G. Hermann, "Testing a Model of Psychological Stress," *Journal of Personality* 34 (September 1966): 381-396; and Richard S. Lazarus, *Psychological Stress and the Coping Process* (New York: McGraw-Hill, 1966).

45. Ole R. Holsti, "Crisis, Stress and Decision-making," *International Social Sciences Journal* 23, no. 1 (1971): 60. See also Holsti, *Crisis, Escalation, War* (Montreal: McGill-Queens University Press, 1972), pp. 11-13.

46. Richard C. Snyder, *Deterrence, Weapons and Decision-Making* (China Lake, Cal.: U.S. Naval Ordnance Test Station, 1961), p. 80.

47. The question given the Foreign Service officers was, "When does a crisis reduce the alternatives for action by decision makers?" The responses were: "Always" 3 (3.8%); "Often" 27 (34.2%); "Sometimes" 47 (59.5%); "Never" 2 (2.5%). Howard H. Lentner, "The Concept of Crisis as Viewed by the U.S. Department of State," in Hermann, *International Crises*, p. 128.

48. Holsti, *Crisis, Escalation, War*, p. 145.

49. Hermann, *International Crises*, p. 294.

50. See especially Richard Smoke, "Toward the Control of Escalation" (Ph.D. diss., M.I.T., 1972) and *War: Controlling Escalation* (Cambridge: Harvard University Press, 1977).

51. Hermann, *International Crises*, p. 287.

52. Hermann, "Maintaining the Quality of Decision-Making," p. 127.

53. Alexander L. George, "Structure, Internal Processes, and Management of Small Groups," *Commission on the Organization of the Government for the Conduct of Foreign Policy Report* 2 (June 1975): 40-53.

54. Irving L. Janis, *Victims of Groupthink* (Boston: Houghton Mifflin, 1972).

55. Cited in George, "Small Groups," p. 40.

56. See, for instance, Richard Head's professional organization model in "Doctrinal Innovation and the A-7 Attack Aircraft Decisions," *American Defense Policy*, 3d ed., pp. 431-445; and "The Sociology of Military Decision-Making," *Pacific Sociological Review* 16 (April 1973): 209-227.

57. John D. Steinbruner, *The Cybernetic Theory of Decision*, and "Models of Decision in the Social Sciences," in Arnold L. Horelick, A. Ross Johnson, and John D. Steinbruner, *The Study of Soviet Foreign Policy: Decision-Theory-Related Approaches*, vol. 4 (Beverly Hills, Cal.: Sage Publications, 1975).

58. Steinbruner, *The Cybernetic Theory of Decision*, pp. 62ff; and Horelick, Johnson, and Steinbruner, *The Study of Soviet Foreign Policy*, p. 15. Steinbruner adapted the concept of "satisficing" from Herbert A.

Simon and James G. March, *Organizations* (New York: Wiley, 1958), pp. 140-141.

59. Steinbruner, "Models of Decision in the Social Sciences," p. 27.

60. Raymond Tanter, *Modelling and Managing International Conflicts: The Berlin Crises* (Beverly Hills, Cal.: Sage Publications, 1974), Vol. 6, Sage Library of Social Research.

61. J. Stein and R. Tanter, *International Crisis Management: Decision-Making in Israel 1967 and 1973* (forthcoming).

CHAPTER 2

1. See, for instance, Dina A. Zinnes, Joseph L. Zinnes, and Robert D. McClure, "Hostility in Diplomatic Communication: A Study of the 1914 Crisis," in Charles F. Hermann, *International Crises* (New York: Free Press, 1972), pp. 139-162.

2. This definition builds on several earlier constructs of Charles Hermann and James Robinson, and it benefits from the work of Michael Brecher in "Toward a Theory of International Crisis Behavior," *International Studies Quarterly* 21 (March 1977): 44.

3. Ibid.

4. Surprise, itself, can be analyzed as a variable factor in the onset of crisis situations. Glenn Paige identified at least three types of surprise and noted their differential impact on policy makers. The first was AGUS (Anticipated Generally, Unanticipated Specifically), which he compared to BATO (Betrayed Assurances to the Opposite) and which tends to be viewed with more alarm by decision makers. The latter is exemplified by President Kennedy's reaction of startled anger, "He can't do that to me!" upon learning of the Soviet implacement of missiles in Cuba, after Ambassador Gromyko had specifically denied their intention to do such a thing. Paige also noted the possible existence of third type of surprise, NEATA (Not Expected At All). See Glenn D. Paige, "Comparative Case Analysis of Crisis Decisions: Korea and Cuba," in Hermann, *International Crises*, pp. 53-54.

5. The term "model" often implies rigorous, mathematical statements or equations and deterministic propositions. No such rigor is intended in this usage, but only the more general specification of an analytical system where the logical relationships among the parts correspond roughly to those in the empirical world. Such a model is weaker than the rigorous mathematical model, but it exchanges the power of simplicity for some of the scope of relevancy. To be more specific, our use of the term "model" is much more general and less rigorous than a mathematical model; it is more closely related to an analytical paradigm or general conceptual framework. The specific limitations that prevent its incorpora-

tion as a formal model are: (1) the inability in the current milieu to specify the laws of interaction of the elements unambiguously; and (2) the lack of a calculus which precisely relates the elements and laws of interaction to those of the real world. See Lawrence C. Mayer, *Comparative Political Inquiry* (Homewood, Ill.: Dorsey Press, 1972), Chapter 4.

6. Gabriel A. Almond, "Approaches to Developmental Causation," in *Crisis, Choice and Change*, eds. Gabriel A. Almond, Scott C. Flanagan, and Robert J. Mundt (Boston: Little, Brown, 1973), pp. 5-8.

7. The point of President Kennedy's skepticism after the Bay of Pigs is documented in Arthur M. Schlesinger, Jr., *A Thousand Days* (Boston: Houghton Mifflin, 1965), Chapter 11.

8. For a more complete description of the application of cybernetics to national policy making, see John D. Steinbruner, *The Cybernetic Theory of Decision*.

9. The factor of organizational procedures has been examined by many analysts as an essential part of policy making. For a more complete study, see Morton H. Halperin, *Bureaucratic Politics and Foreign Policy* (Washington, D.C.: Brookings Institution, 1974).

10. Ideally, procedures are tested before they are put into practice. One notable exception is in the area of strategic nuclear operations, where it is impossible to test organizational procedures completely. Simulations and tests of parts of the system are conducted regularly, but the strategic nuclear crisis situation bears unusually high uncertainty.

CHAPTER 3

1. Roger Hilsman, "The National Security Policymaking Process," *Perspectives in Defense Management*, May 1971, p. 32.

2. For a broad review of the role of the assistant for national security affairs, see I. M. Destler, "National Security Advice to U.S. Presidents: Some Lessons from Thirty Years," *World Politics* 29 (January 1977): 143-161.

3. U.S. Department of State, Operations Center, "Checklist: Setting Up a Task Force or Working Group," mimeograph (Washington, D.C.: Department of State, December 1976).

4. For additional information on the State Department operations center and Foreign Service officer perceptions of crisis, see Howard H. Lentner, "The Concept of Crisis as Viewed by the United States Department of State," in Hermann, *International Crises*, pp. 112-135.

5. "Reflections on Cuba," *Reporter*, November 22, 1962, p. 21. Although there have been many books written about Henry Kissinger, many of them are polemical and do not add to our understanding of his complex, multifaceted personality. For two versions which outline some

of his beliefs, see Stephen R. Graubard, *Kissinger: Portrait of a Mind* (New York: W. W. Norton, 1973), especially the epilogue; and John C. Stoessinger, *Henry Kissinger: The Anguish of Power* (New York: W. W. Norton, 1976), pp. 7-46.

6. U.S., Congress, *Joint Resolution Concerning the War Powers of Congress and the President*, Pub. L. 93-148, 93d Cong., 1st sess., 1973, H. J. Resolution 542.

CHAPTER 4

1. Thomas Reed, speech to the National Armed Forces Communication and Electronic Association, Washington, D.C., June 1976.

2. U.S. Congress, House, Armed Services Investigating Subcommittee of the Committee on Armed Services, *Review of Department of Defense Worldwide Communications, Phase 1: Report to accompany H.R. 201*, 92d Cong., 1st sess., May 10, 1971, p. 15.

3. Ibid.

4. Irving Luckhom, speech to the National Armed Forces Communication and Electronic Association, Washington, D.C., June 1976.

5. U.S. Department of Defense, *Annual Defense Department Report, FY 1976*, Report of the Secretary of Defense James R. Schlesinger to the Congress, February 5, 1975, p. IV-3.

CHAPTER 5

1. Kenneth M. Quinn, "Cambodia 1976: Internal Consolidation and External Expansion," *Asian Survey* 17 (January 1977): 45. See also John Barron and Anthony Paul, *Murder of a Gentle Land* (New York: Readers' Digest Press, 1977).

2. U.S. Congress, House, Subcommittee on International Political and Military Affairs, Committee on International Relations, *Seizure of the Mayaguez*, Hearings on the *Mayaguez* Incident, pt. 4, *Report of the Comptroller General of the United States*, 94th Cong., 2d sess., October 4, 1976, p. 23. (Hereafter referred to as *GAO Report*.)

3. Roy Rowen, *The Four Days of Mayaguez* (New York: Norton, 1975), p. 15.

4. Ibid., p. 40.

5. *GAO Report*, p. 116.

6. Ibid.

7. Interview with Air Force Chief of Staff, General David C. Jones, April 25, 1977, Washington, D.C.

8. *GAO Report*, p. 117.

9. Interview with former President Gerald R. Ford, April 29, 1977, Palm Springs, California.

10. This detail was to present one of the most significant intelligence uncertainties of the entire crisis. The initial message from the ship and the message sent by Mr. Neal indicated that the ship was proceeding "to an unknown Cambodian port." The U.S. embassy in Jakarta reportedly indicated that the ship was headed for Kompong Som, although this was proven incorrect from later events. (See *GAO Report,* page 32.)

11. Ford interview.

12. *New York Times,* May 13, 1975, p. 19.

13. The words "we assumed" are used by Commander J. A. Messagee in, " 'Mayday' for the *Mayaguez:* The Patrol Squadron Skipper," *U.S. Naval Institute Proceedings* 102 (November 1976): 95.

14. Ford interview.

15. Dr. Kissinger was also assistant to the president for national security affairs at this time.

16. Jones interview.

17. Ford interview.

18. Ibid.

19. Message, " 'Mayday' for the *Mayaguez,*" p. 95.

20. Rowen, *Four Days of Mayaguez,* p. 82. The following discussion was derived from personal material and comments made available by General Scowcroft.

21. U.S. Congress, House, Subcommittee on International Political and Military Affairs of the Committee on International Relations, *Seizure of the Mayaguez,* Hearings on the *Mayaguez* incident, pt. 2, 94th Cong., 1st sess., 1975, p. 249. (Hereafter referred to as *Mayaguez Hearings.*)

22. Ford interview.

23. Rowen, *Four Days of Mayaguez,* p. 90.

24. *New York Times,* May 16, 1975, p. 16.

25. Rowen, *Four Days of Mayaguez,* pp. 141-142. This view that one of the targets of the strategic bargaining "signal" was North Korea tends to be confirmed by other high administration officials who apparently greatly feared another Korean crisis. See *New York Times,* May 16, 1975, p. 14.

26. Ford interview.

27. Jones interview.

28. The Joint Chiefs of Staff were placed in the operational chain of command by the DOD Reorganization Act of 1958. The JCS can give orders to the combatant forces, but the orders are issued under the authority of and in the name of the secretary of defense. See Paul Y. Hammond, *Organization for Defense* (Princeton: Princeton University Press, 1961),

and Lawrence J. Korb, *The Joint Chiefs of Staff* (Bloomington, Ind.: Indiana University Press, 1976).

29. General Richard H. Ellis and Lieutenant Colonel Frank B. Horton, "Flexibility—A State of Mind," *Strategic Review* 4, no. 1 (Winter 1976): 33.

30. On this point, a misunderstanding inadvertently occurred between the navy and the White House. The navy assigned the first flight of attack aircraft a "time over target" on the mainland which was after the scheduled arrival of the marine assault force on Koh Tang. The attack aircraft were also assigned the mission of "armed reconnaissance"—"not to expend ordnance unless attacked." The White House had expected that the first strikes would deliver ordnance on the mainland targets on or about the time of the marine assault.

31. Major J. B. Hendricks, " 'Mayday' for the *Mayaguez:* The Battalion Operations Officer," *U.S. Naval Institute Proceedings* 102 (November 1976): 104.

32. Jones interview.

33. Jules Witcover, "The *Mayaguez* Decision, Three Days of Crisis for President Ford," *Washington Post*, May 17, 1975.

34. *New York Times*, May 15, 1975, p. 18.

35. Ibid.

36. The majority of the information in this section is derived from the DOD chronology in the *GAO Report;* the detailed account of the operation compiled by Captain Thomas D. Des Brisay and the staff of the Pacific Air Forces, *Fourteen Hours at Koh Tang*, USAF Southeast Asia Monograph Series, vol. 3, no. 5, (Washington, D.C.: U.S. Government Printing Office, 1975); and the five-part article, " 'Mayday' for the *Maya-guez*," *U.S. Naval Institute Proceedings* 102 (November 1976): 93-111.

37. CH-53 and HH-53 helicopters were used. They are armor plated and have 7.62 rapid-firing miniguns, providing more fire power than most cargo helicopters. In addition, both carry external fuel tanks which extend their range, and the HH-53 is air refuelable from an HC-130 tanker.

38. Eight helicopters carried marines directly to Koh Tang, and one attempted a rescue after landing marines on the U.S.S. *Holt*.

39. The full text of the Cambodian broadcast can be found in *New York Times*, May 16, 1975, p. 15.

40. Ford interview.

41. *Mayaguez Hearings*, pt. 1, p. 70.

42. *New York Times*, May 15, 1975, p. 18.

43. Ibid.

44. Des Brisay, *Fourteen Hours at Koh Tang*, p. 149.

45. *New York Times*, May 16, 1975, p. 1.

46. *Mayaguez Hearings*, pt. 1, p. 89.

47. See *Mayaguez Hearings*, pt. 2, June 25, 1975, pp. 161-182.

48. "The Seizure of the *Mayaguez*—A Case Study of Crisis Management," in *GAO Report*, pp. 58-127.

49. The Eagleburger letter is reprinted in Appendix 3 to the *GAO Report*, pp. 108-109.

50. Ibid., p. 76.

51. Lewis Perdue, "Florida Democrat Abuses Chairmanship, Releases Report to Bias Presidential Debate," *Congress Today* 11 (November 1976): 4.

52. Kenneth N. Waltz, "Electoral Punishment and Foreign Policy Crises," in *Domestic Sources of Foreign Policy*, ed. James N. Rosenau (New York: Free Press, 1967), p. 273.

CHAPTER 6

1. The reader is cautioned that the events portrayed were not observed by all the participants. The result is that the case study may present history in a more logical pattern than was apparent to any of the participants at the time. Specific mention will be made where certain events were not known to major participants.

2. Cited in U.S. Department of Defense, *Annual Defense Department Report, FY 1977*, Report of Secretary of Defense Donald H. Rumsfeld to the Congress, 94th Cong., 2d sess., January 27, 1976, pp. 8-9.

3. Ralph N. Clough, *Deterrence and Defense in Korea: The Role of U.S. Forces* (Washington, D.C.: Brookings Institution, 1976), p. 5.

4. *Annual Defense Department Report, FY 1977*, p. 9.

5. U.S. Congress, House, Committee on International Relations, *Activities of the Korean Central Intelligence Agency in the United States*, pt. 1, 94th Cong., 2d sess., March 17 and 25, 1976.

6. Robert R. Simmons, *The Strained Alliance: Peking, Pyongyang, Moscow, and the Politics of the Korean Civil War* (New York: Free Press, 1975), p. 32.

7. Gregory Henderson, Richard Ned Lebow, and John C. Stoessinger, eds. *Divided Nations in a Divided World* (New York: McKay Co., 1974), p. 72.

8. For instance, see *U.S. News and World Report*, September 13, 1976, p. 37.

9. U.S. Department of State, "Korean Question at the U.N.," memorandum submitted to the House Committee on International Relations, 94th Cong., 2d sess., August 1976. The vote on the U.S.-backed resolution was 59 for; 51 against; 29 abstentions; and on the D.P.R.K.-backed one 54 for; 43 against; 42 abstentions.

10. New China News Agency broadcast in English, July 10, 1976.

11. Ibid.

12. North Korean News Agency broadcast, August 5, 1976, reprinted in U.S. Department of State message 182222Z August 1976, pp. 2-3.

13. This campaign position to withdraw U.S. ground forces from Korea was fortified by the analysis and recommendations in the Brookings/ Clough study, *Deterrence and Defense in Korea.*

14. *Washington Post,* August 14, 1976, p. 1.

15. *Pravda,* August 18, 1976, p. 4.

16. *Washington Post,* August 18, 1976, p. A22.

17. Interview with Lieutenant Colonel Victor S. Vierra, April 15, 1977, Washington, D.C.

18. Although many agencies had begun to work on the DMZ "incident," this decision to convene a WSAG set a deadline for bureaucratic action and represents an authoritative recognition of the situation as a "crisis."

19. Interview with former President Gerald R. Ford, April 29, 1977, Palm Springs, California, and material from General Scowcroft.

20. Coauthored with Richard Moorsteen (Cambridge, Mass.: Harvard University Press, 1971).

21. Secretary of Defense Rumsfeld was away from Washington through most of the crisis period. The acting secretary in his absence was Deputy Secretary William Clements.

22. Korea Herald, *Axe-Murders at Panmunjom* (Seoul: Korea Herald, 1976), p. 19.

23. Department of State, Transcript of Press, Radio, and Television News Briefing, August 18, 1976, 1:45 p.m., pp. 1-5.

24. Ibid, p. 12.

25. Statement by Press Secretary Ron Nessen, Kansas City, Missouri, August 18, 1976. White House, *Weekly Compilation of Presidential Documents* 12, no. 34 (August 23, 1976): 1263.

26. "U.S. Crisis Unit Takes Up DMZ Killings," *New York Times,* August 20, 1976, p. 3.

27. Ibid.

28. The *New York Times* article on August 20 read, "The group, an official said, discussed at length the incident in the demilitarized zone yesterday and speculated on the motivation for the attack. All the participants agreed that it seemed premeditated, the official said. 'Frankly, we're a bit baffled,' another official said afterward."

29. Clough, *Deterrence and Defense in Korea,* pp. 5, 9-10.

30. These actions have been described variously in the *New York Times* and *Washington Post* on August 20 and 21, 1976.

31. Interview with General Richard G. Stilwell, U.S. Army (Ret.),

commander in chief, United Nations Command, March 9, 1977, Washington, D.C.

32. Ibid.

33. Ibid.

34. *New York Times,* August 20, 1976, p. 3.

35. U.S. Department of State, Operations Center, *Checklist: Setting Up a Task Force or Working Group,* n.d.

36. U.N. Command News Release, August 19, 1976.

37. *Washington Post,* August 20, 1976, p. 3.

38. U.N. Command News Release, August 19, 1976.

39. *Washington Post,* August 20, 1976, p. A3.

40. Ford interview.

41. United Press International release, August 20, 1977, reprinted in Korea Herald, *Axe-Murders at Panmunjom,* p. 22.

42. Ibid., p. 23.

43. Ibid., p. 24.

44. Ibid.

45. Ford interview.

46. Stilwell interview.

47. Proposed remarks by the chairman of the Joint Chiefs of Staff before the Bull Elephant Club, Washington, D.C., September 16, 1976.

48. *Washington Post,* August 22, 1976, p. A1.

49. Unclassified message, "21 August 1976 Informal Meeting between the Military Armistice Commission (MAC) Senior Members," from CINCUNC to JCS, August 22, 1976. Also quoted in Korea Herald, *Axe-Murders at Panmunjom,* p. 28; *Washington Post,* August 23, 1977, p. 24; and Department of State answers to questions, Press Briefing, August 23, 1976.

50. Department of State, Transcript of Press, Radio, and Television News Briefing, August 23, 1976.

51. *Washington Post,* August 21, 1977, p. A2.

52. Ibid.

53. Stilwell interview.

54. Associated Press, as quoted by the Korea Herald, *Axe-Murders at Panmunjom,* p. 27.

55. *Washington Post,* August 23, 1976, p. A1.

56. Ibid.

57. U.S. Department of State, transcript of Press, Radio, and Television News Briefing, August 23, 1976.

58. *Washington Post,* August 24, 1976, p. 1.

59. Ibid.

60. General Richard G. Stilwell, "CINCUNC Statement to Command

Personnel," August 31, 1976.

61. *New York Times,* September 2, 1976, p. C5. The *Times* reported that the flights stopped on August 30, but were resumed on September 2.

62. The idea of separating the U.N. and North Korean security forces had been proposed by the U.N. Command in 1970, but it had been rejected at that time and ever since by the North Korean representative.

63. Interviews at the JCS, ISA, NSC, State Department, and the U.N. Command.

64. *Washington Post,* August 24, 1976, p. 16.

65. *New York Times,* August 24, 1976.

66. *New York Times,* August 23, 1976.

67. *Chicago Defender,* August 25, 1976.

68. *Chicago Sun Times,* August 24, 1976.

69. *San Diego Union,* August 25, 1976.

70. *Milwaukee Journal,* August 24, 1976.

71. *Pittsburgh Press,* August 24, 1976.

72. *Chicago Tribune,* August 24, 1976.

73. *Cleveland Plain Dealer,* September 5, 1976.

74. Joseph C. Harsch, "North Korean Primitives," *Christian Science Monitor,* August 24, 1976, p. 27.

75. Joseph Kraft, "The U.S. Stance in Northeast Asia," *Washington Post,* August 24, 1976, p. 17.

76. U.S. Congress, House, *House Resolution 506,* 94th Cong., 2d sess., August 31, 1976.

77. *Executive-Legislative Communications and the Role of the Congress During International Crises* (Washington, D.C.: General Accounting Office, 1976).

78. The GAO Report carefully noted the representation of the members responding to the survey. The respondents tended to: have less tenure than the average; be Democrats; be House members; and be from the Northeast section of the United States. Ibid., p. 4.

79. U.S. Congress, House, Committee on International Relations, *Deaths of American Military Personnel in the Korean Demilitarized Zone,* before the Subcommittee on International Political and Military Affairs and the Subcommittee on International Organizations, 94th Cong., 2d sess., September 1, 1976. (Hereafter referred to as the *Korean Crisis Hearings.*)

80. Ibid., pp. 14-15. (See also the War Powers Resolution, Appendix C.)

81. For full text, see Appendix D.

82. *Korean Crisis Hearings,* p. 18.

83. Cited by U.S. Information Agency in *Worldwide Treatment of*

Current Issues 62 (August 26, 1976), p. 7. (Hereafter referred to as *Current Issues.*)

84. Ibid.

85. *Current Issues,* August 20, 1976, p. 8.

86. *Current Issues,* August 26, 1976, p. 8.

87. Ibid.

88. Ibid., p. 11.

89. *Current Issues,* August 23, 1976, p. 20.

90. P. Dalnov, "Peace and Security for the Korean Peninsula," *Izvestiya,* August 29, 1976, p. 3.

91. "N. Korea Allies Withdraw Draft," *Newsreview,* September 25, 1976.

CHAPTER 7

1. Graham T. Allison, *Essence of Decision* (Boston: Little, Brown & Co., 1971), pp. 101-143.

2. Speech by former President Gerald R. Ford, University of Kentucky, April 11, 1977, reported in the *Washington Post,* April 12, 1977, p. 5.

3. On this vital point, Thomas Belden writes perceptively on the bureaucratic barriers that separate analysts, policy makers, and action organizations. See T. G. Belden, "Indications, Warning, and Crisis Operations," *International Studies Quarterly* 21 (March 1977): 183.

4. For this suggestion of intentions staircases, we are most thankful to Thomas Belden.

5. "It was assumed that Egypt would not attack Israel unless it achieved the capability to strike Israel's centers of population by air and neutralize Israel's air force." See *The Agranet Report* (Tel-Aviv: Am Oved, 1975), pp. 19-20, as cited in Abraham Ben-Zvi, "Hindsight and Foresight: A Conceptual Framework for the Analysis of Surprise Attacks," *World Politics* 28 (April 1976): 381-395.

6. Charles F. Hermann and Robert E. Mason, "Identifying Behavioral Attributes of Events that Trigger International Crises: An Events Data Approach to Short-term Forecasting," a paper delivered at the 18th Annual Convention of the International Studies Association, St. Louis, Missouri, March 16-20, 1977.

7. Glenn D. Paige, *The Korean Decision* (New York: Free Press, 1968), p. 285.

8. Interview with former President Gerald R. Ford, April 29, 1977, Palm Springs, California.

9. For example, after the ill-fated Bay of Pigs invasion of 1961,

President Kennedy's popularity soared to an all-time high of 83 percent, compared to his average of 70 percent during his administration and a peak of 74 percent after the Cuban missile crisis. President Eisenhower's popularity similarly increased after the 1960 U-2 incident and the collapse of the U.S.-Soviet summit meeting. See Kenneth N. Waltz, "Electoral Punishment and Foreign Policy Crises," in *Domestic Sources of Foreign Policy,* ed. James N. Rosenau (New York: Free Press, 1967), p. 273.

10. As cited in Roy Rowen, *The Four Days of Mayaguez* (New York: Norton, 1975), p. 223.

11. Transcript of speech by former President Gerald R. Ford, University of Kentucky, April 11, 1977.

12. These points derive from discussions with Colonel John C. Fryer, Jr., USAF.

Selected Bibliography

Adomeit, Hannes. *Soviet Risk-Taking and Crisis Behavior: From Confrontation to Coexistence?* Adelphi Papers, no. 101. London: Institute for Strategic Studies, 1973.

Allison, Graham T. "Conceptual Models and the Cuban Missile Crisis." *American Political Science Review* 63 (September 1969):689-718.

——. *The Essence of Decision: Explaining the Cuban Missile Crisis.* Boston: Little, Brown, 1971.

—— and Halperin, Morton H. "Bureaucratic Politics, a Paradigm and Some Policy Implications." In *Theory and Policy in International Relations,* eds. Raymond Tanter and Richard Ullman, pp. 40-79. Princeton: Princeton University Press, 1972.

Andriole, Stephen J. and Young, Robert A. "Toward the Development of an Integrated Crisis Warning System." *International Studies Quarterly* 21 (March 1977):107-150.

Art, Robert J. "Bureaucratic Politics and American Foreign Policy: A Critique." *Policy Sciences* 4 (1973):467-490.

Association of the U.S. Army. "Murder at Panmunjom." *Army,* September 1976, p. 9.

Atkeson, Edward B. "The Impact of Crises on the Evolution of Strategy and Forces in an Era of Detente." In *National Security and Detente,* ed. faculty members of the Army War College. New York: Thomas Y. Crowell Co., 1976.

Averch, H. and Lavin, M. M. *Dilemmas in the Politico-Military Conduct of Escalating Crises.* Rand Paper P-3205. Santa Monica, Cal.: Rand Corporation, 1965.

Axelrod, Robert, ed. *Structure of Decision: The Cognitive Maps of Political Elites.* Princeton: Princeton University Press, 1976.

Bartlett, Tom. "Mayaguez." *Leatherneck Magazine* 58, no. 9 (September 1975):50-55.

Bauer, Charles J. "Military Crisis Management at the National Level." *Military Review,* August 1975, pp. 3-15.

Belden, T. G. *Crisis Conferencing and the Pueblo Case.* Research Paper P-580. Arlington, Va.: Institute for Defense Analyses, 1970.

Betts, Richard K. *Soldiers, Statesmen, and Cold War Crises.* Cambridge, Mass.: Harvard University Press, 1977.

Blechman, Barry M. and Kaplan, Stephen S. "The Use of the Armed Forces as a Political Instrument." Washington, D.C.: Brookings Institution, 1977.

Bobrow, Davis B. "Communications, Command and Control: The Nerves of Intervention." Paper presented at the Interuniversity Seminar on Armed Forces and Society Conference, Chicago, Ill., June 17-19, 1976.

Bock, Edwin A. *Essays on the Case Method.* Brussels: International Institute of Administrative Sciences, 1962.

Brecher, Michael. "Toward a Theory of International Crisis Behavior." *International Studies Quarterly* 21 (March 1977):39-74.

Brzezinski, Zbigniew. "How the Cold War Was Played." *Foreign Affairs* 51 (October 1972):181-209.

Carlile, Donald E. "The Mayaguez Incident: Crisis Management." *Military Review* 56 (October 1976):3-14.

de Rivera, Joseph. *The Psychological Dimension of Foreign Policy.* Columbus, O.: Merrill Publishing Co., 1968.

de Sola Pool, Ithiel and Kessler, Allen. "The Kaiser, the Tsar, and the Computer: Information Processing in a Crisis." *American Behavioral Scientist* 8 (May 1965):31-38.

Des Brisay, Thomas D., Captain. *Fourteen Hours at Koh Tang.* USAF Southeast Asia Monograph Series, vol. 3, monograph 5, Washington, D.C.: U.S. Government Printing Office, 1977.

Destler, I. M. "National Security Advice to U.S. Presidents: Some Lessons from Thirty Years." *World Politics* 29 (January 1977):143-161.

——. *Presidents, Bureaucrats and Foreign Policy.* Princeton: Princeton University Press, 1972.

Dougherty, James E. and Pfaltzgraff, Robert L., Jr. "Decision-Making Theories." In *Contending Theories of International Relations.* New York: Lippincott, 1971, p. 312ff.

Dror, Yehezkel. *Crazy States—A Counterconventional Strategic Problem.* Lexington, Mass.: Heath Lexington Books, 1971.

Druzhinin, V. V. and Kontorov, D. S. *Concept, Algorithm, Decision (A Soviet View).* Soviet Military Thought, no. 6. Washington, D.C.: United States Air Force, 1975.

Ellis, Richard H. and Horton, Frank B. "Flexibility—A State of Mind." *Strategic Review* 4 (Winter 1976):26-36.

Freedman, Lawrence. "Logic, Politics, and Foreign Policy Processes: A Critique of the Bureaucratic Politics Model." *International Affairs,* July 1976, pp. 434-449.

George, Alexander L. "The Case for Multiple Advocacy in Making Foreign Policy." *American Political Science Review* 66 (1972):751-785, 791-795.

———. "The 'Operational Code': A Neglected Approach to the Study of Political Leaders and Decision-Making." *International Studies Quarterly* 13 (1969):190-222.

———. *Propaganda Analysis.* Evanston, Ill.: Row, Peterson, 1959.

———; Hall, D. K.; and Simons, William R. *The Limits of Coercive Diplomacy.* Boston: Little, Brown, 1971.

Graubard, Stephen. *Kissinger: Portrait of a Mind.* New York: Norton, 1973.

Halperin, Morton H. *Bureaucratic Politics and Foreign Policy.* Washington, D.C.: Brookings Institution, 1974.

———. "Why Bureaucrats Play Games." *Foreign Policy,* Spring 1971, pp. 70-90.

Handel, Michael I. "The Yom Kippur War and the Inevitability of Surprise." *International Studies Quarterly,* September 1977, pp. 461-501.

Harris, Don R. *The Flow Lines of Information, Intelligence, and Policy Inputs to National Security Decision Making.* Arlington, Va.: Consolidated Analysis Centers, 1974.

Hazelwood, Leo; Hayes, John J.; and Brownell, James R., Jr. "Planning for Problems in Crisis Management." *International Studies Quarterly* 21 (March 1977):75-106.

Head, Richard G. and Rokke, Ervin J., eds. *American Defense Policy.* 3d ed. Baltimore: Johns Hopkins University Press, 1973.

———. "Doctrinal Innovation and the A-7 Attack Aircraft Decisions." In *American Defense Policy,* edited by R. G. Head and Ervin J. Rokke, 3d ed., pp. 431-445. Baltimore: Johns Hopkins University Press, 1973.

Hermann, Charles F. *Crises in Foreign Policy: A Simulation Analysis.* Indianapolis: Bobbs-Merrill, 1969.

———. "Impact of Organizational Arrangements on Crisis Management." In *Research Tasks for International Crisis Avoidance and Management,* pp. 80-91. Advanced Research Projects Agency, 1975.

———. "International Crisis as a Situational Variable." In *International Politics and Foreign Policy,* edited by James N. Rosenau, rev. ed. New York: Free Press, 1969.

———. "Some Consequences of Crisis which Limit the Viability of Organizations." *Administrative Science Quarterly* 8 (June 1963):61-82.

———, ed. *International Crises.* New York: Free Press, 1972.

———, and Mason, Robert E. "Identifying Behavioral Attributes of Events that Trigger International Crises: An Events Data Approach to Short-Term Forecasting." Paper delivered at the 18th Annual Convention of the International Studies Association, St. Louis, Mo., March 16-20, 1977.

Hermann, Margaret G. and Hermann, Charles F. "Maintaining the Quality of Decision Making in Foreign Policy Crises: A Proposal." *Report of the U.S. Commission on the Organization of the Government for the Conduct of Foreign Policy*, June 1975. Washington, D.C.: U.S. Government Printing Office, 1976. Vol. 2:86-93.

Hilsman, Roger. *To Move a Nation*. New York: Doubleday, 1967.

Holsti, Ole R. "The Belief System and National Images: A Case Study." *Journal of Conflict Resolution* 6 (1962):244-252.

——. "The Belief System and National Images: John Foster Dulles and the Soviet Union." Ph.D. dissertation, Stanford University, 1962.

——. *Crisis Escalation War*. Montreal: McGill-Queens University Press, 1972.

——. "Foreign Policy Formation Viewed Cognitively." In *Structure of Decision*, edited by Robert Axelrod, pp. 18-54. Princeton: Princeton University Press, 1976.

——. "The 'Operational Code' Approach to the Study of Political Leaders: John Foster Dulles' Philosophical and Instrumental Beliefs." *Canadian Journal of Political Science* 3 (1970):123-157.

——; Brody, Richard A.; and North, Robert C. "The Management of International Crisis: Affect and Action." In *Theory and Research on the Causes of War*, edited by Dean G. Pruitt and Richard C. Snyder, pp. 62-79. Englewood Cliffs, N.J.: Prentice-Hall, 1969.

——; Brody, Richard A.; and North, Robert C. "Measuring Effect and Action in International Reaction Models: Empirical Materials from the 1962 Cuban Crisis." *Journal of Peace Research* 1 (1964):170-189.

Horelick, Arnold L.; Johnson, A. Ross; and Steinbruner, John D. *The Study of Soviet Foreign Policy: Decision-Theory-Related Approaches*. International Studies Series No. 02-039, Vol. 4. Beverly Hills, Cal.: Sage Publications, 1975.

Janis, Irving L. *Victims of Groupthink: A Psychological Study of Foreign-Policy Decisions and Fiascoes*. Boston: Houghton Mifflin, 1972.

Jefferies, Chris L. "Defense Decision-Making in the Organizational-Bureaucratic Context." Mimeograph. Colorado Springs, Colo.: U.S. Air Force Academy, 1976.

Jervis, Robert. *The Logic of Images in International Relations*. Princeton: Princeton University Press, 1970.

Kahn, Herman. *On Escalation: Metaphors and Scenarios*. New York: Praeger, 1965.

Kettelhut, M. C. *The Crisis Situation and National Response.* Washington, D.C.: National War College, 1973.

Kissinger, Henry A. *American Foreign Policy: Three Essays.* New York: W. W. Norton, 1969.

———. "Domestic Structure and Foreign Policy." *Daedalus* 95, no. 2 (Spring 1966):503-529.

Kissinger, Henry A. and Brodie, Bernard. *Bureaucracy, Politics, and Strategy.* Security Studies Paper No. 17. See especially "Bureaucracy and Policymaking: The Effect of Insiders and Outsiders on the Policy Process," by Henry A. Kissinger, pp. 1-14. Los Angeles: University of California, 1968.

Korb, Lawrence J. *The Joint Chiefs of Staff: The First Twenty-five Years.* Bloomington, Ind.: Indiana University Press, 1976.

Kronk, Arthur. *Memoirs.* New York: Funk & Wagnalls, 1968.

Lanyi, George A. and McWilliams, Wilson C., eds. *Crisis and Continuity in World Politics.* New York: Random House, 1973.

Leites, Nathan. *The Operational Code of the Politburo.* New York: McGraw-Hill, 1951.

Lentner, Howard H. "The Pueblo Affair." *Military Review* 49 (July 1969): 55-66.

McClelland, Charles A. "The Acute International Crisis." In *The International System,* edited by K. Knorr and S. Verba. Princeton: Princeton University Press, 1961.

———. "The Anticipation of International Crises." *International Studies Quarterly* 21 (March 1977):15-38.

March, James G. and Simon, Herbert. *Organizations.* New York: Wiley, 1958.

May, Ernest R. *"Lessons" of the Past: The Use and Misuse of History in American Foreign Policy.* New York: Oxford University Press, 1973.

"Mayaguez, The President, and History." *Armed Forces Journal International* 112 (June 1975):31.

Messegee, J. A., Commander, et al. " 'Mayday' for the *Mayaguez.*" *U.S. Naval Institute Proceedings* 102 (November 1976):93-111.

Milburn, Thomas W. "The Management of Crisis." In *International Crises: Insights from Behavioral Research,* edited by Charles F. Hermann, pp. 259-280. New York: Free Press, 1972.

Nathan, James A. "The Missile Crisis: His Finest Hour Now." *World Politics* 27 (January 1975):256-281.

Neustadt, Richard E. *Alliance Politics.* New York: Columbia University Press, 1970.

———. *Presidential Power.* New York: New American Library, 1964.

Nicholas, Jack D., et al. *The Joint and Combined Staff Officers Manual.* Harrisburg, Pa.: Telegraph Press, 1959.

Quinn, Kenneth M. "Cambodia 1976: Internal Consolidation and External Expansion." *Asian Survey* 17 (January 1977):43-54.

Rosenau, James N. "The Premises and Promises of Decision-Making Analysis." In *Contemporary Political Analysis,* edited by James C. Charlesworth. New York: Free Press, 1967.

——. "Pre-Theories and Theories of Foreign Policy." In *Approaches to Comparative and International Politics,* edited by R. Barry Farrell. Evanston, Ill.: Northwestern University Press, 1966.

Rosi, Eugene J. *American Defense and Detente.* New York: Dodd, Mead & Co., 1973.

Rowan, Roy. *The Four Days of Mayaguez.* New York: Norton, 1975.

Sandefer, Howard L., Lieutenant Commander. "Proper Prior Planning and the Next *Mayaguez.*" *U.S. Naval Institute Proceedings* 101 (August 1975):85-86.

Schelling, Thomas C. *The Strategy of Conflict.* Cambridge, Mass.: Harvard University Press, 1960.

Schilling, Warner R.; Hammond, Paul Y.; and Snyder, Glenn H. *Strategy, Politics and Defense Budget.* New York: Columbia University Press, 1962.

Shapiro, Michael J. and Bonham, G. Matthew. "Cognitive Processes and Foreign Policy Decision-Making." *International Studies Quarterly* 17 (1973):147-174.

Shlaim, Avi. "Crisis Decision-Making in Israel: The Lessons of October 1973." In *The International Yearbook of Foreign Policy Analysis* 1. London: Croom-Helm, 1975.

——. "Failures in National Intelligence Estimates: The Case of the Yom Kippur War." *World Politics* 28 (April 1976):348-380.

Simmons, Robert R. *The Strained Alliance: Peking, Pyongyang, Moscow and the Politics of the Korean Civil War.* New York: Free Press, 1975.

Simon, Herbert. *Administrative Behavior.* New York: Macmillan, 1947.

Singer, J. David. "The Level-of-Analysis Problem in International Relations." *World Politics* 14 (1961):77-92.

Smoke, Richard. *War: Controlling Escalation.* Cambridge, Massachusetts: Harvard University Press, 1978.

Snyder, Glenn H. "Crisis Bargaining." In *International Crises,* edited by C. D. Hermann, pp. 217-256. New York: Free Press, 1972.

——, and Diesing, Paul. *Conflict among Nations: Bargaining, Decision Making and Systems Structure in International Crises.* Princeton: Princeton University Press, 1977.

——. *Deterrence and Defense.* Princeton; Princeton University Press, 1961.

Snyder, Richard C.; Bruck, H. W.; and Sapin, Burton. *Foreign Policy Decision Making.* New York: Free Press, 1962.

—— and Paige, Glenn D. "The United States Decision to Resist Aggression in Korea: The Application of an Analytical Scheme." *Administrative Science Quarterly* 3 (1958):341-378.

Steinbruner, John D. *Cybernetic Theory of Decision.* Princeton: Princeton University Press, 1974.

——."The Mind and the Milieu of Policy Makers: A Case History of the MLF." Ph.D. dissertation, M.I.T., 1968.

——. *Some Effects of Decision Procedures on Policy Outcomes.* Cambridge, Mass.: Arms Control Project, M.I.T. Center for International Studies, 1970.

Stoessinger, John G. *Nations in Darkness: China, Russia, and America.* New York: Random House, 1971.

Tanter, Raymond. "Crisis Management: A Critical Review of the Academic Literature." *Jerusalem Journal of International Relations* 1 (Fall 1975):71-101.

——. "International System and Foreign Policy Approaches: Implications for Conflict Modelling and Management." In *Theory and Policy in International Relations,* edited by Raymond Tanter and Richard Ullman, pp. 7-39. Princeton: Princeton University Press, 1972.

——. *Modelling and Managing International Conflicts: The Berlin Crises.* Beverly Hills, Cal.: Sage Publications, 1974.

Triska, Jan F. and Finley, David D. *Soviet Foreign Policy.* New York: MacMillan, 1968.

U.S. Congress, House, Committee on Armed Services. *Inquiry into the U.S.S. Pueblo and EC-121 Plane Incidents.* Report, 91st Cong., 1st sess., July 28, 1969.

——, House, Committee on Armed Services. *Review of Department of Defense Worldwide Communications, Phase I.* Report, 92d Cong., 1st sess., May 10, 1971.

——, House, Committee on International Relations. *Congress and Foreign Policy.* Washington, D.C.: Government Printing Office, 1976.

——, House, Committee on International Relations. *Seizure of the Mayaguez.* Hearings before the Committee on International Relations and its Subcommittee on International Political and Military Affairs. 94th Cong., 1st sess., 1975.

——, House. *Executive-Legislative Communications and the Role of the Congress during International Crises.* Report of the Comptroller General of the United States. Washington, D.C.: General Accounting Office, 1976.

Walker, Stephen G. "Cognitive Maps and International Realities: Henry A. Kissinger's Operational Code." Paper prepared for the annual meeting of the American Political Science Association, San Francisco, September 1975.

Walton, Richard J. *Cold War and Counter Revolution.* New York: Viking, 1972.

Waltz, Kenneth N. *Man, the State and War: A Theoretical Analysis.* New York: Columbia University Press, 1959.

Warner, Edward L. III. "Bureaucratic Politics: A Thematic Outline." In *Study Guide to American Defense Policy,* by Richard G. Head, 3d ed. Baltimore: Johns Hopkins University Press, 1973.

Weiner, Anthony J., and Kahn, Herman, eds. *Crisis and Arms Control.* New York: Hudson Institute, 1962.

Weintal, Edward and Bartlett, Charles. *Facing the Brink: An Intimate Study in Crisis Diplomacy.* New York: Scribner, 1967.

Wilensky, Harold L. *Organizational Intelligence: Knowledge and Policy in Government and Industry.* New York: Basic Books, 1967.

Williams, Phil. "Crisis Management." In *Contemporary Strategy: Theories and Policies,* by John Baylis, Ken Booth, John Garnett, and Phil Williams, pp. 152-171. New York: Holmes and Meier, 1975.

Wohlstetter, Roberta. *Cuba and Pearl Harbor: Hindsight and Foresight.* Santa Monica, Cal.: Rand Corporation, 1965.

——. *Pearl Harbor: Warning and Decision.* Palo Alto, Cal.: Stanford University Press, 1962.

"WWMCCS: Worldwide Military Command & Control System." *Commanders Digest* 15 (February 1974).

Young, Oran. *The Intermediaries: Third Parties in International Crisis.* Princeton: Princeton University Press, 1967.

——. *The Politics of Force: Bargaining During International Crises.* Princeton: Princeton University Press, 1968.

Zinnes, Dina A. "A Comparison of Hostile Behavior of Decision-Makers in Simulation and Historical Data." *World Politics* 18 (April 1966): 474-501.

——. "The Expression and Perception of Hostility in Prewar Crisis: 1914." In *Quantitative International Politics,* edited by J. D. Singer, pp. 85-119. New York: Free Press, 1968.

——. "Hostility in Diplomatic Communications: A Study of the 1914 Crisis." In *International Crises,* edited by C. F. Hermann, pp. 139-162. New York: Free Press, 1972.

Index